MEDICALLY ASSISTED DEATH

Does a competent person suffering from a terminal illness or enduring an otherwise burdensome existence, who considers his life no longer of value but is incapable of ending it, have a right to be helped to die? Should someone for whom further medical treatment would be futile be allowed to die regardless of whether he has expressed a preference to be given all possible treatment? Do the answers to these moral questions have any legal implications? These are some of the questions that are asked and answered in this wide-ranging discussion of both the morality of medically assisted death and the justifiability of making certain instances legal. A case is offered in support of the moral and legal permissibility of specified instances of medically assisted death, along with responses to the main objections that have been levelled against it. The philosophical argument is bolstered by empirical evidence from The Netherlands and Oregon where voluntary euthanasia and physician-assisted suicide are already legal.

ROBERT YOUNG is Reader in Philosophy at La Trobe University, Melbourne, Australia.

MEDICALLY ASSISTED DEATH

ROBERT YOUNG
La Trobe University

CAMBRIDGE
UNIVERSITY PRESS

CAMBRIDGE UNIVERSITY PRESS

Cambridge, New York, Melbourne, Madrid, Cape Town, Singapore, São Paulo, Delhi

CAMBRIDGE UNIVERSITY PRESS
The Edinburgh Building, Cambridge, CB2 8RU, UK

Published in the United States of America by Cambridge University Press, New York

www.cambridge.org
Information on this title: www.cambridge.org/9780521706162

© Robert Young 2007

First published 2007

Printed in the United Kingdom at the University Press, Cambridge

A catalogue record for this publication is available from the British Library

ISBN 978-0-521-88024-4 hardback
ISBN 978-0-521-70616-2 paperback

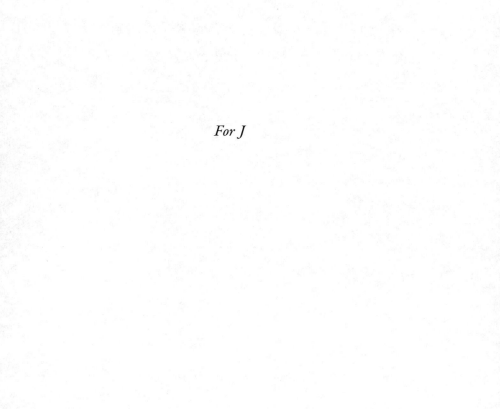

For J

Contents

Acknowledgments

There is by now a vast literature dealing with the issues discussed in this book. I have learned much from that literature and am very happy to acknowledge the fact here. I have also benefited from the comments of audiences at the Australian National University, Charles Sturt University, La Trobe University, the University of Melbourne and the University of Sydney where I read earlier versions of some of the chapters. It has also been my good fortune to receive valuable written feedback from friends and colleagues on earlier drafts of some of the material included in the book. So, I take this opportunity to thank: John Campbell and Norvin Richards for their comments on various draft chapters; Will Barrett, Andrew Brennan, Steve Buckle, Norva Lo and Catherine McDonald for their comments on a draft of chapter five; Michael Ashby, Alec Hyslop and David Lyons for their comments on a draft of chapter six; Arthur Kuflik and Janna Thompson for their comments on a draft of chapter seven; Steve Clarke for his comments on a draft of chapter eight; Lynda Burns for her comments on a draft of chapter ten; and Jennifer Poole for her comments on a draft of chapter eleven. Their constructive criticisms and encouragement contributed greatly to the quality of the final product. Finally, I wish to thank the anonymous readers for the Press whose detailed critiques helped me to produce a far better work than would otherwise have been the case.

CHAPTER I

Introduction

Various sorts of decisions made about end-of-life medical care are known to culminate in death. They range from the relatively uncontroversial, like the many decisions that are made (with or without the patient's consent) concerning the withdrawal or withholding of life-prolonging measures, sometimes in concert with the use of 'terminal sedation';[1] through decisions by patients to refuse artificial nutrition and hydration, kidney dialysis, vital organ transplants, donated blood and life-prolonging surgery; to the controversial, like physician-assisted suicide and voluntary euthanasia; and on to the very controversial, like non-voluntary euthanasia. Even though it will include some reflection about the less controversial modes of bringing about death, this book is chiefly about the more controversial forms of medically assisted death, namely, physician-assisted suicide, voluntary euthanasia, and non-voluntary euthanasia. My central thesis is that there is a strong case for legalising physician-assisted suicide and voluntary euthanasia but that it is neither justifiable nor necessary to do so for non-voluntary euthanasia.

Briefly, when a person (typically, a doctor) carries out an act of *euthanasia* she brings about the death of another person because she has good reason to believe *either* that the effects of illness or disability have made the latter's present existence so bad that he would be better off dead, *or* that, unless she intervenes, illness or disability will lead to such deterioration that a point will soon be reached where he would be better off dead. Though it is necessary to allow for 'mixed motives', the agent's belief that euthanasia will benefit the one whose death is brought about has to constitute a primary element in her motivation, because euthanasia

---

[1] The name given to the medical practice of administering drugs (usually benzodiazepines, or, benzodiazepines in combination with morphine) to relieve the suffering of a dying patient in the knowledge that they will have the further effect of sedating the patient during what remains of his life. A patient who is terminally sedated is denied nutrition and hydration. For an impressive discussion of some of the strategic inadequacies of terminal sedation see Orentlicher (1998).

is (in Philippa Foot's words) 'for the sake of the one who is to die'.[2] The same holds for instances of *physician-assisted suicide*, but this term is restricted to forms of assistance which stop short of the doctor 'bringing about the death' of the patient. Instead, the doctor provides the patient with the means to end his life and the latter must then decide when to use them.

Much of the book is concerned with medically assisted death at the request of the dying. I will be focusing mainly, but not exclusively, on *voluntary euthanasia*, that is, those instances of euthanasia in which a competent person makes a voluntary and enduring request to be helped to die, and *physician-assisted suicide*. In relation to the former, I will consider not only the direct means of ending life but also the use of indirect means (as in the withholding and withdrawing of medical and other treatment). I will not be considering the justifiability of suicide for those who are able to end their own lives without medical assistance, a category which includes at least some who choose to do so for reasons unconnected with the impact of illness or disability on the value their lives have for them.[3] Prior to Chapter 11, I will not consider *non-voluntary euthanasia* – where death is procured for a person who is neither competent, nor able, to request euthanasia, and for whom there is no proxy authorised to make a substituted judgment[4] – except when investigating the claim that legalising voluntary euthanasia will lead inexorably to non-voluntary euthanasia. Non-voluntary euthanasia will, however, be the sole focus of Chapter 11. *Involuntary euthanasia* – in which a competent person's life is brought to an end despite an explicit rejection of euthanasia – will receive no further comment beyond the following: no matter how honourable the perpetrator's motive in bringing about such a death, it constitutes homicide.

I

Debate about the morality and legality of physician-assisted suicide and voluntary euthanasia has, for the most part, been serious only in the last hundred years. By way of contrast, debate about the morality and legality

---

[2] Foot (1977: 87).

[3] See Battin (1995) for a thorough consideration of the ethical issues raised by suicide.

[4] In a substituted judgment a proxy decision-maker chooses on behalf of a no longer competent patient in accordance with how the patient would have chosen were he still competent to do so. The status of substituted judgments varies between jurisdictions: for example, they are recognised for various purposes in the United States; under Australian law their use is confined to the management of property under guardianship; while British law prohibits their use.

of suicide has been occurring for far longer. With the well-known exception of the Hippocratic school,[5] the ancient Greeks and Romans did not consider life needed to be preserved at any cost and were, in consequence, tolerant of (rational) suicide in cases where no relief could be offered to the dying, or to avoid the humiliation of military defeat or execution, or to show loyalty to a dead husband or master.[6] Opposition to suicide based on Neoplatonic thinking subsequently became entrenched in Judaeo-Christian and Islamic thought and has held sway ever since, even if individual thinkers within these traditions have sometimes challenged the supposed immorality of suicide. For example, in the sixteenth century Thomas More envisaged a utopian community that would facilitate the death of those whose lives had become burdensome as a result of 'torturing and lingering pain'.[7] Some modern scholars have claimed that More's use of irony means that he cannot be taken as having endorsed assisted dying. According to their reading, Book II of *Utopia* ridicules it.[8] Others acknowledge its ironic temper but believe *Utopia* 'shows Christian humanism's most attractive face',[9] and expresses qualified admiration for many of the practices it describes. John Donne's defence of suicide in *Biothanatos* was more straightforward, but despite being prepared to countenance it in a narrow range of circumstances he was not willing to have the work (which was originally written *c.* 1606) published until after his death. It was eventually published in 1644. David Hume's essay 'On Suicide', which he never authorised for publication in his lifetime, received its first publication in a French translation in 1770. It was published under Hume's name in English in 1783 and constitutes a landmark in that it attacked the prevailing religious opposition to suicide and offered the first defence of it on grounds of personal autonomy.

---

[5] See, for example, Temkin (1991: 34, 252).

[6] The Greeks were more inclined to write about suicide in plays and mytho-poetry while maintaining a discreet silence about the practice in real life, but some philosophical support can be found in the writings of Cynics like Antisthenes and Diogenes. Plato's *Phaedo* 62b-c and Aristotle's *Nicomachean Ethics*, Book 5.11 are well-known sources for philosophical criticism of suicide. There was greater philosophical support for the practice among the Romans. See, for example, Seneca, *Epistulae* 70.4 and 70.14 and *De Ira* 3.15.4, along with Epictetus, *Discourses* 1.24–1.25. For a comprehensive treatment of Graeco-Roman thought on these matters see van Hooff (1990). For a comprehensive study of ancient Greek and Roman medical views see Nutton (2004).

[7] See More (1516: 187).

[8] A suggestion that is said to gain support from his having written *A Dialogue of Comfort: Against Tribulation*, in which he explicitly criticises assisted death, during his period of imprisonment prior to his execution. See More (1535).

[9] Kenny (1983: 102).

In the last hundred years there has been sporadic discussion and debate about the moral and legal propriety of assisting dying people (and some severely disabled people who, strictly, are not dying) to die, but it has only been in the past several decades that it has been widely and publicly discussed.[10] The increasing interest in medically assisted death can be attributed, at least in part, to the fact that, whereas in the past little could be done to prolong the lives of the seriously ill, nowadays, at least in the developed world, large numbers of people face the unwelcome prospect of dying at an advanced age after a prolonged period of suffering from a degenerative and terminal condition.[11] This has undoubtedly increased reflection within the medical and legal professions in various countries, as well as by philosophers and theologians, about the right of competent patients to refuse medical treatment when that is tantamount to choosing to die, and to request voluntary medical assistance with dying. A further significant stimulus has been a series of landmark court hearings, particularly in The Netherlands, the United States, Canada and the United Kingdom.

I will briefly elaborate on each of these points. First, I will highlight a few of the more important court cases to illustrate how legal views have evolved. There is space only to mention a few of the relevant cases but those I have selected reveal that assisted death is not just about the relief of pain, nor merely an issue for those who are terminally ill. Second, I will offer a snapshot of the legislative initiatives that have been taken in favour of assisted death.

One, perhaps the chief, stimulus for these initiatives has been the legal toleration, followed recently by the legalisation, in The Netherlands of certain instances of medically assisted death. In the early 1970s a Dutch doctor, Geertruida Postma, was charged with murder after she eventually acceded to her elderly mother's persistent requests to be helped to die. Dr Postma ended her mother's life by administering a lethal dose of morphine. She was convicted of murder but was given only a token suspended sentence along with a brief period of probation. The court's lenient sentence was widely approved by the Dutch.[12] In 1976 the Royal Dutch Medical Association issued a statement in favour of (voluntary) euthanasia[13] remaining a criminal offence, but

---

[10] There has also been debate outside the public domain. The most significant instance has been among sub-communities in Western countries afflicted with AIDS. See, for instance, Magnusson (2002).
[11] Cf. Battin (2003).
[12] For a clear account of the *Postma* case and its aftermath see Griffiths, *et al.* (1998).
[13] The Dutch use the term 'euthanasia' to signify what is elsewhere referred to as 'voluntary euthanasia'.

urging that doctors be permitted to administer drugs for the purpose of pain relief despite knowing they would be hastening death, and to withhold or withdraw life-prolonging treatment in cases they deemed medically futile. In 1984 the Supreme Court heard an appeal by Dr Schoonheim against the judgment of the Court of Appeals which, having set aside an earlier judgment of the District Court in Alkmaar, had found him guilty of 'taking the life of another person at that person's express and earnest request'.[14] Schoonheim had hastened the death of a ninety-five year old, bed-ridden patient (who, though she was not, strictly, terminally ill, had asked to be helped to die because she found her dependent state intolerable). The Court of Appeals imposed no penalty despite its finding of guilt. The Supreme Court rejected several of the grounds on which the defendant based his appeal but accepted his contention that he was entitled to rely on a defence of 'necessity', that is, that he *had* to break the law because he was faced with a conflict between his duty to alleviate suffering and his duty not to bring about a patient's death, but could only fulfil one of them.[15] It ruled that he exercised his medical judgment properly in concluding that his duty to alleviate suffering should take precedence over his duty not to bring about his patient's death, and so reversed the finding of guilt. The case led ultimately to an agreement being drawn up between the Royal Dutch Medical Association and the Ministry of Justice on a series of guidelines that medical practitioners were required to follow in order to avoid a prosecution similar to that in *Schoonheim*. Though the agreement was not codified by Parliament until 1994 it played a significant role in the legal toleration of voluntary euthanasia and physician-assisted suicide for the best part of two decades, including a period prior to the codification, and another beyond it leading up to the introduction of legislation in 2001.[16]

In the United States, debate about assisted death has also been stimulated by various court cases. In 1975 Karen Ann Quinlan became a *cause célèbre* when she collapsed after a party at which she had imbibed alcohol and other drugs. She was subsequently diagnosed as having entered a persistent

[14] For details in English of this and two later landmark cases in The Netherlands see Griffiths, *et al.* (1998: 321–351).

[15] The Court distinguished this sense of 'necessity' from another, viz., that of being under duress. The notion of having to act out of necessity has been cited as a defence by those charged with a criminal offence in several celebrated cases involving euthanasia.

[16] There is a helpful account of the factors leading up to the introduction of legislation in Griffiths *et al.* (1998) and, more briefly, in Cosic (2003: ch. 7).

vegetative state,[17] connected to a respirator, and provided with hydration and nutrition via a nasogastric tube. Her parents sought to have her artificial respiration discontinued and when the matter eventually reached the New Jersey Supreme Court it found in their favour.[18] Despite being taken off the respirator she remained in a persistent vegetative state for a further nine years until her death. In 1983 Nancy Cruzan was severely injured when she lost control of the car she was driving. She, too, entered a persistent vegetative state but was able to live without a respirator. When her bodily condition deteriorated over a period of several years her parents gave up hope of any recovery and petitioned the Missouri Supreme Court to have her artificial feeding and hydration stopped. This was a step beyond what had been sought in *Quinlan*. After the court refused the request the matter went to the United States Supreme Court which recognised the right of competent patients to refuse life-preserving treatment – even where this may lead to death from an under-lying disease – but upheld the right of the State of Missouri to insist on clear evidence that Ms Cruzan would have exercised that right had she been in a position to do so.[19] In 1997 attention was again focused on the Supreme Court when it heard two test cases to do with the existence of a constitutionally protected right to die – *Washington et al. v. Glucksberg et al.*[20] and *Vacco et al. v. Quill et al.*[21] It reaffirmed the position it supported in *Cruzan*; ruled that it was legally permissible to make use of terminal sedation and to give palliative care to terminally ill patients even if this hastened death; but rejected the proposition that such patients have the right to control the manner and time of their death.

Around the same time as important cases like *Cruzan* were being fought out in the United States, there were similar issues being faced in the United

---

[17] For a taxonomy of vegetative and related states see Jennett (2002). According to it, someone is in a vegetative state when, in the immediate period after an acute brain insult, there is dissocia-tion between arousal and awareness such that there are periods of wakeful eye opening but no evidence of a working mind. A continuing vegetative state is one that has lasted for more than four weeks. A persistent or, as it is sometimes called, a permanent vegetative state is one that, in light of agreed criteria, is considered irreversible. The key indicator is lack of awareness (or, more technically, cognitive function). A patient who is in a vegetative state will have first been in a coma, that is, in a state in which her eyes are continuously closed and she cannot be aroused to consciousness. A comatose patient who regains consciousness never enters a vegetative state.

[18] *In re Quinlan* [1976] 137 NJ S. Ct. 227, 348 A2d 801, modified and remanded, 70 NJ 10 355 A2d 647, 429 S. Ct. 922.

[19] *Cruzan v. Director, Missouri Department of Health* [1990] 497 U.S. 261, 110 S. Ct. 2841.

[20] [1997] 117 S. Ct. 2258.   [21] [1997] 117 S. Ct. 2293.

Kingdom. In an important case in 1993, *Airedale N.H.S. Trust v. Bland*,[22] a request by a doctor to withdraw artificial feeding was found to be lawful. The decision was made on the basis of Anthony Bland's *best interests* rather than on what, given the opportunity, he would have chosen. In the eyes of many commentators this introduced a significantly different position from that taken in the United States. Notwithstanding their commentary, the later case of *R v. Cox*[23] reaffirmed that causing death with the intention of relieving a patient's intolerable pain remains murder under current British law. Subsequent events have supported that conclusion while showing at the same time that juries are unwilling to convict doctors who help the terminally ill to die. In 1999 Dr David Moor was charged with murder after he gave diamorphine to his eighty-five year old patient, George Liddell, who was dying an agonising death from bowel cancer. Despite the prosecution's claim that his intention was to end Liddell's life via a lethal overdose of diamorphine, the jury acquitted him. More recently, in 2005, Dr Howard Martin was charged with murder on similar grounds to Moor (in his case in connection with the deaths of three of his patients). He, too, was acquitted by a jury.[24]

It has, however, not only been the findings of various courts that have shaped the debate. An English journalist, Derek Humphry,[25] had a significant impact on the public debate in the 1980s, first in the United Kingdom and subsequently in the United States. In the early 1990s, two medical

---

[22] [1993] 1 All ER 821. Anthony Bland was crushed in an incident at a football stadium in April, 1989 and suffered severe anoxic brain damage. He lapsed into a persistent vegetative state but his ventilation, nutrition and hydration were technologically sustained for some three and a half years before being removed in 1993 following the decision of the final court of appeal, the House of Lords.

[23] [1992] 12 BMLR 38. Dr Cox administered an injection of potassium chloride to relieve the intolerable rheumatic pain being suffered by his patient, Lillian Boyes. He was charged only with attempted murder (apparently because it was considered to be too difficult to establish conclusively that the injection caused Boyes' death). The key issue on which his conviction seems to have turned was the identification of his primary purpose, namely, whether it was to relieve Boyes' pain or to end her life. Cox received only a suspended sentence and was allowed to continue to practise medicine.

[24] The pattern was repeated in 2001 in Western Australia when a jury deliberated for only ten minutes before acquitting a urologist, Dr Daryl Stephens, of murdering a woman who had died after being given an intravenous injection of drugs which ended her intense suffering and her life. (The patient's brother and sister were also acquitted of the same charge.) Court decisions like these were no doubt among the factors that influenced Lord Joffe in 2005 to try to legislate for medically assisted death in the UK via the introduction to the House of Lords of his *Assisted Dying for the Terminally Ill Bill*. The Bill's progress in the House of Lords was blocked by opponents in May, 2006 so as to stymie debate, but Lord Joffe has pledged to reintroduce the Bill at a later date.

[25] His impact was achieved initially through the publication of Humphry and Wickett (1978), in which an account is given of how he assisted his wife, Jean, to commit suicide to foreshorten the ravages of cancer. Subsequently, he migrated to the United States where he founded an activist organisation, The Hemlock Society, to promote reform of laws prohibiting assisted death, and published his (1981) and (1996).

activists joined the public debate in the United States with similar effect. Jack Kevorkian[26] became notorious for openly admitting to lending medical assistance with dying to numbers of terminally ill and disabled patients, while Timothy Quill, a far more distinguished medical practitioner, outlined in a prestigious medical journal how he had prescribed a lethal dose of drugs to one of his adult patients (who was suffering from leukaemia) when she requested help to facilitate her suicide.[27]

Disability advocacy groups have also contributed importantly to the recent debates and in the process have shown that medically assisted death is not simply about the relief of the pain and suffering of the terminally ill. Among those who made submissions in the now famous cases of *Washington et al. v. Glucksberg et al.* and *Vacco et al. v. Quill et al.*, to which I referred a moment ago, were various disability advocacy groups. They opposed the idea of there being a right to control the manner and time of one's death, as disability advocacy groups had done previously in 1993 in a Canadian case *Rodriguez v. British Columbia (Attorney General).*[28]

Sue Rodriguez was a forty-two year old sufferer from motor neurone disease (amyotrophic lateral sclerosis), who knew that her desire to be able to control the manner and time of her death would be compromised once she could no longer commit suicide without assistance. She petitioned the Supreme Court of British Columbia under the Canadian Charter of Rights and Freedoms for a court order to allow a qualified medical practitioner to provide her with physician-assisted suicide. Her argument was that the severely disabled were disadvantaged as compared with able-bodied people in not being able to exercise the right to control their own bodies. She was denied her request at trial, had her appeal rejected by the Court of Appeal, and, finally, lost a further appeal to the Supreme Court

---

[26] He was acquitted on three occasions, had a further trial declared a mistrial, and was eventually found guilty in 1999 of unlawfully killing a patient suffering from amyotrophic lateral sclerosis, a progressive neuro-degenerative disease (a form of motor neurone disease) that attacks nerve cells in the brain and spinal cord. The progressive degeneration of the motor neurones, which reach from the brain to the spinal cord and from there to the muscles throughout the body, leads to loss of voluntary muscle control and, eventually, total paralysis and death. The minds of sufferers remain unaffected. It is the most common of the group of diseases collectively known as motor neurone disease and is often known as 'Lou Gehrig's disease', after a famous baseballer who was one of the first to be diagnosed with it. Kevorkian openly broke the law to draw attention to the need for law reform so as to permit assistance with dying to be given to competent individuals who requested it. He publicised what he had done on a national television programme, was imprisoned, and will be eligible for release on parole in 2007.

[27] Quill (1991).   [28] [1993] 107 D.L.R. (4th) 342.

of Canada (by a margin of 5–4). She was illegally assisted to die by a doctor within months of this last defeat.

In the years since, there have been several further high profile instances involving victims of motor neurone disease who have sought to be assisted to die. Thus, for example, in 2001 Diane Pretty, a forty-one year old suffering from motor neurone disease, petitioned the Director of Public Prosecutions (DPP) in England for an assurance that her husband would not be charged with the criminal offence of assisting a suicide if he helped her to die (which they intended he would do before her condition deteriorated to the point where she would die of suffocation).[29] The DPP rejected her request. The couple went, in turn, to the High Court, the House of Lords and the European Court of Human Rights,[30] but, despite expressions of sympathy from the presiding judges and law lords, each of their requests was turned down. Mrs Pretty died in a hospice a couple of weeks after the European Court published its decision. Her case contrasts starkly with that of another Briton, Ms B, who was also suffering from an irreversible neurological disease and likewise wanted to be assisted to die. Ms B had suffered bleeding into her spinal cord, leaving her paralysed and dependent on a ventilator. She asked to have the ventilator turned off but her medical team refused her request despite her being judged to be competent. Ms B challenged the legality of the decision and won.[31] She was placed in the care of a different medical team, permitted to have the ventilator withdrawn, and died within weeks. The handling of these two cases is directly relevant to an issue I will consider below in Chapter 6, namely, that of the supposed moral permissibility of letting die, and the supposed moral impermissibility of killing. For the moment, though, I simply draw attention to the way in which Ms B was able to fulfil her desire to end her life whereas Diane Pretty was not. The only relevant difference between their cases was that, unlike Mrs Pretty, Ms B was dependent on mechanical life-support (and thus could end her life by discontinuing her medical treatment).[32]

Finally, I draw attention to several recent instances from my own neck of the woods where individuals have felt compelled to take drastic action in order to highlight the inadequacies of the legal situation with medically assisted death. In Australia in 2002, in an instance that did not go before a court but did achieve notoriety, another sufferer from motor neurone

[29] *R (Pretty) v. Director of Public Prosecutions (Secretary of State for the Home Department Intervening)* [2001] 3 WLR 1598.
[30] *Pretty v. United Kingdom* [2002] ECHR (application no. 2346/02).
[31] *Re B (adult: refusal of medical treatment)* [2002] FD.
[32] For further discussion see Boyd (2002).

disease, Sandy Williamson, publicly declared her intention to suicide while she remained able, in order to draw attention to the need to legalise voluntary euthanasia and physician-assisted suicide for those in similar circumstances. Her attempt did not go entirely to plan and she was rendered comatose, but died in hospital a week later.

In 2004 in New Zealand, Lesley Martin, an experienced intensive care nurse, was sentenced to fifteen months in prison for the attempted murder of her mother in 1999. Martin wrote a book, *To Die Like a Dog* (New Plymouth: M-Press, 2002), in which she detailed how she had given a 60 mg dose of morphine to her mother after her mother had requested help to die. When her mother lingered, she used a pillow to end her life. Martin's mother had had surgery early in 1999 for rectal cancer. During the surgery a tumour on her liver was discovered. She elected not to have further surgery but instead to be cared for at home by her daughter. Martin was prosecuted on the evidence of her book even though she had previously informed the police about what had transpired and they had taken no action. Yet, also in 2004, just across the Tasman Sea in Tasmania, Australia, John Godfrey was given a suspended sentence of twelve months for assisting his eighty-eight year old mother to commit suicide. She had been an outspoken campaigner for law reform in relation to voluntary euthanasia and physician-assisted suicide.

Undoubtedly, it has not just been cases like those mentioned above that have contributed to the fomentation surrounding the issue of medically assisted death during the past few decades in Australasia, Europe, North America and elsewhere. The impact of the cases that have been before the courts has been significant, but the contributions to the wider public debate of medical and other activists, some of whom I have had occasion to mention, have also had an impact. Nonetheless, there has been no direct path from any of these factors to what has happened legislatively (except perhaps in The Netherlands). It should, therefore, help if I detail what the situation is as regards legislation in favour of assisted death (and, where there is no legislation, its legal toleration).

In Switzerland, assisted suicide (in general, not merely in the guise of physician-assisted suicide) has been legally tolerated for some decades. As already noted, for a period of about two decades, medically assisted death was legally tolerated in The Netherlands before legislation was enacted in 2001 to permit both voluntary euthanasia and physician-assisted suicide under strict medical guidelines. However, it is perhaps less well known that the Northern Territory of Australia was the first jurisdiction to *legislate* in favour of voluntary medically assisted death. The legislation was agreed to in 1995 and came into effect for a brief period in 1996. During this period, an activist doctor, Philip Nitschke,[33] assisted four people to die. He developed a computer-based machine to enable the dying to self-administer a lethal dose of pharmaceutical drugs. But the statute was short-lived because, within a matter of months, it was nullified by the Australian Federal Parliament. In the Australian federal structure there are six States and two Territories. The States have sovereignty over a number of designated areas of power, but, under the constitution, certain kinds of legislation enacted in the Territories may be over-ridden by federal legislation. So, when the Federal Parliament voted to take away the power of the Legislative Assembly of the Northern Territory to make laws 'which permit or have the effect of permitting . . . the form of intentional killing of another called euthanasia (which includes mercy killing) or the assisting of a person to terminate his or her life', it acted constitutionally, albeit contrary to the democratic will of Northern Territorians. The powers of the Legislative Assembly to make laws with respect to the withdrawal or withholding of medical treatment, and the provision of palliative care, were not affected, as long as these practices did not involve the intentional killing of patients.

In 1997 the State of Oregon in the United States passed legislation in favour of physician-assisted suicide. The legislation was authorised by a referendum held in 1994 but its implementation was delayed by court action. The legality of the legislation is still being challenged in the courts by the federal government at the time of writing.[34]

In 2003 Belgium followed the example of its Dutch neighbours and legislated to permit medically assisted dying.

II

In this book I will not be attempting to cover all of the issues that have been raised in the debate about medically assisted death. Some of these are technical medical and legal issues that are properly the province of those with greater medical and legal knowledge than mine. However, even though

---

[33] See Nitschke and Stewart (2005).
[34] In the US, opponents of physician-assisted suicide legislation have not only made legal challenges to it but have attempted by other means to prevent physicians from facilitating suicide, perhaps most notoriously via the 1999 federal *Pain Relief Promotion Act*, which made it illegal to use scheduled drugs for the purpose of causing death. By way of response, some who support physician-assisted suicide have endeavoured to defeat such tactics by developing technological means of assisted death that do not require the active involvement of physicians. Cf. Battin (2005a). Battin sees the technological developments as having the potential to produce 'wins' for both opponents and proponents of assisted death.

my focus is on the *philosophical* (and, to a lesser extent, the *theological*) issues raised by medically assisted death, I make reference more frequently than is common in philosophical works to relevant medical and legal matters because I believe that credible work in bioethics needs to be in contact with the medical and legal realities. My consideration of the philosophical issues is more comprehensive than is common elsewhere, because I cover some aspects of the debate about medically assisted death that have been given insufficient attention (e.g. the issue of professional integrity for medical practitioners in the event that medically assisted dying becomes legal), and some more fully than has been common hitherto (e.g. what requirements have to be satisfied for someone who seeks assisted dying to be competent to do so). My attempt at a comprehensive coverage of the issues necessitates retracing territory covered in previous contributions to the relevant literature (including those I have made) but I hope that readers will think this only a minor imposition.

Though the book is an essay in applied philosophy, it is intended to be accessible to those from cognate disciplines as well as to those directly involved in the formulation of public policy. It behoves the latter, in particular, to familiarise themselves with the range of matters covered in the essay because public policy on medically assisted death lags behind not only scholarly debate but public opinion. This has been evident for several decades in the public opinion polls taken in Australia, Canada, Japan, New Zealand, the United Kingdom, the United States of America and various European countries, which have consistently shown substantial majorities of citizens in favour of legislation to permit assisted dying for competent dying patients. Yet, apart from the Northern Territory, Oregon, The Netherlands and Belgium there has been no legislative action to match the high levels of public support. Many activists, and some philosophers, attribute this legislative inaction to the influence of religious opponents.[35] I doubt that this is the sole explanation. In at least some of the countries just mentioned, legislation to permit abortion has been introduced despite opposition from religious institutions and orchestrated campaigns by conservative religious groups. The same institutional opposition exists toward the legalisation of medically assisted death because it, too, supposedly breaches the sanctity of human life. Given that abortion is legally permitted, religious opposition to the legalisation of assisted dying seems incapable on its own of accounting for the relative lack of legislative activity in relation to assisted dying. However, the situation in the United States

[35] Cf. Stutsman (2004).

appears to be exceptional in the extent to which lobbying by religious individuals and bodies has had an effect on legislative activity in the broad domain of bioethics, including medically assisted dying. As in other countries, lobbying by professional medical organisations has also played a significant role in persuading legislators not to take their cue from the convictions of the wider public. In my view, lobbying by professional medical bodies has probably been more significant in influencing the legislative position in Australia than has lobbying by religious groups. However, well-informed commentators claim that in the United States the evidence is clear that religious lobbyists have had a far greater impact than have medical lobbyists.

Undoubtedly, a good deal of traditional medical practice is premised on values that have become enshrined in the law in many jurisdictions, and those values are at odds with the idea of medically assisted death. (Witness, for example, the way in which 'the doctrine of double effect' – discussed below in Chapter 6 – has underpinned the notion that administering pain relieving drugs, even when it is foreseen that this will lead to death, is an acceptable medical practice provided that it involves no negligence, whereas intentionally assisting a patient to die who competently requests such assistance in order to escape from a painful existence is not.)

Some might claim that even the conservative medical values embedded in the practices just alluded to ultimately originated from religious ideas. I think this is implausible because there is no reason to trace either moral or medical values exclusively to religiously based norms, as the claim assumes. Consider, for example, the influence of ancient Greek thought on moral ideas, including medico-moral ideas. Or, consider the extent of moral agreement across various cultures despite their having been influenced by quite diverse religious traditions. In the legal sphere, as well, the situation is more complex than the objection allows: consider, for example, the influence of Roman law on English law. No doubt, religious thought, specifically, the Judaeo-Christian tradition, has been influential in the development of Western medical law and ethics, but it is quite a leap from this to the claim that the conservatism evident in Western medical law and ethics had its origins entirely, or even largely, in the ideas of that religious tradition.

Whatever the correct explanation of why it has been the case, it is the case that public policy on assisted death has remained unchanged in many of the countries where it might reasonably have been expected to undergo change so as to reflect the strength of community conviction. With that in mind, it is my hope that this essay will help change the legal status of medically assisted dying, especially, but not only, in my own country.

As previously indicated, the book deals chiefly with medically assisted death when voluntarily requested by competent dying persons, and only secondarily with non-voluntary euthanasia. I will argue that, despite claims to the contrary by critics of the legalisation of voluntary euthanasia and physician-assisted suicide, the stance taken on them carries no entailment about the stance to be taken on non-voluntary euthanasia. The chapters that follow have been arranged so as to keep the matters as separate as possible.

In Chapter 2 I offer a positive case for legalising forms of medically assisted death, in particular voluntary euthanasia and physician-assisted suicide, whose legalisation would require changes in much current medical practice and law. In Chapter 3 I argue that medical treatment can sometimes be said to be futile, thereby removing one obstacle to medically assisted death, particularly when the assistance consists in withholding, or withdrawing, further (life-prolonging) medical treatment. Chapter 4 is devoted specifically to the issue of physician-assisted suicide. In subsequent chapters I look closely at objections to the legalisation of voluntary forms of medically assisted death based on: the supposed sanctity of human life; the claim, in effect, that it is morally permissible, in certain circumstances, to allow a dying person to die but never morally permissible to kill such a person; the claim that the doctrine of double effect shows that it is not necessary for competent dying individuals ever to have their lives ended intentionally; the claim that the legalisation of these practices would be at odds with the goals of medicine and thus would be incompatible with the maintenance of professional integrity among medical professionals; the claim that the requirements for someone competently to request voluntary euthanasia or to participate in physician-assisted suicide are not able to be met in cases of terminal illness even via the device of an advance directive; and, finally, the claim that their legalisation would propel us down a slippery slope leading inevitably to non-voluntary euthanasia.

Then, in Chapter 11, I will consider whether, and, if so, when non-voluntary euthanasia is morally defensible. I will give consideration both to cases involving those, like infants and young children, who have never been competent, as well as to cases involving those who are no longer competent but who gave no indication while competent of the sorts of circumstance in which they would wish to be assisted to die. It will be my contention that advocates of the legalisation of voluntary euthanasia should not support the legalisation of non-voluntary euthanasia even if, on occasion, the practice would be morally justifiable, because, even then, it is unnecessary.

In the concluding chapter I briefly re-trace the course of my argument.

CHAPTER 2

A case for the legalisation of voluntary medically assisted death

In this chapter I will develop a case for the legalisation of voluntary medically assisted death. It has two elements. First, I will offer two grounds for the moral permissibility of voluntary medically assisted death and, second, I will contend that even though the moral case I develop is, on its own, insufficient to justify legalisation there are good public policy reasons to legalise voluntary euthanasia and physician-assisted suicide. Because of the importance of being clear about exactly what each of them involves, in section I I will explain in detail how voluntary euthanasia and physician-assisted suicide are best characterised, and, through a comparative analysis of their advantages and disadvantages, how they differ. In the following section I will set out a case for the moral permissibility of these voluntary forms of medically assisted death. In the final section I will show that the legalisation of voluntary medically assisted death represents the most appropriate public policy response to this moral case out of the available options. Once the positive case for legalisation has been stated the way will be open to investigate the various reasons that have been given for not legalising medically assisted death. In subsequent chapters I will show that these negative considerations do not overwhelm the positive ones.

I

As mentioned in the previous chapter, when someone who needs assistance to end his own life requests voluntary euthanasia he is requesting medical help to die because he would prefer to die than to endure his illness or disability. To establish its seriousness, the request must be enduring, not made on a whim. A doctor who performs an act of euthanasia in response to such a request must be motivated primarily by a desire to benefit her patient. In the absence of such a motive what she does will not constitute euthanasia.

(It is here assumed that it is possible to benefit someone by bringing about his death, but the objection that this is not a coherent possibility will be taken up later.) Since the characterisation I have given is consistent with death being brought about either by act or by omission, it avoids begging the important moral question of whether it is morally acceptable to respond to a competent request for assisted dying by way of allowing the requester to die, but *not* by killing him.

It may be worth acknowledging here that the characterisation of voluntary euthanasia I have given does not preclude a more elaborate taxonomy in which an instance brought about via an act is classified as *active* voluntary euthanasia, and one brought about via an omission, or, more usually, a refraining, as *passive* voluntary euthanasia. Nevertheless, later, in Chapter 6, I shall argue that even though there is a legitimate distinction to be drawn between an act and an omission, the distinction has far less moral significance than it has traditionally been ascribed. Indeed, I shall suggest that what makes the moral difference in a particular context are the contextual considerations. In the meantime, I will simply make the point that the classification of certain occurrences as passive voluntary euthanasia is, anyway, not entirely straightforward.[1] Consider the fact that it is legally permissible in most jurisdictions for a terminally ill person who remains competent to refuse, or forego, life-sustaining medical treatment, including, for example, artificial nutrition and hydration. Because such a refusal may be tantamount to hastening death, some believe that it should be classified as suicide.[2] Others think of such a refusal as, instead, an instance of passive voluntary euthanasia.[3] However, like Jeff McMahan, I believe that whether we regard this as an instance of suicide – on the ground that the patient refuses to be kept alive and so is assisted to die by the doctor – or one of passive voluntary euthanasia – on the ground that the doctor allows the patient to die with the intention of benefiting him – is moot.[4] So, I will generally distinguish passive voluntary euthanasia and active voluntary euthanasia only when others allege that the distinction has moral significance.

If voluntary euthanasia is to be legalised, a more formal statement of the conditions that will have to be satisfied by those who are candidates for voluntary euthanasia will be required than has hitherto been given. My starting point will be a set of individually necessary conditions typical

---

[1] For an interesting discussion of attempts in several recent United States cases to maintain that there is a clear line between suicide and refusal of life-sustaining medical treatment see Stell (1998: 226ff).
[2] Cf. Siegel (1998: note 146).   [3] Cf. Mojica and Murrell (1991).   [4] McMahan (2002: 459f).

of those proposed by advocates of the legalisation of voluntary euthanasia. In the course of considering the set I will suggest some necessary modifications so as to reach a more acceptable proposal.

Medical assistance with dying to facilitate a request by a competent person who wants to die (either by being allowed to die or by being killed) should legally be permitted provided the person:

1. is suffering a terminal illness;
2. is unlikely to benefit from the discovery of a cure for the illness during what remains of his life expectancy;
3. is, as a direct result of the illness, *either* suffering intolerable pain, *or* an unacceptably burdensome existence (because the illness has to be treated in ways which make him so dependent on others, or on technological means of life support, as to cause severe distress);
4. has an enduring, voluntary and competent wish to die, or, in the event that he is no longer competent, has previously, while competent, given appropriate expression to his desire to die should conditions 1–3 be satisfied; and
5. is unable, without assistance, to commit suicide.

It should be noted that at least two of these conditions (the first and fifth) are quite restrictive; indeed, more restrictive than I, and many others, believe appropriate. The first condition would allow access to voluntary euthanasia only for those who are *terminally ill*. An illness is commonly regarded as terminal if it is progressive and will cause death to occur within twelve months. Nonetheless, it is well to remember that medical professionals cannot always be sure that a particular patient will die within a specified period of time. Still, it seems reasonable to apply it to those in the last stages of various cancers and illnesses like AIDS and chronic obstructive pulmonary disease, but not to those rendered quadriplegic as a result of traumatic injury, or those with motor neurone disease, or those in the early stages of Alzheimer's disease.[5] Of course, some in these latter categories do request help with dying. In The Netherlands, for example, requests to be helped to die by persons suffering various forms of motor neurone disease have figured prominently in the courts in recent years, and have, in fact, been a specific focus for study and documentation.[6] I believe, therefore,

---

[5] Alzheimer's disease is the most common form of dementia, a group of conditions in which gradual destruction of brain cells leads to progressive decline in mental function.

[6] In a study of victims of a common form of motor neurone disease – amyotrophic lateral sclerosis, or, Lou Gehrig's disease – which was conducted in The Netherlands during the period when assisted death was legally tolerated, about one in five of those in the study was helped to die on request and a further one in four had their lives foreshortened as a result of the medical treatment they received. See Veldink, *et al.* (2002).

that eligibility for voluntary euthanasia should extend not only to those with a terminal illness but also to those with an incurable medical condition that results in them finding life intolerably burdensome.[7] However, others who agree that making voluntary euthanasia available only to those with a terminal illness may be too restrictive believe that attempting to extend coverage to those with incurable medical conditions whose deaths are not imminent would, at least in the first instance, make it harder to persuade legislators to legalise any acts of voluntary euthanasia, and thus would be tactically unwise. On its own, of course, that does not entail that legal provision for medically assisted death should be denied to those who, strictly, are not dying, and yet are unable without assistance to end their unbearably burdensome lives. At most, it has tactical significance for attempts to effect legal change. Hence, the first condition should be modified to include those for whom life has become intolerably burdensome (*vide* the third condition). For that reason I think it a deficiency in the Oregon statute that it restricts access to physician-assisted suicide to those who are expected to die within the ensuing six months (which is already a lesser period than is commonly indicated for terminal conditions).

The second condition is intended simply to reflect the fact that whether someone's health status is curable is usually determinable. So-called 'miracle' cures may be given sensationalist coverage by journalists, but progress toward medical breakthroughs is typically painstakingly slow. Should there be instances where miracles are wrought by God, the need for assisted dying in those instances would be forestalled, but it is clear that not everyone's death is thus to be postponed. If the incurability specification is considered too restrictive, an alternative would be to limit access to those unlikely to receive effective treatment in their lifetime.

The third condition recognises what many who oppose the legalisation of voluntary euthanasia do not, namely, that it is not only release from pain that leads people to want to be allowed, or helped, to die. In The Netherlands, for example, it has been found to be a less significant reason for requesting assistance with dying than have other forms of suffering, like frustration with loss of independence. Indeed, in several court cases it has been accepted that some people are afflicted with 'unbearable mental suffering' that will only be relieved upon death.[8] In Oregon, too, the evidence is that dying patients are more concerned about loss of autonomy, as evidenced by their inability to participate in activities they care about

---

[7] Cf. Miller, *et al.* (1994).
[8] The Court of Appeal in *Schoonheim*, for example, referred to this as 'an established fact'.

and in lost independence.[9] Be that as it may, there is much wider agreement about the fact that sufferers from some terminal conditions may, in having their pain relieved, have to endure side effects that, for them, make life unbearable. In addition, there are those (e.g. victims of multiple sclerosis[10] and motor neurone disease) who do not have to cope with pain they cannot endure, but find it intolerable to have to depend on technological forms of support that rob their lives of quality.

The fourth condition requires that the choice to die not only be voluntary and competent, but also an enduring (rather than transitory) choice. The choice is such as to require discussion as well as time for reflection, and so should not be settled in a moment. Normal adults are presumed to be competent to make choices of this kind. The onus of establishing lack of competence (e.g. because of the presence of defeating considerations) is on those who refuse to accept the person's choice. There is no need to deny that it is sometimes possible to establish that a person is neither competent nor able to act in a voluntary fashion (e.g. if he is in a state of clinical depression). But the onus is on those who believe an adult's choice is incompetent to show that it is. The point is just the familiar one that competent individuals are free to engage, without interference, in risky pursuits, whether they be everyday ones, like crossing the street, or exceptional ones, like sky-diving.[11]

Finally, the fifth condition (like the first) may also be considered too restrictive. It limits access to voluntary euthanasia to those incapable of ending their lives. Those who think physician-assisted suicide is preferable to voluntary euthanasia, perhaps because they are convinced that health care practitioners may never justifiably *kill* their patients but may nonetheless assist with dying, are likely to believe the restriction is desirable. By contrast, those who question the psychological capacity for suicide of many competent persons who wish to die may consider it too restrictive. It is legitimate in this context again to raise the issue of whether to regard the refusal of nutrition and hydration as tantamount to suicide. For those who think such a refusal is tantamount to suicide, the drawn-out process that it involves has to be taken into account in assessing its comparative merits. (I return to this issue in section III.)

I turn now to whether there are any significant differences for our purposes between voluntary euthanasia and physician-assisted suicide,

---

[9] Cf. Ganzini, *et al.* (2003a), and Steinbock (2005: 235f).
[10] Multiple sclerosis is an auto-immune disease that damages the myelin sheath that coats nerve cells. This impairs communication between the cells and leads to progressive physical disability.
[11] Cf. Feinberg (1986) and Chapter 8 below.

and, if so, what they are. This much can be agreed: with voluntary euthanasia, but not physician-assisted suicide, the physician performs the act that is the final cause of death. A competent dying person who wishes to die but who is *either* not willing to attempt unassisted suicide (e.g. because he is aware of the risks of failure and hence of the possibility that he may be left in an even more parlous condition if he attempts suicide and fails),[12] *or* unable to bring about his own death by refusing medical treatment, might, in consequence, request help from a physician by asking for the means (e.g. drugs) to enable him to suicide. This would be a request for physician-assisted suicide. By contrast, if he asks his physician to end his life (including via the administration of drugs), that constitutes a request for active voluntary euthanasia. I shall assume from now on that this much is agreed.

There is less agreement, though, about whether the physician must *intend* death in either circumstance. Some philosophers maintain that a physician must intend her patient's death in performing voluntary euthanasia, but in offering physician-assisted suicide need only intend to facilitate her patient's choice (despite knowing that it is to commit suicide).[13] By contrast, the majority of the judges in two recent landmark cases before the United States Supreme Court, which I mentioned in Chapter 1, appeared to believe that a physician who assists in suicide necessarily intends the death of her patient.[14] (While I happen to agree with Brock and Kamm, rather than the majority of the judges, as far as I can tell nothing in this book depends on that agreement.[15])

Several recent studies[16] suggest that physicians consider that even though there is no significant moral difference between physician-assisted suicide and voluntary euthanasia (especially, though not just, in its active variant), the former has one major advantage from their perspective over the latter, namely, it empowers a competent patient to hasten his death, in much the same way as he may already legally do by refusing life-prolonging medical treatment.[17] From the patient's point of view,

---

[12] Cf. Wellman (2003: 23). It is also true that a dying person may, out of concern for others, seek a medically assisted death because the non-medical options (shooting, gassing, hanging, etc.) are so violent.

[13] Cf., for example, Brock (1999) and Kamm (1999).

[14] See *Washington et al. v. Glucksberg et al.* [1997] 117 Sup. Ct. 2258 and *Vacco et al. v. Quill et al.* [1997] 117 Sup. Ct. 2293.

[15] For a helpful account of the state of the law concerning assisted suicide, including physician-assisted suicide (especially in the United Kingdom and Australia, but with consideration also given to the legal situation in the United States), see Otlowski (1997: ch. 2).

[16] See, for example, van der Maas, *et al.* (1995); Bachman, *et al.* (1996); and Lee, *et al.* (1996).

[17] That there is any close resemblance is challenged by many opponents of the legalisation of (active) voluntary euthanasia and physician-assisted suicide. Cf. Kamisar (1995).

when a physician provides a patient with access to barbiturates, opioids, or other lethal medications, or to a 'suicide machine', that is, a machine which delivers a lethal dose to a patient once that patient activates the machine (usually by entering the required key stroke into a computer), their provision enables the patient to decide when his suffering is unbearable, and thus permits him to choose when to administer a lethal dose. With voluntary euthanasia, the timing of death may not be so directly within the patient's control because of the need to rely on another (or, others). From the point of view of the medical practitioner who assists with a patient's suicide there need be no direct involvement with the patient's death. Some practitioners see this as enabling them to think of their role as at least akin to the way the role of the physician has traditionally been conceived. Irrespective of the justifiability of this rationalisation, the legalisation of physician-assisted suicide would still require a modification of the traditional conception of physician care since it is no part of that conception that patients be provided with lethal doses of drugs to enable them to end their lives. That being so, any advantage that physician-assisted suicide has over even active voluntary euthanasia seems slight. However, as previously mentioned, there are physicians to whom it matters that they need only intend to give a patient the option of taking his own life. Unfortunately, this has the consequence that they feel morally unable to assist with the deaths of severely disabled individuals, for whom suicide without more hands-on assistance is impossible.[18]

II

In this section I will develop a moral case for legalising voluntary euthanasia and physician-assisted suicide based on the two key arguments that supporters of these practices have offered, in the full knowledge that neither argument in isolation can make the moral case and that it, in turn, is insufficient on its own to justify their legalisation.

The first of the key arguments in support of the moral permissibility of medically assisted death is that respect for persons demands respect for their

---

[18] Interestingly, even though the Royal Dutch Medical Association recommended in 1995 that physician-assisted suicide be chosen over voluntary euthanasia, in part because of considerations to do with its understanding of the role of the physician, the rate of physician-assisted suicide remains remarkably low in The Netherlands as compared with that for voluntary euthanasia. See Onwuteaka-Philipsen, *et al.* (2003). The researchers infer that even patients capable of ending their own lives need to be reassured that unforeseen possibilities will not intervene to prevent death and hence prefer direct medical assistance with dying. Obviously, those unable to suicide even with assistance must rely on voluntary euthanasia.

autonomous choices, as long as those choices do not result in harm to others.[19] It will sometimes be necessary to appeal to law to ensure that choices are respected. This first argument is directly connected with the requirement that any request for medical assistance with dying be competently made because autonomy presupposes competence. It is in the interests of competent persons to make important decisions about their lives in accordance with their conceptions of how they want to lead those lives. In exercising autonomy, or self-determination, each of us takes responsibility for our life and, since dying is a part of life, choices about the manner of our dying, and the timing of our death, are part of what is involved in taking responsibility for our life. It is quite natural for each of us to be concerned about what the last phase of our life will be like, not merely because of fears that our dying might cause us great suffering, but also because of our desire to avoid dependency, to retain our dignity, and, more generally, to retain as much control over our life as is possible during its final phase.[20]

Developments in modern medicine have highlighted the significance of control over end-of-life decision-making because life-saving and life-prolonging interventions made possible by new technologies have had a dramatic impact on the extent to which dying can be drawn out and life extended. Sometimes this added life is an occasion for rejoicing; sometimes it stretches out the period of significant physical and intellectual decline so as to impair and burden an individual's life and render it no longer worth living. There is, in consequence, no single, objectively correct answer, applicable to every individual, as to whether, and, if so, when, life becomes an unwanted burden. But that fact simply points up the importance of individuals being able to decide autonomously for themselves whether their own lives retain sufficient quality and dignity for them to judge that further life will be worthwhile. In making such decisions, competent individuals are entitled to decide about the mix of self-determination and personal well-being that suits them. Even when a competent person is critically ill and in the typically severely compromised and debilitated state that that

---

[19] For present purposes I rely on Joel Feinberg's analysis of *harm* as consisting in wrongful or unjust invasion of a being's interests. See Feinberg (1984: ch. 1). I grant that, even among the liberal-minded, there is not universal agreement that harm to others is the only ground for limiting the exercise of people's autonomy. Indeed, I think that seriously offensive behaviour should, under certain circumstances, also be considered a basis for restricting people's autonomy. However, in the present context, the relevant ground for placing limits on the exercise of individual autonomy is whether it will result in harm to others. The issue of whether behaviour that is seriously offensive to others should be restricted is given a superbly balanced discussion in Feinberg (1985).

[20] There are fuller accounts of personal autonomy along these sorts of lines in, for example, Young (1986) and Dworkin (1988).

involves, it is, other things being equal, his judgment of whether continued life is a benefit to him that should carry the greatest weight.

Suppose, as is generally agreed in liberal societies, that a person's exercise of his autonomy warrants our respect, at least in the absence of overriding social concerns about harm to others (as, for instance, would be the case if a person's autonomous behaviour risked spreading an epidemic). If medical assistance is to be provided to help a person achieve his autonomously chosen goal of an easeful death (because he cannot end his own life unaided), the autonomy of the assisting professional, or team of professionals, must also be respected. The value (or, perhaps, right) of self-determination does not entitle a patient to demand of a medical professional that she act contrary to her personal health or her moral and professional values. What implications, if any, does this have for the legalisation of medically assisted death? It has this obvious implication: if medically assisted death is to be legally permitted it must be against a backdrop of respect for professional autonomy. That is why I will later argue in greater detail (in Chapter 7 below), that if a doctor cannot both fulfil her moral or professional responsibilities and facilitate a request for euthanasia, provision should be made, other things being equal, for the transfer of the patient's care to a doctor who faces no such conflict.

Other objections to the appeal to individual autonomy as a ground for the moral permissibility of medically assisted death have to do with whether autonomy is to be considered a more important value than, for instance, the sanctity of human life, and with whether permitting autonomous individuals to seek help with dying would have damaging consequences for others. These objections will be considered in detail in Chapters 5 and 10, respectively.

The second key moral reason for legalising medically assisted death is based on compassion[21] for the suffering of patients. Those who appeal to this argument believe that laws requiring people to endure pointless suffering should be abolished. Because the argument from compassion places more emphasis on the role of the carer than does the argument from autonomy, it seems likely to figure prominently in the thinking of those who see medically assisted death as a last resort, to be contemplated only when nothing further can be done to relieve suffering.[22]

---

[21] This term is to be preferred because it portrays the relevant emotion more accurately than does 'mercy'. Some do, however, speak of 'mercy killing'. See, for example, Battin (2003: 686–690).
[22] Cf. Angell (1998).

Those who reject this argument do so for one or more of the following reasons. First, it is sometimes claimed, especially by those within the hospice movement, but also by those who believe palliative care can satisfactorily meet the needs of the dying, that it is possible with modern drugs to relieve the pain and distress experienced by all dying patients. To the reply that it is untrue that *all* such pain and distress can be relieved, a second consideration is apt to be introduced, namely, that where pain and distress prove intractable patients can be sedated, usually with barbiturates and benzodiazepines, so that they enter a pharmacological oblivion from which they will not exit prior to death. Such patients die of dehydration, or electrolyte imbalance, or medical complications of their diseases because no life-prolonging interventions are made. To supporters of voluntary medically assisted death this state (sometimes known as 'terminal sedation') seems either indistinguishable from death, or to represent 'a fate worse than death'.[23] A different consideration altogether is invoked by those who contend that a painful or distressing death may be a valuable experience for an individual, in that it may foster moral virtues, enhance religious understanding, deepen relationships with loved ones, or bring a sense of completion to a life. Supporters of voluntary medically assisted death need not dispute that these benefits may sometimes accrue to a dying individual – they can counter that not every dying person experiences them but, more importantly, that it should be the patient's choice whether to endure pain and suffering in quest of such benefits.

I need to issue a caution: from the perspective of advocates of the legalisation of voluntary medically assisted death, the argument from compassion should not be considered in isolation from the argument from autonomy. The reason is that the argument from compassion applies equally to dying persons who have not competently requested medically assisted death as well as to those who have. Advocates of the legalisation of voluntary medically assisted death argue that these are entirely different matters (see Chapter 11 below) and so insist that the argument from compassion not be employed in isolation but only in harness with the argument from autonomy.

Earlier I noted that it does not follow from an act's being morally permissible that it ought to be made legal. In the next section I seek to strengthen the positive case for the legalisation of medically assisted death by introducing some additional public policy reasons in favour of legalisation.

---

[23] Cf. Orentlicher (1998).

III

The legalisation of voluntary medically assisted death clearly has important implications for health care practice, both within and outside hospitals (as is evident from the recent medical history of Australia's Northern Territory, The Netherlands and Oregon). But legalisation is not the only possible public policy that might be adopted. It might, for example, be held that even though voluntary medically assisted death is morally permissible in at least some instances, it should still not be legalised because its legalisation would be symbolic of a diminished respect for human life (this despite the fact that even some who are wedded to the idea of the sanctity of human life agree that *in extremis* life may not be worth living). Alternatively, it might be thought impossible to produce legislation that will contain sufficient safeguards against the possibility of abuse. Or, that even when it would be morally permissible to help someone to die, it still could not be a legitimate part of *medical practice* to help and so should not be afforded legislative protection. Those who hold such views often propose other options for public policy than legalisation, including: leaving the law as it is but encouraging public prosecutors to use their discretion as regards mounting a prosecution; leaving the law as it is but taking the motive of any person who assists in bringing about a death into account in sentencing; providing for a new offence of 'compassionate homicide' which would attract a much lighter sentence than a wrongful killing; and, re-drafting relevant laws to allow for a defence of compassionate motive against a charge of assisting a death.[24]

In practice, it has been rare for compassionate killers of the terminally ill (including the few who have acted without first seeking to obtain a competent request for assistance) to be visited with the full force of the law.[25] Sometimes defendants have been permitted to plead that they acted with diminished responsibility; often juries have been loath to find defendants guilty of any offence, and when they have it has been for manslaughter rather than murder; judges have typically refused to impose severe sentences unless required by mandatory sentencing provisions;[26] and governments

---

[24] Even some of those who are in no doubt about the moral permissibility of voluntary euthanasia, like James Rachels (1986: 182ff), have supported the idea of a special plea of compassionate killing. Rachels' proposal is criticised by Feinberg (1986: 347ff).

[25] Lanham (1993: 174).

[26] In *Gilbert v. State* [1986] 487 So.2d 1185, a minimum sentence of twenty-five years was imposed because the court was not permitted discretion in sentencing. In Chapter 11 I will discuss a recent Canadian case, *R v. Latimer* [2001] 1 S.C.R. 3, where the harsh sentence handed down led to the case becoming a *cause célèbre*.

have sometimes exercised clemency because of public outcry over punishment that is considered too harsh. Law reform commissions in various countries, including Canada[27] and Australia,[28] have investigated both the idea of a special category of offence and the idea of permitting a defence based on the existence of a motive of compassion. Neither proposal has been supported. The lack of support can be traced to a variety of reasons, which, as Lanham points out, have included 'the problem of abuse, difficulty in establishing motive, the problem of mixed motives and the incongruity if other motives, such as necessity, [are] not also recognised'.[29]

It is quite likely that those whose objection to the legalisation of voluntary medically assisted death is that it would result in a lowering of respect for human life would have no higher regard for the introduction of a special offence of compassionate killing. Hence, they would prefer to leave juries to probe the credibility of someone's claim to have acted out of compassion rather than allow for a specific defence based on compassionate motive, because a defendant whose motive is found to be genuine would then be spared the opprobrium that goes with being convicted of unlawful killing. (As noted in Chapter 1, the track record of juries is that they have been unwilling to convict doctors charged with compassionately ending the lives of their dying patients.)

An overarching concern about proposals for bypassing the legalisation of voluntary medically assisted dying, in favour of giving legal recognition to compassionate motive, is that they would leave anyone who assisted a death exposed to the risk of serious punishment (notwithstanding the history of leniency in these matters). Medical professionals, in particular, have reason to be concerned about this prospect since they stand not only to lose their careers, but their liberty, too, should a defence of compassionate motive fail to be accepted. Even though neither relied on a defence of compassionate motive, David Moor and Howard Martin spoke after their acquittals not just about the relief they felt on hearing the respective verdicts, but also about the toll on their lives. Moor, in fact, died in his early fifties shortly after his trial. It seems particularly invidious to expect medical professionals to put themselves at risk for assisting someone to die who wants to die but cannot do so unaided, when there is no such jeopardy attaching to their withdrawing or withholding life-prolonging medical treatment from those who request that they do so.

[27] Law Reform Commission of Canada (1983: 31).
[28] Victorian Law Reform Commission (1984: 24–29).   [29] Lanham (1993: 175).

Moreover, as Gerald Dworkin has pointed out,[30] if the key arguments that are advanced against the legalisation of physician-assisted suicide were effective against it, they would be equally effective against allowing competent patients to refuse life-prolonging medical treatment (which, as has already been noted, is widely endorsed as a means of ensuring that unwanted medical treatment, and, indeed, unwanted life, is not imposed on competent patients). He cites a number of the reasons that were canvassed by the New York State Task Force on Life and the Law, which recommended in 1994 against changing the state's laws prohibiting euthanasia and assisted suicide.[31] Among the reasons given, the following were the most important: that the state has an interest in preventing the error and abuse that would *inevitably* follow the legalisation of assisted death; that to overturn the existing laws – no matter what safeguards were subsequently put in place – would run counter to the state's responsibility to ensure that its laws do not endanger the lives of those vulnerable persons who would avail themselves of assisted death because they are depressed, or are being coerced, or are suffering pain that is amenable to treatment; that since laws which prohibit assisted death not only encourage the active care of the dying, but also protect the vulnerable (who might otherwise seek to die because of depression, or coercion, or the effects of treatable pain) and the incompetent against being killed, the state ought to continue to uphold those laws; that, given the escalating cost pressures of caring for the dying, if laws permitting assisted death were introduced the dying would be persuaded or coerced into being assisted to die rather than continue to receive care.

Crucially, however, as Dworkin highlights, each of these supposedly strong reasons for not legalising medically assisted death could equally be deployed to oppose the right of competent patients to refuse life-prolonging medical treatment when suffering terminal or incurable illnesses. But, since none of them shows that such a right should be set aside, there is no reason to count them as any more decisive in relation to the legalisation of assisted dying. This is a powerful reply. In response it might be said that historically a major reason why the law has excluded the consent of the victim as a justification for killing has been the difficulty of establishing the genuineness of the consent. However, this is unconvincing because establishing suitable procedures for ensuring the genuineness of consent to medically assisted

---

[30] Dworkin, *et al.* (1998: 66–70). Similar sentiments are expressed in Jackson (2004). For further discussion of public policy concerning medically assisted dying see Kamisar (1958); Rachels (1986); Feinberg (1986); Battin (1994d); Kuhse (1996); and Keown (2002).

[31] New York State Task Force on Life and the Law (1994).

death should be no harder than establishing procedures to ensure the competence of refusals of burdensome, or otherwise unwanted, medical treatment.

Since many of the same considerations that have been canvassed above are as central to the objections made against voluntary medically assisted death as they are to the debate about its legalisation, I will supplement my responses to them in subsequent chapters in an attempt to persuade those unconvinced by the preceding considerations. There is an additional point I want to add to my comments about public policy options, namely, that studies conducted in The Netherlands, which has had the most extensive experience in these matters, have made it clear that decisions to discontinue treating the dying (including the incompetent) far outnumber decisions to provide medically assisted death to those who competently request it.[32] Even if questions about the clarity of the distinction between deaths that have been competently requested, and those that have not, are set to one side, unless it can be shown that voluntary medically assisted death is significantly morally more objectionable than withholding or withdrawing life-prolonging medical care, it is quite unreasonable to deny legal protection to those who practise the former while affording it to the latter. The question of whether the former is significantly morally more objectionable will be answered in subsequent chapters.

In the next chapter I begin my replies to the important objections that have been raised against the legalisation of voluntary medically assisted death by arguing against those who claim that to continue the provision of life-prolonging medical treatment can never be futile.

---

[32] See, for example, van der Maas, et al. (1996) and Onwuteaka-Philipsen, et al. (2003). For comparable Australian findings see Kuhse, et al. (1997).

CHAPTER 3

Medical futility

Medical professionals sometimes appeal to the idea of its being *medically futile* to continue to offer life-sustaining treatment to certain patients. The idea is invoked in connection with permanent loss of consciousness by a patient, with permanent dependence on a life-support system, with permanent loss of consciousness *and* permanent dependence on a life-support system, as well as when death is held to be imminent. Staunch opponents of the legalisation of voluntary medically assisted death have been known to claim that life-sustaining medical care is never futile, but it is more common for them to contend that if, and when, further medical treatment becomes futile, physicians may only withdraw or withhold further life-sustaining care. I will argue that neither of these contentions need be accepted.

Since what it is for a medical treatment to be futile is contested my first task is to clarify the concept. I will begin by briefly referring to two significant legal cases in which medical futility was a key issue, albeit they had different outcomes. Those looking after Mrs Helga Wanglie in the Hennepin County Medical Centre in Minnesota in 1989 considered that to continue to provide her with life-sustaining treatment was medically futile. Her husband objected to the treatment being withdrawn.[1] As mentioned in Chapter 1, in 1992 the Airedale National Health Service Trust in the UK sought the discontinuation of all life-sustaining treatment for

---

[1] *In re Conservatorship of Wanglie* [1991] Minn. Dist. Ct., Prob. Div., No. PX-91-283. Mrs Wanglie was eighty-five years old when she fractured her hip. While recovering from the fracture she developed respiratory failure. After some months on the respirator she suffered a cardio-pulmonary arrest that caused a lack of oxygen to her brain and she entered into a persistent vegetative state. The attending staff eventually sought to have the respirator removed because it was no longer serving her medical interests. For further details of the case see Miles (1991a). It was Miles who petitioned the court for the removal of Mrs Wanglie's respirator. The legal situation in the US is, however, fluid. In *Gilgunn v. Massachusetts General Hospital* [1995] Mass. Sup. Ct., No. 92-4820, verdict 21, the prerogative of medical professionals to decline medical interventions they consider futile was upheld after the daughter of a comatose seventy-two year old complained about a DNR order for her mother on the ground that her mother would value continued life even in an impaired condition.

Anthony Bland – treatment to which the patient was unable to consent (because his injuries had led to him becoming incompetent).[2] When a competent patient is treated without having given his informed consent the treatment amounts to *medical trespass* except where it is a matter of *necessity*. In Bland's case necessity was ruled out – by reason of further treatment's being futile. Where a patient is *temporarily* incompetent (e.g. he is unconscious but will recover), or not likely to regain lost competence, or has never been competent,[3] consent does not have to be obtained. Nonetheless, it is customary, when a patient has not made an advance directive while competent, for there to be consultation with his family, friends or guardian in such cases. Bland had neither made an advance directive nor would he ever regain competence, and his family supported the discontinuation of treatment.

---

[2] *Airedale NHS Trust v. Bland* [1993] 1 All ER 821. The decision of the Law Lords that treatment could lawfully be discontinued was not welcomed by all. See, for example, Finnis (1993). There have been two controversial recent cases in which (unlike *Bland*) the families have opposed the discontinuation of life-sustaining treatment. In 2004, the parents of a brain-damaged child, Charlotte Wyatt, sought to challenge her medical team's view that further treatment would be futile. The original trial judge ordered that the medical team did not have to resuscitate, but on appeal (a year later) that order was lifted on the ground that the child's 'best interests' should be the final determinant of what was appropriate – see *Wyatt v. Portsmouth Hospitals NHS Trust* [2005] EWCA (Civ) 1181. In February 2006 Charlotte's condition deteriorated and the original trial judge ruled *inter alia* that 'the medical professionals should be free to refrain from intervention by way of intubation and resuscitation' because a treatment's being 'intolerable' to a child represents a valuable guide to her best interests. Even more recently, in *An NHS Trust v. MB and Anor* [2006] EWHC (Fam) 507, Justice Holman ruled that even though a court cannot countermand a doctor's considered judgment, MB's best interests would be served if his artificial ventilation were continued despite his treating doctors wishing to withdraw it on futility grounds. MB suffers from one of the severest forms of spinal muscular atrophy (SMA), a congenital condition resulting from a genetic abnormality that is degenerative and progressive. It affects the voluntary muscles (but not the involuntary ones like those of the heart). Since the affected muscles include the respiratory muscles, death is inevitable in the absence of artificial ventilation. In MB's case an invasive endotracheal tube had to be passed through his nostrils, down his windpipe and into his lungs. By contrast, Sir Mark Potter, in *Re K*, which was heard around the same time as that involving MB, made a declaration to enable medical staff to remove the feeding tube from an infant and only provide palliative care so as to allow her to die peacefully. Despite acknowledging certain parallels with MB's case he emphasised the singularity of each case. K suffered an inherited condition, congenital myotonic dystrophy, which causes chronic muscle weakness. She had to be mechanically ventilated and tube fed; suffered several life-threatening bouts of septicaemia; and was significantly intellectually disabled. See *Re K (A minor)* [2006] EWHC 1007 (Fam).

[3] In the UK, the enactment in 2005 of the *Mental Capacity Act* was intended to govern decision-making on behalf of those who have lost competence, or never had it. The Act is underpinned by five key principles. First, there is a presumption that every adult has the capacity to make his or her own decisions; second, individuals are to be given all practicable help to make their own decisions; third, an 'unwise' decision made by an individual does not on its own establish a lack of capacity; fourth, any decision on behalf of someone judged to lack capacity must be taken with a view to promoting or protecting his or her best interests; and, fifth, anything done on behalf of a person who lacks capacity should be done in such a way as to be least restrictive of his or her basic rights and freedoms. Some other jurisdictions have made similar legislative provision, while others rely on case law to the same effect.

Even though the same point may be variously expressed in different jurisdictions, the issue of whether health care providers are obliged to offer treatment which they judge to be futile (or even needlessly burdensome to a patient), has become both increasingly significant and disputed. It obviously bears on whether, and when, life-sustaining treatment may be withdrawn or withheld, but also on the rights of a patient (or his proxy decision-maker) to insist on treatment regardless of cost and of whether the insistence is realistic (though it is worth mentioning that these latter considerations can only provide *additional* reasons for not treating if the chief reason given is the futility of doing so[4]). For all its importance, medical futility is nonetheless a hotly contested and far from clear idea. I will consider a number of suggestions as to how it is best characterised. It will emerge that it has various distinct senses, and that these distinct senses have differing implications for medical and legal thinking about the care of the dying. I will argue that it remains useful when appropriately employed. Given its usefulness, it will sometimes be justifiable to appeal to it in connection with a request for medical assistance with dying.

I

Intuitively, medically futile treatments are incapable of achieving the purpose for which they are used, whether that is curative, restorative or palliative. But there are many critics who have complained about the inadequacy, as they see it, of this intuitive account.

A widely voiced objection to the intuitive account is that it does not distinguish between what is (quantitatively) *physiologically futile* and what is *qualitatively futile* and that some such distinction is needed if the idea of medical futility is to have a serious role. Lawrence Schneiderman, Nancy Jecker and Albert Jonsen[5] contended in an important paper that a proper understanding of medical futility has to be agent-benefit centred and so must take into account both quantitative and qualitative considerations. According to their original account, physicians should regard a treatment as futile on quantitative grounds when the chances of its benefiting the patient are less than one in a hundred (as shown by relevant empirical data), and futile on qualitative grounds when it fails to end total dependence on intensive medical care or merely preserves unconsciousness. Subsequently, they added that the empirical data must be used in harness with socially endorsed value judgments if physicians are to arrive at

---

[4] See Gampel (2006: 102f).   [5] Schneiderman, *et al.* (1990) and Schneiderman, *et al.* (1996).

appropriate quantitative assessments. Some of their critics[6] urged that because the idea of the medically futile is value-laden the only way it can be made clinically useful is to understand it in a value-free way, in particular as what is physiologically futile. For those of such a mind, a medical intervention is physiologically futile if it is incapable of achieving the physiological outcome desired by the patient (or, the patient's surrogate), no matter how many times it is repeated. The idea found favour with some professional bodies, for example the American Heart Association and the Council for Ethical and Judicial Affairs of the American Medical Association.[7]

Second, it has been contended that a treatment does not have to be *incapable* of serving its intended purpose to be futile; it is enough that it be *very unlikely* that it will do so. This criticism is often based on a belief that in clinical medicine nothing, strictly, is certain. Accordingly, the view has been advocated that, in a clinical setting, if a particular therapy or treatment has only a very low probability of success it is futile to employ it. But, as I will show, accounts of the medically futile that are grounded in statistically based (or probabilistic) analyses are open to serious objections.

Third, the intuitive account has been criticised for being of little value in the clinical setting because it allegedly lacks nuance. Its critics contend that, once this is acknowledged, the ambiguities in the idea that a treatment is medically futile detract from its operational usefulness.

I will consider these three criticisms consecutively, beginning with the claim that medical futility must be understood strictly in terms of the physiologically futile. It will be my contention that such accounts are indefensible: medical futility cannot be confined to the realm of the quantitative. First, whether a medical intervention is worthwhile is not to be judged merely by reference to a physiological outcome.[8] Benefit to the patient has to be taken into account, and, once it is, a medical intervention must, at least, be capable of producing an outcome acceptable to the patient if it is to avoid being futile. Once that is acknowledged it becomes untenable simply to cite the achievement of a particular physiological effect (e.g. the preservation of organ function) to rebut a charge of offering futile

---

[6] Truog, *et al.* (1992).
[7] See Emergency Cardiac Care Committee and Subcommittees of the American Heart Association (1992) and Council on Ethical and Judicial Affairs, American Medical Association (1999). The Council contends that decisions about medical futility are value-laden and hence that there can be no universal consensus about it. It therefore declines to define the concept and, instead, advocates a process, first, for determining instances in which futility is at issue and, second, for subsequent responses.
[8] Gampel (2006: 95).

treatment. Second, the idea of the physiologically futile is incapable of resolving the issue of whether health care professionals may override a patient's (or, a surrogate's) request for treatment to be continued in the event that the professionals consider the requested treatment inappropriate. Those who think a patient's remaining alive, albeit in a persistent vegetative state, is a beneficial outcome will, of course, reject any move to have treatment discontinued no matter that it is judged to be futile by medical personnel.

Even though the distinction between quantitative and qualitative aspects of futility has been widely supported, Baruch Brody and Amir Halevy[9] have shown that it is far too broad-brushed to be clinically helpful. Thus, for instance, they point out that it is necessary to refine the idea of the physiologically futile by reference to whether the desired physiological effect is unachievable because the patient's demise is imminent, or because the patient is suffering a condition that will prove lethal and any intervention will, therefore, have no bearing on the patient's life expectancy. They also show, by reference to their more fine-grained analysis of types of medical futility, that many of the accounts of medical futility put forward by professional medical organisations and legislators in seeking to clarify the ethical status of judgments of medical futility are seriously unclear and so of little practical use; in this vein they roundly criticise various proposed guidelines for cardio-pulmonary resuscitation (CPR).[10] I agree in large measure with their schema for understanding the different senses of medical futility, but there is at least one aspect of it that is open to criticism.

According to their schema, there are at least eight possible ways of understanding the idea of medical futility. Despite successfully showing that medical futility is much more complex than is often acknowledged, their introduction of various patient dependent senses of the term needlessly

---

[9] Brody and Halevy (1995). They argue that there are at least eight possible ways of characterising medical futility. With the first four, the relation between a medical intervention and its possible outcomes is key; with the second four, patient input is key. The eight categories are as follows: patient independent physiological futility; patient independent imminent demise futility; patient independent lethal condition futility; patient independent qualitative futility; patient dependent physiological futility; patient dependent imminent demise futility; patient dependent lethal condition futility; and, patient dependent qualitative futility. So, for example, an intervention will be an instance of patient independent imminent demise futility if the patient will die soon despite the intervention, and so forth. Whereas Brody and Halevy think medical futility is a complex, but still useful, notion, Wilson (1996) contends that the burden of proof should be on the physician to show that a judgment of medical futility signifies more than a disagreement about treatment goals or about whether further treatment will be hard to endure, and that having to bear this burden can prove an aid to communication with patients and their relatives.

[10] Brody and Halevy (1995: 134ff).

complicates matters. In consequence, several of the senses they identify should be jettisoned. Thus, for example, a patient dependent sense of physiological futility cannot resolve disputes about what is, or is not, medically futile. Moreover, neither a patient dependent sense of imminent demise futility nor a patient dependent sense of lethal condition futility is capable of being rendered operationally useful. Consider the former. Suppose a patient were to say that he would, for example, regard his death as imminent if it were to occur within a week, whereas his medical attendants consider imminence implies a different time frame. As Brody and Halevy acknowledge, a patient dependent imminent demise sense of medical futility would, in such a circumstance, be intelligible. But, in reality, patients rely overwhelmingly on their medical attendants for information on which they can base an informed judgment about the imminence of their death, so what reason could there be for medical attendants to defer to any judgment made independently by a patient about the imminence of his demise? This will be particularly clear if the patient's view about the likely time of his death is seriously inaccurate and he is resistant to attempts to correct his view.[11] There is surely no reason for attending medical staff to decide the appropriateness of continuing treatment by reference to his (seriously inaccurate) belief about how soon he will die. At best, his conviction might be construed as an expression of his belief that futility is a patient dependent qualitative matter. As such, it would have significance because among patient dependent futility judgments only the qualitative ones need be taken seriously. So, though I believe that Brody and Halevy have performed a great service in revealing the complexity of the idea of medical futility, their introduction of patient dependent understandings of medical futility that go beyond the qualitative only muddies the waters.

I now turn to the second objection to the intuitive idea that medically futile treatments are those that are incapable of achieving the purpose for which they are administered, namely, that because clinical conclusions lack certainty, talk of futile outcomes can amount to no more than talk of unlikely outcomes. Critics conclude that if the idea of something's being medically futile is to have a clinical role it must be understood probabilistically. The broader the statistical base for something's being judged medically futile, the less likely that a judgment reached by an individual physician acting unilaterally on the basis of her own clinical experience can be considered reliable. It will be advisable, therefore, for an individual medical professional to rely on statistically well-founded claims where

[11] See further Tomlinson and Brody (1990) and Daar (1993).

they are available, since the alternative would be for each clinician to rely on a very restricted range of clinical experiences, namely, her own and those of her close associates.[12] But, even though probabilistic accounts of medical futility (in particular, those having to do with patient independent physiological futility) have had their supporters,[13] they are open to serious objections.

First, the broader the statistical base that is utilised the more individual variations will have been ironed out in gathering the information used to form that base. Hence, it will always be the wiser course to be cautious about the application of such broadly based statistics to a particular case.

Second, problems can arise in connection with setting a threshold of probability. How low can the probability of success be set before a treatment is considered futile? As previously noted, a figure of one per cent has sometimes been advocated in clinical circles but such statistically based proposals necessarily rely on studies of numbers of patients from different circumstances and so cannot be guaranteed to apply in particular circumstances to any given individual. Thus, even if there is, say, less than a one per cent recovery rate overall from triple organ failure, the possibility cannot be ruled out that a particular patient will recover from such a failure, and, hence, that continuing to treat him should not be deemed medically futile.

Third, determining when a sufficient number of applications have been made of a life-prolonging treatment poses a problem for those wishing to rely on rates of successful application for the purpose of determining when they may give up. Even when a mode of treatment is thought to have a statistically well-founded likelihood of success, the question remains of how many attempted applications of the treatment should be made before it is appropriate to give up. Suppose, for instance, that CPR requires multiple attempts (as in fact it frequently does). How many failed attempts must there be before it is appropriate to conclude that it is futile to continue with CPR for a particular patient? The higher the number, the less likely that any reliance can be placed on the statistical evidence since, even with an oft employed strategy like CPR, it is unlikely that there will be enough supporting evidence available from studies involving high numbers of applications of CPR. (It is worth bearing in mind that, unlike the situation with CPR, there is a dearth of reliable data for many medical interventions. So, if the case for CPR is unsupported, the same

[12] See, for example, Griener (1995: 210f).   [13] Cf. Schneiderman, *et al.* (1990).

will certainly be true for other forms of life-sustaining treatment like che-motherapy and radiotherapy for patients with various forms of cancer. The more untried and experimental a form of treatment, the less reliable information about its efficacy will be, and the more reasonable a patient's insistence that the treatment should be given a go rather than deemed futile.)

Fourth, there is a question about what is to count as a successful outcome. Requiring that a patient be able to be discharged after a course of treatment produces a very different picture compared with requiring that a patient survive the treatment, spend a considerable time in hospital, but die without ever being discharged. There is no need to labour the point further: statistically based accounts of medical futility and, in particular, of patient independent physiological futility – the account of medical futility most favoured among clinicians and their professional bodies – are seriously problematic. But that does not show that the intuitive account should be rejected.

The third objection to the intuitive account of medical futility was that once the various meanings of medical futility have been disambiguated the idea proves to be of little use clinically. Consider again the idea of (patient independent) physiological futility. Brody and Halevy show by reference to examples provided by the American Heart Association, the American College of Physicians, and the American Medical Association, that the evi-dence needed to establish that particular life-sustaining interventions are physiologically futile is very difficult to come by, and that such evidence as there is lacks the required precision.[14] However, in many instances where further medical treatment appears futile, strictly this will not be because the treatment is physiologically futile, but because the demise of the patient is so imminent. In such a circumstance a judgment by a clinician that a form of treatment is physiologically futile will not be the decisive consideration.

Should our understanding of medical futility, then, be based on the imminent demise of the patient? There are at least three reasons against an affirmative answer. First, if a patient makes a judgment about what

---

[14] Brody and Halevy (1995: 134–137). They cite the American Heart Association's suggestion that for patients for whom 'no physiological benefit from BLS [basic life support] and ALS [advanced life support] can be expected', CPR is not recommended, because it will not restore circulation where a patient has suffered a cardiac arrest despite optimal treatment for progressive septic or cardiogenic shock. As they point out, this recommendation cannot properly be made unless it is known (or, believed to be highly probable), *in advance*, that in such cases circulation cannot be restored. But such knowledge (or, belief) would require supporting evidence, and the American Heart Association fails to provide any.

amounts to imminent death *without regard to the advice of his medical attendants* there is an immediate problem with taking the patient's judgment as the measuring stick, because he (or, his surrogate) may insist on continued treatment (as in *Wanglie*). Second, if the measuring stick is one that is independent of the judgment of the affected patient, any attempt to extrapolate from statistical data to a conclusion that the particular patient's demise is imminent will be problematic.[15] Third, in countries where the citizens believe (as, in the West, they have been encouraged to believe) in the capacity of modern technological medicine to prolong lives, it is hard to sell the idea that death will continue to be imminent for some patients regardless of medical intervention. This is particularly the case when the efficacy of emergent technologies is played up by, for example, the pharmaceutical industry or by clinical bodies that rely on receiving ongoing research grants.

A similar point can be made in relation to any understanding of medical futility that is couched in terms of the futility of treating patients with underlying lethal conditions, even ignoring that a criterion of lethal condition futility can be no more reliable than the advice given to patients about their life expectancies. There is no need to dwell for long on the point to see the potential for dispute if a doctor claims that it would be futile to offer life-prolonging or life-sustaining treatment to a patient with a lethal condition despite life expectancy being uncertain. Such a patient might still have available a period of life that he would regard as worth living. Consider, for example, someone suffering from a cancer that has metastasised, who would nevertheless be able to enjoy whatever life remains available to him once discharged from hospital.[16]

Finally, what about the idea of understanding the medically futile as the qualitatively futile? Brody and Halevy[17] urge that even in the case of patients in persistent vegetative states it is not possible to be definitive as to whether a particular treatment, say, CPR, will be medically futile. They hold that claims to the contrary face a dilemma that cannot be evaded: *either* we cannot be confident that any individual in (what is believed to be) a persistent vegetative state will remain in such a state (since studies reveal a number of such persons regain consciousness),[18] *or*, if we wait until there is virtual certainty that a patient will not regain

---

[15] Brody and Halevy (1995: 138–139).   [16] Brody and Halevy (1995: 139f).
[17] Brody and Halevy (1995: 140ff).
[18] See, for example, the evidence gathered by Cohen-Almagor (2001: 42–51).

consciousness (e.g. we wait several years, as Cohen-Almagor (2001) advocates), the number of patients who then remain alive but in a permanent vegetative state will be so small that no statistically reliable conclusion will be able to be drawn about the qualitative futility of continued treatment. So, any hope of evading the dilemma will have to be based on escaping the second horn. But, as *Wanglie* shows, a sufficiently determined relative may refuse to accept that it is futile to prolong the life of a patient who has been in a vegetative state for several years, and base the refusal on a qualitative judgment that reflects the patient's values and priorities. Should that happen, even the second horn of the dilemma will not be evadable.

The preceding discussion of objections to the intuitive idea of medical futility leads to the conclusion that not one of the proposed replacements offers an adequate basis for the unilateral withdrawal or withholding of life-sustaining medical treatment, or a ground on which a request may be made for medically assisted death. Nonetheless, it is too soon to dismiss the idea of medical futility. For all that it is both contested and ambiguous, the idea has had a significant role in both clinical and legal thought concerning the care of the dying. It seems unduly sceptical, therefore, to deny it a continuing role in clinical assessments or in the determination of appropriate moral and legal responses. Moreover, the absence of a single, agreed analysis of the idea of medical futility may not, in reality, pose insuperable operational difficulties. It may, for instance, be possible to render operational a disjunctive account of medical futility with one sense being appropriate on a particular occasion and another on a different one. In the next section I will show how providing opportunity for medical staff to discuss with patients, or their surrogates, whether further treatment would be futile has the potential to result in greater clarity about just which sense of futility is being claimed in any particular case. If that can be achieved it should be possible, at least, to reduce the number of seemingly irresolvable disputes about futility (which necessitate action in the courts, or in specially established tribunals in those jurisdictions where matters are decided more informally[19]). Furthermore, it should enable competent dying persons to make more considered assessments of how they wish their deaths to be managed.

---

[19] In the State of Victoria, Australia, for example, there is no case law relating to these matters. At least part of the explanation is that cases involving those who are deemed not to be competent come under the guardianship arrangements established by the legislature. The Office of the Public Advocate is charged with conciliating and, if that fails, arbitrating any such cases.

II

Even though there is no single, agreed analysis of medical futility, the idea may still be a guide to competent dying persons making decisions about abatement of treatment. This will be so irrespective of whether medically assisted dying is sought. Suppose the issue of withholding or withdrawing treatment on grounds of futility is raised. Discussion ought then to follow between the attending medical team and the patient (or, proxy) about the appropriateness of withholding or withdrawing treatment.[20] It is the responsibility of the medical team to reach a view about the medical appropriateness of initiation, or continuation, of a particular form of treatment and to inform the patient. It is the patient's responsibility to consider that information. Though it is a key obligation for doctors to provide appropriate care, they are not obliged to provide care they judge medically inappropriate. Hence, any decision on their part to initiate or continue treatment has to be made in the belief that it is appropriate.[21]

Where the medical team think further treatment inappropriate they must explain to the patient (or, the patient's surrogate) in an intelligible way their belief that treatment should be abated. The team need to be clear about the status of their clinical judgments, and about the sense in which further treatment would be futile. The patient (or, proxy), equally, has to be clear about why he rejects the judgment that further treatment would be futile, and has to be clear about what it is that he wants done. It may be said that if patient autonomy is to be taken seriously this entails that the patient's judgment must prevail.[22] Since my support for the autonomy of competent patients is made clear throughout this book, I need to respond lest it seem that I think doctors must forego their professional autonomy if there is any dispute about the futility of further treatment. Later, in Chapter 7, I will show how the use of referrals and transfers can solve some of the problems these matters pose for the integrity of medical professionals, but for now I will highlight two further considerations.

First, in practice, there are very few instances in which even though doctors are adamant that further treatment would be futile, and thus

---

[20] For a discussion of how such a strategy can work in practice see Wear and Logue (1995).

[21] In the event that a proxy wishes to insist on continued treatment, but there is evidence that the patient, when competent, expressed a clear preference for treatment to be discontinued in the prevailing circumstances, the patient's earlier autonomous preference should be considered authoritative. This takes the matter out of the realm of judgments about medical futility – see Chapter 9 below on 'Advance Directives'.

[22] Cf. Gampel (2006: 102). But see Skene (2006).

medically inappropriate, patients (or, surrogates) insist on further treatment, with the result that no resolution is achievable.[23] The ones that have reached the courts are not *causes célèbres* for nothing.

Second, it would be needlessly defeatist to think that dispute resolution procedures cannot be invoked to handle such disputes *or* resolve them. Mostly it will be possible to use the opportunity such procedures provide to air views and to reach agreement about how to proceed. For example, in some instances it will be possible to agree on a time limit for continued treatment in order to determine beyond any reasonable doubt whether continuing to treat will be futile. In others it may be possible to reach agreement that while further treatment would be futile, treatment should be continued to allow the patient time to settle important matters prior to death, or to permit distant relatives to visit him before death, or to give time to his family to come to terms with the imminent demise of their loved one. Suppose, though, that agreement cannot be reached. If death does not bring a resolution, the medical team may sometimes opt not to push the issue of the futility of further treatment with the patient (or, his proxy), because of the risk that the disagreement will end up in court. At other times, the issue may be seen as crucial to how the medical staff understand their implicit duty not to act in ways they consider futile.[24] That may lead to a referral or transfer of the patient (which, as indicated, I will consider in detail in Chapter 7), but it may also raise issues about the efficient use of scarce medical resources. I will not consider the former suggestion further here, but I do need to say something briefly about the latter.

Much modern medical practice is based on a presumption that resources are available to carry out whatever the attending practitioner decides is necessary. For this reason many medical practitioners are loath to accept that it is any part of their task as a professional to ration beneficial medical treatments, which results in clinical decisions being made *in isolation* from any concern about their likely impact on the allocation of medical resources elsewhere in the health care system. Nonetheless, it would obviously be glib to suggest that resources are available regardless of the wealth or other circumstances of patients. Even in the United States where health care expenditure is proportionately greater than in other developed nations, many are denied access to basic health care, let alone the best available health care. I only wish to make the point that

---

[23] See, for example, the study undertaken by Curtis, *et al.* (1995). For a British study see Way, *et al.* (2002). For a discussion of how the law can help see Fine and Mayo (2003).
[24] Cf. Miles (1992: 311f).

many health care practitioners focus on the patient in their immediate care to the exclusion of other considerations. This professional stance is unsustainable because, at least as far as opportunity costs are concerned, health care resources are scarce even in the wealthiest nations. When resources are scarce, to waste them, or to allocate them inefficiently, is surely morally objectionable. Should a clinician judge that continuing treatment in a particular case would be futile, say, because it would involve patient independent physiological futility, she has a moral responsibility to take this into account in raising the issue of the justifiability of further treatment with the patient (or, the patient's proxy). The devotion of scarce resources to a patient whose circumstances do not warrant them renders them unavailable to others whose circumstances do warrant them.

It would, however, be a mistake to think that this shows that resource considerations ultimately drive decisions about futility. The matters are quite distinct and should be kept that way. It is clearly open to a clinician to judge that giving further treatment to a particular patient would be futile (on grounds, say, of patient independent physiological futility), *and* for her to believe that it would be an unjustifiable waste of resources to provide such treatment, without her having to appeal to the latter consideration to justify the futility judgment. The issue of how best to allocate scarce medical resources is properly a matter of what would constitute the most beneficial use of the available resources given that it is not possible to treat all those who could benefit from them.[25] Considerations of futility are, and need to be kept, independent from considerations of resource allocation.

Of course, a patient (or, his proxy) may still insist that treatment be continued.[26] In that event the issue will have to be resolved by one of the parties giving way (as discussed above), or, failing that, the matter will have to be taken to the courts to resolve the disagreement over the futility of continuing treatment. Since there have been quite a few cases to do with medical futility that have ended up in the courts, I will now look at how the courts have handled them.

---

[25] Cf. Hope, *et al.* (1993) and Gampel (2006: 102f).

[26] As happened recently in the widely publicised British case of Jaymee Bowen, who had had non-Hodgkin's lymphoma when she was six, and was subsequently diagnosed at age nine with acute myeloid leukaemia. She was given a bone marrow transplant and chemotherapy. Within nine months she relapsed and her paediatricians recommended that she be given only palliative care during the remaining weeks they estimated she would live. Her father refused to accept this advice and eventually asked the Cambridge and Huntingdon Health Authority to fund further treatment. The Health Authority refused. The Court of Appeal upheld the Health Authority's right to refuse to fund further treatment that it considered futile. See *R v. Cambridge Health Authority, ex parte B* [1995] 2 All ER 129 (CA).

III

In relation to Anthony Bland, Lord Goff said that 'it is the futility of [Bland's] treatment which justifies its termination'.[27] In attempting to elucidate when treatment may justifiably be considered futile and, hence, abated, the Law Lords focused on the idea of 'necessity'. Since Bland was no longer competent it was ruled that his care was to be guided by his best interests.[28] Once Bland entered a persistent vegetative state (his cerebral cortex having liquefied), any hope of recovery was lost, and the Law Lords were able to hold that there could be no justification for the further use of invasive medical treatments: it was not in his best interests to be given unnecessary treatment. In the United States, too, courts have held that in the absence of an expression by the patient (while competent) of a view about the continuation of life support, such support may be discontinued if further treatment is considered futile by those in charge of the patient's care. Thus, in re Fiori,[29] Mr Fiori's mother was permitted to authorise the withdrawal of his gastrostomy feeding tube. Mr Fiori, who had been in a vegetative state for fifteen years, was being fed by tube, but was not being ventilated.

So, at least in those jurisdictions (and, almost certainly, in others, too), it is clear that there is no obstacle in principle to withholding or withdrawing life-sustaining treatment if further medical treatment is agreed to be futile. There have, of course, been cases, like that of Helga Wanglie, where the courts have sided with patients (or, their proxies) against medical professionals who judged further treatment to be futile. Typically, in those cases, the medical professionals have been allowed to transfer the patient to the care of other willing and available professionals.

Despite the fact that the idea of medical futility could not settle the dispute in *Wanglie*, I believe it has an important role in clinical assessment. The fact that the courts have been prepared to allow a role for the idea of medical futility, even without an agreed analysis, lends some strength to this position. Those who insist that, in the absence of an absolutely certain diagnosis and prognosis, all stops must be pulled out to keep patients alive (lest the clinician's values prevail), and those who insist that, in the absence of a socially unanimous view on the allocation of scarce medical resources, medical professionals must make resources available to all who request

---

[27] [1993] 1 All ER 821 at 870.
[28] Mason, *et al.* (2002: 403ff) challenge the validity of relying on a best interests test and advocate a substituted judgment test.
[29] [1995] 652 A 2d 1350 Pa.

them, will, no doubt, be unpersuaded. But neither of these standpoints is plausible, so to adopt either of them will be no service to those dying patients for whom nothing further can be done to provide them with either a quantitative or qualitative medical benefit.

Since the extreme view that continuing with medical treatment can never be futile lacks credibility, the wiser course is to proceed on the basis that it is sometimes futile. For those persons for whom any further medical treatment would be futile, and whose deaths would follow straightforwardly from its discontinuation, it may be relatively easy to achieve an acceptable death. However, for those for whom the discontinuation of futile treatment would not produce that result but would, instead, unacceptably prolong their dying, it remains to be established whether the legalisation of voluntary medically assisted death offers the hope of avoiding a fate some of them consider worse than death.

CHAPTER 4

Physician-assisted suicide

Even if physician-assisted suicide has certain advantages over active voluntary euthanasia (and, in some instances, over passive voluntary euthanasia), it has been a specific target for some opponents of medically assisted death.[1] This chapter will be devoted to consideration of the reasons for their opposition. In subsequent chapters I will consider objections that have been levelled against voluntary medically assisted death more generally.

Among the more important concerns specifically raised about physician-assisted suicide are the following: whether it is appropriate to place potentially lethal doses of barbiturates, opioids, and other medications in the hands of the terminally ill; whether medical practitioners may with propriety agree not to play a supervising role at the time when a patient chooses to take a lethal dose of such drugs; whether physician-assisted suicide is of any use to sufferers from severely disabling conditions like multiple sclerosis or motor neurone disease (who would be unable to suicide in the way envisaged in physician-assisted suicide); whether (as opponents of physician-assisted suicide claim) there are available equally efficacious but less contentious strategies – like the refusal of food and fluids – which would enable competent terminally ill persons to end their lives; whether legalising physician-assisted suicide would pose any serious risks to others, especially those who constitute the more vulnerable members of society; and, whether requests for assistance with dying made in advance of the onset of incompetence by, for example, victims of Alzheimer's disease, may legitimately be honoured through physician-assisted suicide.

I will consider these issues consecutively in the following sections.

---

[1] For a collection of essays critical of physician-assisted suicide see Foley and Hendin (2002).

I

The first two questions raised above are best taken together. Under, for example, Oregon's *Death With Dignity Act* a competent terminally ill patient may request that medication be prescribed to enable him to end his life in a 'humane and dignified manner'. Like other similar instruments it permits competent terminally ill persons to determine the manner and time of their death by enabling them to obtain the means to end their lives (typically via the use of lethal prescription drugs like barbiturates). The distinguishing feature of physician-assisted suicide is that the drugs are to be self-administered. This enables medical practitioners to distance themselves from the action and be legally protected against prosecution for assisting a suicide (a criminal offence in many jurisdictions). The self-administration can be mechanically assisted (as with some of Kevorkian's early cases in Michigan), computer assisted (as with Nitschke's patients in the Northern Territory of Australia during the operation of the Territory's *Rights of the Terminally Ill Act*), or manual. Which of those forms self-administration takes is, however, mere detail. For our purposes, the more important concern is whether serious risks are introduced by distancing the medical practitioner from the proximate cause of the patient's death.

Perhaps what critics of the idea of providing dying patients with lethal doses of drugs fear most is that the drugs may be used to kill others, not the person who has procured them. This certainly seemed to be a relevant consideration when the idea of establishing a suicide clinic was proposed in Switzerland a decade or so ago, despite it having been legally permissible in Switzerland for many years for assistance with suicide to be rendered not only by those with medical qualifications but also by those who lack them, as long as they do so for humane reasons and do not stand to gain personally from the death. The proposed suicide clinic was to be a venue for persons who would: attend the clinic; be given sufficient lethal drugs to bring about their own deaths; and, self-administer them away from the clinic. The total lack of supervision over the use of the lethal drugs that this would have involved brought howls of protest because of the risk that the drugs might be used for some other purpose than to facilitate the client's suicide. Even allowing for the fact that those envisaged as legitimately able to obtain a lethal dose of drugs for the purposes of suicide were not likely to wish to use the drugs for any other purpose, the risks of nefarious misuse by others, or of accidental misuse, or even of the drugs being inappropriately used for suicidal purposes by someone else, were deemed to be too serious for the proposed clinic to be countenanced.

Since society has to ensure that the security of lethal drugs is not compromised, the legalisation of physician-assisted suicide requires facing squarely the desire of some medical practitioners to take an arms-length approach to patient suicide. It might seem obvious that the way to avoid any such compromise would be to insist that medical practitioners supervise the administration of lethal drugs that they have prescribed for their dying patients. But this is not at all obvious. Medical practitioners cannot always be available to supervise the taking of lethal drugs by their patients. Moreover, patients can stockpile drugs, even at the cost of enduring greater suffering because they aren't taking drugs prescribed for pain relief or to help with sleep. There is no way a medical practitioner could guard against such a practice if a patient were sufficiently determined. (This would be so even for a patient who is hospitalised but not subject to an around-the-clock watch.) Consider a case like that of Diane's, as reported by Timothy Quill.[2] Quill was aware that Diane, who was dying of leukaemia, was saving up some of the barbiturates he had prescribed for her – ostensibly to help her sleep but, in fact, in the knowledge that she was preparing to suicide – but he did not find out until two days after her death that she had chosen her moment. (In the circumstance that Quill was confronted with, namely, the illegality of physician-assisted suicide, he felt obliged to give Diane a wide berth because of the legal risks to which he would otherwise have been exposed. He subsequently acknowledged the regret he felt about having to adopt that strategy.)

Despite its being impractical for medical practitioners who prescribe potentially lethal drugs to dying patients to closely supervise the use of those drugs, and despite the low risk of nefarious or accidental misuse, or other inappropriate use of such drugs, it is incumbent on those prescribing lethal drugs to educate their patients about the risks associated with drug misuse. The situation is precisely like that concerning other potentially lethal items that may be in private hands (for instance, poisons and firearms). In many jurisdictions, records are kept, or registrations required, because of the risks of misuse. No one should believe, though, that it is possible to eliminate the risks entirely. The risks of misuse are almost certainly going to be much lower for lethal drugs prescribed for terminally ill patients; but risks will remain and so efforts need to be made to minimise those risks.

There is a second and quite separate issue raised by allowing dying patients to commit suicide with drugs in a medically unsupervised setting. In such a setting things may not go to plan. A suicide attempt may be botched and

---

[2] Quill (1991).

cause distress to those who find, or care about, the would-be suicide. This possibility is far more likely to eventuate, it seems to me, than are the ones previously mentioned (of nefarious or accidental misuse of prescription drugs). It is a sufficiently serious possibility that medical practitioners would be well advised to endeavour to be present, or be contactable, when their patients attempt (physician-assisted) suicide.[3] This advice is, however, subject to at least one exception. Even where physician-assisted suicide is legal it is likely that at least some dying individuals will crave privacy on the occasion of their death, and so not want their physicians to be present. If the autonomy of dying patients is to be respected this will have implications both for their privacy and for societal qualms about allowing lethal drugs to be used in an unsupervised setting. So, on occasion, these qualms may need to be set aside. Accordingly, in those instances where a dying patient who seeks physician-assisted suicide determines that he does not wish his physician to be present, she should abide by his decision. Where a patient prefers his physician not to be present, but is willing to inform her about when he will take the lethal dose, she should, where possible, be available to attend the patient in the event that things do not go to plan.

Finally, it needs reiterating that it is at present possible in only a few jurisdictions for the dying to obtain physician assistance with suicide. In the climate prevailing in the great majority of jurisdictions, a physician who thinks it medically appropriate to offer assistance with suicide will need to take account of the legal risks such a course of action involves and the wisdom of being present at the death. Even so, in circumstances like these, a physician will still have a responsibility to counsel her patient about the nature of the drugs; to give clear directions about dosages; to ensure that there is an adequate supply of the drugs; to explain what should be done if things do not go to plan; and, to be available, in the event that they do not, so as to minimise any ill effects for the would-be suicide or his carers.

II

The availability of a supervisory or, at the very least, supportive doctor is clearly of great importance to patients contemplating physician-assisted

---

[3] One study has indicated that doctors in The Netherlands have sometimes had to deal with failures to accomplish physician-assisted suicide by way of the subsequent administration of lethal injections. See Groenewoud, *et al.* (2000). Roger Magnusson (2002: ch. 10) has documented instances of botched attempts that have occurred in the surreptitious practice of voluntary assisted death in AIDS-affected communities in the United States and Australia.

suicide who would find it physically very difficult, or impossible, to bring about their own death unaided. Thus, sufferers from, for example, motor neurone disease, multiple sclerosis, and progressive supranuclear palsy,[4] strictly, are not dying even when they reach the later, distressing stages in their illness. In the event that such a sufferer does not want to bring about his own death before reaching such a stage, he will lose both the opportunity and the capacity to end his own life. He will, therefore, be differently placed from someone who is on a life-support system and only needs to have it turned off to achieve a speedy death. Moreover, precluding physician-assisted suicide means that the only accessible form of medically assisted death is active voluntary euthanasia.[5] However, it is sometimes said that victims of conditions like those mentioned above are still able to bring about death by refusing food and fluids.[6] Whether refusal of sustenance should be classified as an act of suicide, rather than a rejection of disproportionately burdensome treatment, need not be resolved here (though it is of significance for those who think suicide immoral).[7] Although I will mention one study shortly which reported some 'bad' deaths, the evidence more generally is that patients who refuse food and fluids typically die from electrolyte imbalance and do not suffer. This does not gainsay the fact that it may still be very hard psychologically for patients to undertake to die in such a manner. For this reason, among others, some medical supporters of the idea have advocated that patients who opt to end their lives in this way should be placed in a state of pharmacological oblivion via 'terminal sedation' (which is usually achieved by administering benzodiazepines, or benzodiazepines coupled with morphine).[8]

Some who advocate the strategy of patient refusal of food and fluids believe it represents a socially less risky way of helping dying patients obtain a relatively easy death, despite their thinking physician-assisted suicide is morally acceptable.[9] I will focus on the position of Bernard Gert, Charles Culver and K. Danner Clouser, who consider

---

[4] Progressive supranuclear palsy destroys nerve cells in the parts of the brain that control eye movements, breathing and muscle coordination. The loss of nerve cells causes palsy, or paralysis, that slowly gets worse as the disease progresses.

[5] This was true for at least one of Jack Kevorkian's patients, a man named Youk, who was suffering from motor neurone disease, and so was unable to perform the simple action needed to trigger the delivery of the lethal substance Kevorkian had provided. Kevorkian performed the action for him.

[6] As was advocated, for example, by Dick Sobsey, an opponent of physician-assisted suicide, in his submission to the Special Senate Committee on Euthanasia and Assisted Suicide (Canada).

[7] For a discussion of this issue see Jansen (2004: 63f).

[8] Quill and Byock (2000). For a contrasting view see Hallenbeck (2000).

[9] See, for instance, Bernat, et al. (1993); Teichman (1996: 69); Quill, Lo and Brock (1997); and Miller and Meier (1998).

physician-assisted suicide to be morally preferable to active voluntary euthanasia because the former, unlike the latter, does not require the physician to
kill, but who, nonetheless, advocate withholding nutrition and hydration as
a preferable way of meeting a dying patient's request. They do so because
this avoids 'the serious societal risks of legalising physician-assisted
suicide' without inflicting pain on the patient (at least, if there is appropriate palliative care or pharmacological support); produces a relatively quick
death in that unconsciousness occurs in about a week, and death in
about two weeks; and, allows patients to change their minds prior to slip-
ping into unconsciousness.[10] Thus, they conclude, if the goal is to allow a
patient to choose a relatively painless death at a time of his own choosing,
without giving rise to societal risks, physician-assisted suicide (to say nothing
of voluntary euthanasia) should remain illegal.

For present purposes, I will not question the background assumption
made by Gert, Culver and Clouser that both passive voluntary euthanasia
(withholding or withdrawal of life-sustaining treatment on the request of
a competent patient), and their own preferred strategy of patients refusing
food and fluids, are morally distinct from suicide (and, hence, from
physician-assisted suicide). Instead, I wish to comment on their attitude
to the extra week or two of existence that their preferred strategy would
require dying patients to undergo.[11] Obviously, if a patient is comfortable
with the strategy these authors propose no further comment is necessary.
However, not every patient will prefer to undergo an extra week or two
of what is, from his point of view, pointless existence. Death, for such a
patient, is not 'relatively quick'. Worse still, he is denied his autonomous
preference and made to bear a cost he does not wish to bear to enable
society to avoid legalising physician-assisted suicide. Granted that the legalisation of physician-assisted suicide would require the establishment of procedural safeguards, the suggestion by Gert, Culver and Clouser that their
strategy should be adopted because we do not live in an ideal world,
wherein patients might be safely entrusted with the means to take their
own lives, simply assumes that the unfair burden that would thereby be
imposed on dying patients would be outweighed by lowering the risk of
misuse of lethal medical means.

[10] Gert, *et al.* (1997); and Gert, *et al.* (1998).
[11] There have been few published studies of the impact of hastening death by voluntary refusal of food
and fluids but one study of hospice patients in Oregon offers a comparison between such a strategy
and that of physician-assisted suicide. The researchers reported that most deaths by the former means
were peaceful but that there was a significant minority for whom death was described by carers as
'bad'. See Ganzini, *et al.* (2003b) and Jacobs (2003). Data is also sparse for The Netherlands, but
see Rietjens, *et al.* (2004). For a personal perspective (based on his father's death) see Quill (2004).

If there is an obligation to respect competent and uncoerced refusals of life-prolonging treatment, as Gert, Culver and Clouser, along with many others, contend, why is there not also an obligation to respect competent and uncoerced requests for assistance with dying? From the perspective of the autonomous patient they appear exactly parallel. Perhaps those who wish to endorse competent patients being permitted to refuse food and fluids, but not to request medical assistance with dying, believe that a refusal has the advantage over a request from a medical professional's perspective. However, many opponents of the legalisation of medically assisted death seem to believe that the advantage stems from the fact that the risk of harm to *persons other than those competent dying patients who choose physician-assisted suicide or active voluntary euthanasia* will be higher if society honours their requests for such assistance than if it merely honours their refusals of further medical care. In the next section I will argue that safe-guards can be erected against this alleged risk, and that erecting them would both respect the autonomous choices of competent dying persons to be helped to die, and remove a burden they ought not to have to endure.

III

In Chapter 1, I referred to a striking Canadian case (*Rodriguez v. British Columbia (Attorney General)*), in which Sue Rodriguez, who suffered from motor neurone disease, argued that not only did the prohibition in Canada of physician-assisted suicide deny her liberty interest in committing suicide, it also discriminated against her on the basis of her disabilities.[12] Her argument was that persons who are unable to end their lives without assistance are subject to discrimination when assisted suicide is prohibited because they do not have the option available to able-bodied persons of choosing suicide. Rodriguez was joined in her argument by the largest disability advocacy group in Canada (the Coalition of Provincial Organiz-ations of the Handicapped (COPOH)). By contrast, in the US case of *Vacco et al. v. Quill et al.*, also mentioned previously, another disability advocacy group (Not Dead Yet (NDY)) argued the paternalistic position that to legalise physician-assisted suicide would expose people with disabilities to abuses resulting in wrongful deaths.

These seemingly differing approaches by the two disability advocacy groups turn out, on closer inspection, to be a function of the fact that

---

[12] For more details of the case and the subsequent appeal see Somerville (1994); Weinrib (1994); and Otlowski (1997: 86–94).

COPOH recognised that Sue Rodriguez was clearly autonomous. Hence, it accepted that she was as competent a chooser as an able-bodied person. Nonetheless, like NDY, it considered many disabled people to be vulnerable to having decisions forced upon them or to becoming the victims of socially oppressive attitudes and thus unlikely to be able to exercise autonomy.[13] Their attitude highlights two questions that require consideration. First, is there reason to think that the disabled would be coerced into opting for physician-assisted suicide if it were legally available? Second, is there reason to think the disabled would choose physician-assisted suicide because they have internalised socially oppressive attitudes toward them? An alternative way to think about these matters is to ask whether Rodriguez was so exceptional among the disabled that, as some have claimed, the law and relevant social policy ought not to be framed with her, or her like, in mind.

I am not persuaded that Sue Rodriguez was exceptional. Nor do I think that others like her should have their autonomous decisions disregarded (an experience demeaning in itself). Even if both beliefs are sound, it remains open to dispute as to whether it is possible to ensure that disabled persons who lack autonomy, for either of the reasons mentioned above, should be denied access to physician-assisted suicide. There is also likely to be lingering dispute about whether honouring a decision like the one made by Ms Rodriguez will inexorably impose on other, vulnerable disabled persons the burden of feeling they have to follow suit. I will consider these two disputed points consecutively.

The suggestion that it is impossible simultaneously to protect the vulnerable among the disabled *and* respect the decisions of competent disabled persons should be rejected. Those who lack competence to choose physician-assisted suicide – whether able or disabled – should not be permitted to avail themselves of such assistance. The way to avoid premature deaths among those who seek physician assistance with dying because of choices they have made under duress, or because they have internalised oppressive social attitudes, is to insist that decisions to seek physician assistance with dying must be free, informed and uncoerced. Such legislation as there is in this respect is quite demanding. Oregon's *Death With Dignity Act* is representative. For example, it incorporates stringent requirements for: satisfaction of a residency test; independent confirmation of diagnosis and prognosis; requests for assistance to be repeated on separate occasions to ensure that they are informed and voluntary; a waiting period between

---

[13] Bickenbach (1998: 130) and Mayo and Gunderson (2002).

the making of requests and the provision of assistance with dying to ensure that requests are enduring; psychiatric evaluations when there is any uncertainty about patient competence. Nonetheless, as David Mayo and Martin Gunderson point out,[14] some disability advocacy groups still insist (despite the evidence to the contrary) that it is impossible to put safeguards in place to ensure that the disabled are not coerced into making decisions, or into making decisions that result directly from their oppressive circumstances. Taken at face value this suggests that the interests of the disabled would be best served by society having a policy of maintaining the lives of the disabled for as long as it is possible to do so (regardless of the views of any particular disabled individual). Any such policy would, of course, be at odds with the efforts of disability advocacy groups to have the disabled considered on a par with the able-bodied as regards their independence and autonomy (a point not lost on COPOH when it supported Sue Rodriguez).

I turn now to the second issue in dispute, namely, the issue of whether there is a slippery slope of the sort alleged by opponents of physician-assisted suicide, one which begins with upholding the autonomy of those unable directly to end their own lives without assistance because of physical disability, and ends with the killing of those whose lives are judged by others not to be worth living (that is, ends in non-voluntary euthanasia). In the following paragraphs I will discuss the specific allegation that legalising physician-assisted suicide would have disastrous unintended consequences for the vulnerable (like the disabled). Later, in Chapter 10, I will discuss slippery slope arguments in greater detail because the claim that the legalisation of voluntary medically assisted death will lead down a slippery slope to the approval of non-voluntary euthanasia has been a common refrain of critics of the legalisation of voluntary medically assisted death.

Notwithstanding the remarks I have made in connection with the first point of dispute, many embrace the position of the New York State Task Force on Life and the Law,[15] which concluded that, no matter how carefully guidelines were drawn, physician-assisted suicide would put the vulnerable at greatest risk and, hence, that the 'social risks' of legalising physician-assisted suicide would be too great. The Task Force considered that not even those patients for whom further medical treatment would be futile *and* who request physician-assisted suicide ought to have access to it, since to allow such access would endanger a greater number of vulnerable patients. Clearly, the Task Force was appealing to a version of a 'slippery

---

[14] Mayo and Gunderson (1998: 18–20).
[15] New York State Task Force on Life and the Law (1994).

slope' argument (or what is sometimes known as a 'thin end of the wedge' argument). For the moment it will suffice to say that according to arguments of this form, once a certain step is taken, subsequent steps follow inexorably and lead down a slope to an unacceptable outcome (namely, a foreshortening of the lives of the vulnerable who, but for their vulnerability, would choose to have their lives prolonged).

Let me grant the possibility that, if certain competent persons have the option of choosing physician-assisted suicide, there will be some of doubtful competence who will feel that they, too, should choose physician-assisted suicide (for example, to alleviate any financial impact on family or friends, or because they feel they are a burden to their loved ones, or because of depression). Let me grant, as well, that for such people these pressures may feel coercive and lead them to believe they have no other option but to suicide. This may be the case regardless of whether the pressure is felt to come from family, from medical personnel, or, more generally, from prevailing social attitudes. In addition to the point already made that legislation permitting physician-assisted suicide incorporates safeguards to ensure that those who are not clearly competent to choose physician-assisted suicide are not afforded the opportunity to do so, it is worth reminding those influenced by the Task Force finding that a blanket prohibition on such assistance would have a further effect, namely, of locking out competent, but vulnerable, persons, who have indicated a wish to be helped to die, from being given the assistance they seek.

But there are several further points I believe it is worth making. First, there is, in principle, no difference between a competent patient's uncoerced choice of physician-assisted suicide and a competent patient's choice either to forego life-prolonging measures or to consent to pain relief that has the effect of hastening death.[16] These latter options are, of course, legally protected. Second, given that procedural safeguards have been put in place to respect the autonomy of decision-makers in matters like the purchase of major consumer items, it is surely not beyond us to do the same in relation to physician-assisted suicide. I do not mean to suggest that the same significance attaches to cases in which individuals feel pressured into buying cars and houses as to cases in which individuals contemplate ending their lives, but there is a common thread, namely, the need to respect autonomy. I see no basis for thinking it impossible to implement measures similar to those for consumer protection, to protect the autonomy of those making decisions about physician-assisted suicide. Moreover, it is plain what sorts

---

[16] Brock (1999: 538f).

of procedural safeguards are required: checks to ensure that the patient is competent and free from coercion; checks to ensure that the patient is psychiatrically healthy; and the opportunity, at any time, for a patient to set aside a previous decision (e.g. via a 'cooling off' period). As already noted, these are just the sorts of requirements on which those who have legislated in favour of voluntary medically assisted death in jurisdictions as diverse as the Northern Territory of Australia, Oregon, The Netherlands and Belgium have insisted.

It may be thought that things are different when the pressure on the vulnerable comes not from other people, or from social attitudes, but from their financial circumstances.[17] In countries lacking a universal health care scheme, for example, might the decision-making of someone who lacks health insurance be so compromised that he would opt for physician-assisted suicide rather than have his family financially ruined? To my knowledge no evidence has been uncovered in any of the various studies of legalised medically assisted dying in either The Netherlands or Oregon to suggest that there is any ground for concern on this score, so it can safely be set to one side. However, it has to be added that if attendant medical professionals are not convinced of an individual's competence, or consider that his choice was coerced, they should refuse a request for physician-assisted suicide. Professionals who find themselves faced with such a request obviously have to be able to back up their conviction with relevant evidence of incompetence, or of coercion, since the onus of proof is on them to show that the presumption of competence should be withdrawn. (It should go without saying that the evidence cannot consist simply in the fact that the patient has requested physician-assisted suicide.) In the event that the concerns of the professionals prove groundless, a patient's request for physician-assisted suicide should be honoured. Respect for other people's autonomy is no more dependent on our agreeing with the way they have weighted the various ingredients going into the decisions they make than it is on our agreeing with the decisions they make. So, even those adults (like Sue Rodriguez) whom others think vulnerable because of their disabilities or social circumstances ought to be presumed competent until shown otherwise. If incompetence is shown then there can be no question of facilitating a request for physician-assisted suicide. The slide down a slippery slope predicted to follow from honouring competent requests will thereby be prevented.

[17] Cf. Emanuel (1999).

IV

As has previously been mentioned, some who acknowledge that a case for physician-assisted suicide can be made out on the basis of respect for the autonomous choice of a competent patient nonetheless consider that the *legalisation* of physician-assisted suicide would be a bad thing because it would expose vulnerable sub-groups in the population – people with disabilities, people from disadvantaged backgrounds, and the elderly – to a yet further source of pressure to end their lives.[18] Though such critics agree that having the legal right to choose physician-assisted suicide gives more choice rather than less, they contend that this is one occasion when it is better not to have more choice.[19] An argument that is sometimes given for this startling conclusion is that once physician-assisted suicide becomes an option, a dying person has to convince himself that he should not resort to it, which may be difficult in circumstances where, for example, his continued existence will place extra burdens (financial, emotional, and so forth) on loved ones. Even though I believe that a parallel argument could be offered to show that having the option of refusing further life-prolonging treatment (which competent patients already have) imposes a comparable burden on the dying, I will tackle the argument head on.

Suppose that, in circumstances like those just described, a person comes to believe that, all things considered, it would be better if he availed himself of physician-assisted suicide even though his preference is to go on living. Ought we to conclude that the legalisation of physician-assisted suicide introduces an option whose very availability renders him worse off in virtue of the fact that he has to consider something he would not otherwise have had to consider? Those who think the answer is 'yes' clearly believe that a society that makes legal provision for physician-assisted suicide will suffer worse consequences than if it makes no such provision. For this to be convincing it will have to be the case that more bad consequences than good will stem from making physician-assisted suicide legal. But, in turn, that means it must be the case that more bad will be occasioned by the premature suicides of certain individuals than will be avoided by those whom physician-assisted suicide enables to escape from needless pain and suffering, or an intolerably burdensome existence. Setting aside the complex calculations that would be required to reach such a conclusion,

---

[18] Kamisar (1991); Marquis (1998: 274ff); and Bickenbach (1998).
[19] Velleman (1992). For a contrary view see Gerald Dworkin, 'Public Policy and Physician-Assisted Suicide' in Dworkin, *et al.* (1998: 64–80).

an even more pressing concern is whether the evidence required to sustain such a conclusion would even be obtainable. It seems to me that a better resolution can be achieved by allowing physician-assisted suicide to be chosen by those competent individuals who prefer to have the extra option, while at the same time insisting on the presence of safeguards to protect vulnerable individuals from being pressured into taking their non-preferred option of premature suicide (which, as should be clear from earlier remarks, is precisely what legislation for physician-assisted suicide has sought to ensure wherever it has been introduced).

I recognise that in societies where there is not a universal health care system, as well as those where health care is increasingly delivered in a context of managed care by health maintenance organisations,[20] the devising of such safeguards represents a major challenge, but Oregon, for instance, has not encountered any great difficulty in meeting it. Supporters of physician-assisted suicide have an obligation to remind governments to take seriously the need to regulate the operation of health maintenance organisations, so that, as far as is humanly possible, the choices of dying persons are made in circumstances free of coercive pressure. In that way the safeguards that are instituted can give confidence to the dying that there are acceptable and affordable options in addition to physician-assisted suicide *and* that they may choose from among all end-of-life options.

Some who oppose the legal toleration of physician-assisted suicide have claimed that its availability would have the effect of diminishing efforts to improve the care of the dying. This strikes me as implausible given that physician-assisted suicide (and active voluntary euthanasia) will likely only ever be sought by a small minority of the dying (to judge by what has happened in The Netherlands and Switzerland over decades, the Northern Territory of Australia in 1996, and Oregon since 1997). Nonetheless, it is worth stressing that the need to improve standards of care for the great majority of the dying will remain regardless of what is done about legalising physician-assisted suicide. Accordingly, even were physician-assisted suicide to become legal, and satisfactory safeguards established, no government should allow a minority of the dying to feel that physician-assisted suicide is their only option because their preferred options are unaffordable. Nobody who is dying should be forced either to endure an intolerable death, or to feel cornered into seeking to be helped to die, simply because they lack financial resources or the opportunity to access facilities that would offer them better management of their end-of-life care.

---

[20] Wolf (1996). But see Emanuel and Battin (1998) and Matthews (1998).

No member of a civilised society should have to experience such a sense of societal abandonment.[21] Unfortunately, as things stand at present, in some wealthy societies (perhaps most notably the United States) poor and dispossessed individuals are given cause to think they have been abandoned, in that they are denied essential medical treatment while political pressure is simultaneously exerted to ensure that resources are devoted to prolonging the lives of individuals in persistent vegetative states.

V

Some have raised what is claimed to be a separate issue arising out of the idea of respecting the autonomous choices of some physically disabled individuals to access physician-assisted suicide. They argue that if autonomy is to be protected even when its exercise results in the ending of an autonomous person's life, it must be irrelevant whether such a person has a severe disability, is terminally ill, is in pain, or is suffering in other ways. Yale Kamisar, for instance, thinks that the logic of giving support to the principle of self-determination commits us to assisting any competent individual who firmly requests help with suicide regardless of the individual's reasons.[22] Since he thinks the supreme value of human life takes precedence over individual self-determination, he concludes that physician-assisted suicide should be legally banned (as, of course, should active voluntary euthanasia and non-voluntary euthanasia). Like many who believe that the distinction between an act and an omission, or, in this context, between killing someone (at their request) and letting them die (at their request), is of critical moral significance, Kamisar believes it is consistent to respect patients' wishes to put an end to a burdensome existence by ending futile medical treatment, while denying them active help to end their lives.

I will go into greater detail in Chapter 6 as to why these distinctions between acts and omissions, and killings and lettings die, do not have the moral significance supposed by Kamisar and others (including Chief Justice Rehnquest in his widely cited judgment in *Cruzan v. Director, Missouri Department of Health*). For now, though, the following will have to suffice. Implicit in the traditional position is the idea that killing and letting die differ morally only if the properties that define an instance of one of them are morally significant *and* those properties are never

---

[21] Cf. Brock (1999: 541ff).   [22] Kamisar (1995: 758), but see Stell (1998).

present in an instance of the other. For example, it has often been claimed that intending the cause of a death is a definitional property of killing that has fundamental moral significance, whereas in instances of letting die this morally significant feature plays no role. However, this is mistaken because people can intentionally be allowed to die. Various opponents of the traditional view who contend that consequences are what matter morally have claimed that in all properly equalised cases, that is, in all pairs of cases (consisting of a killing and a letting die) where intention, motive, effort, and other commonly present variables are equalised, the same moral judgment should be made about each member of the pair and thus that killing and letting die are morally equivalent. Those, like me, who deny that consequences are all that matter in morality, can still consistently affirm that, *on occasion*, killing and letting die are morally equivalent (as I shall show in Chapter 6). There is no inconsistency in judging that certain instances of physician-assisted suicide, or active voluntary euthanasia for that matter, are morally on a par with certain instances of passive voluntary euthanasia. If killing and letting die are morally equivalent in those instances, the distinction between killing and letting die cannot lend moral legitimacy to passive voluntary euthanasia but deny it to physician-assisted suicide and active voluntary euthanasia. Without this cornerstone there is no credibility in Kamisar's (and others') belief that the only way to prevent a situation occurring where every competent individual is entitled to have access to physician-assisted suicide, and thus to prevent an 'opening of the floodgates', is legally to prohibit it in all circumstances.

Notwithstanding this, it may be claimed that I have not fully answered the criticism that the legalisation of physician-assisted suicide would commit society to agreeing to physician-assisted suicide for *every* competent individual no matter why they want to die. There are cogent grounds for rejecting this criticism. First, Kamisar misunderstands the argument from autonomy in connection with voluntary medically assisted death. He interprets it as claiming that whenever autonomy is respected, a *sufficient* moral justification exists for assisting death or hastening it. But proponents of the legalisation of voluntary medically assisted death do not think that an autonomous request for assistance with dying is, or even should be, reason enough to render such assistance legal. That is why they insist that other conditions have to be satisfied – for example, that the person be terminally ill, or be suffering a burdensome existence that precludes suicide. Indeed, in The Netherlands, which provides us with the best empirical evidence on the issue, the great majority of competent requests for medical assistance with dying are rejected.[23] Second, there is no pressing need for physician assistance in many, if not most, instances in which an intention to suicide is formed. So, even if physician assistance with suicide were to become legally permissible for those suffering from a condition that they find intolerable (like motor neurone disease), it would not follow that the same sort of assistance should be available to those not suffering intolerably, or those not facing imminent death. Assisting someone to die can be a legitimate part of a doctor's promotion of the health interests of her patients, since there will be occasions when these are best fostered, or, perhaps, can only be fostered, by way of medically assisted death. But that does not establish a completely general entitlement to such assistance. No society need consider itself obliged to divert medical resources to provide for such a general entitlement, and no individual medical practitioner need see herself as obliged to assist someone to die regardless of whether he is either terminally ill or the victim of a condition which precludes suicide.

VI

One of the previously mentioned objections to physician-assisted suicide questioned the coherence of making it available to those dying persons who in the past competently requested that they be given such assistance but who have in the meantime become incompetent (for example, because of the impact of dementia).[24] In other words, in the event that physician-assisted suicide becomes legally permissible, will advance directives be countenanced, or will many dying persons simply be precluded from taking advantage of physician help with dying because they lack competence at the very time when they need that help?

Early on in this chapter, I made the point that physician-assisted suicide is seen by some medical practitioners as closely resembling in important respects the refusal of (life-prolonging) medical treatment. The point is relevant to the present concern because it seems feasible for an advance directive to provide *either* for a refusal of medical treatment in specified circumstances *or* for a request for assistance with dying in the selfsame circumstances. Where a dying individual's choices accord with his settled and fundamental values, his choices should be respected, whether they are for continuation of life-prolonging medical treatment, refusal of medical treatment, or physician assistance with dying. In the case of a no longer

---

[23] Onwuteaka-Philipsen, *et al.* (2003).   [24] Marquis (1998).

competent individual, physician-assisted suicide would, strictly, be inappropriate, but the withdrawal or withholding of life-prolonging medical treatment would remain an option provided that a proxy entrusted with an enduring medical power of attorney for the no longer competent individual could cite an advance directive in support of such a course. Such directives are now entrenched as legally appropriate instruments for the expression of patient autonomy. In Chapter 9 I will elaborate further on why it is justifiable to appeal to them in the context of medically assisted death, and on why they can incorporate options other than the withdrawal or withholding of life-prolonging medical treatment.

CHAPTER 5

The sanctity of human life

Those opposed to the legalisation of medically assisted death often contend that its legalisation would violate the requirement to respect the sanctity of human life and that this constitutes a decisive reason against legalisation. In order to assess whether respect for the sanctity of human life provides us with a decisive reason, or even, more weakly, a prima facie reason, for opposing the legalisation of medically assisted death, the meaning of the idea of the sanctity of human life must first be clarified. Even among its supporters it is acknowledged that the idea has not been articulated in rigorous philosophical terms.[1] I would go further and contend that this lack of precision ensures that there is not even a single agreed meaning. In the absence of a canonical account of the idea I will attempt to present it in its most convincing guise and to make explicit the various moral foundations that its supporters have proffered. I will conclude that none of the foundations justifies the sort of regard given to human life by those who believe that voluntary medically assisted death must violate the sanctity of human life.

Not only is belief in the idea of the sanctity of human life widespread, it is integral, particularly in Western societies, to legal structures and, via those structures, integral to the practice of medicine authorised by them.[2] Attempts to revise those well-entrenched features of the law that are founded on it tend to meet with resistance. Despite the significant contribution to respect for human life that it has made, I will argue that the idea should be afforded only a restricted application. Instead of a blanket claim in support of the inviolability of human life, the most that can be justified is a presumption in favour of protecting human life, a presumption that may, nevertheless, sometimes justifiably be set aside.

---

[1] See, for example, Boyle (1989) and Devine (2000).

[2] Consider, for example, how in some recent United States cases (like *Cruzan v. Director, Missouri Dept. of Health* [1990] 497 U.S. 261 and *Washington et al. v. Glucksberg et al.* [1997] 117 S. Ct. 2258), the courts have made appeal to the state's interest in preserving human life even at the expense of the autonomy of an individual seeking assistance with dying.

If I am right about the indefensibility of the blanket claim, it becomes imperative to determine when the presumption may be set aside. I will suggest that the presumption may be set aside when the quality of a human life is diminished to a degree that is unacceptable to the individual in question (or, if the individual is in no position to judge, when his surrogate judges that he would find it unacceptable). An alternative way of putting the same point is that the presumption may be set aside when an individual's quality of life fails to reach a certain threshold. This is, of course, not a new suggestion, but it contrasts markedly with the claim by supporters of the traditional idea of the sanctity of human life that it is the presence, other things being equal, of a particular property or of particular properties that is fundamental to the protection of human life. Various properties have been nominated to fill the role, ranging through religiously grounded ones like the possession of a soul; biologically based ones such as having reached a certain stage of foetal development; simply having been born; having become self-conscious; to having properties essential to being a person (as distinct from a human being). I will argue that protection for human life is not warranted in virtue of the presence of any of these nominated grounds for the sanctity of human life, but rather that it is when a human life is of an appropriate quality that such protection should be afforded. Accordingly, the permissibility of voluntary medically assisted death will turn on the quality of human life. But before this contention can be substantiated the idea of the sanctity of human life, and whether it is defensible, must first be investigated.

I

Those who invoke the sanctity (or, in religious terms, the sacredness[3]) of human life, contend that it always affords a reason for human life to be protected against intentional killing. The same contention can be put in non-religious terms as the idea that a human being has a moral status that affords protection against being killed intentionally. With either formulation there is much that cries out both for further explanation and justification,

[3] There can be little doubt that the idea of the sanctity of human life originated in the Judaeo-Christian tradition even if tracing its formation is far more complicated than many contemporary writers claim. For helpful discussion see Frankena (1976). The Islamic tradition within monotheism is disposed toward a similar view, albeit it is less clearly articulated. Perhaps of most interest is that some Islamic opinion opposes even the withdrawal of life-sustaining treatment. The Hindu, Jain and Buddhist traditions emphasise the sacredness of life, rather than the sacredness of human life, though, of course, the former implies the latter. Because of the religious origins of the idea some who are committed to it think it isn't possible wholly to characterise it in moral terms. See, for instance, Boyle (1989: 245); contra Donagan (1977: 76–77).

including even what it is to be a member of the species *homo sapiens sapiens*. This may seem obvious,[4] but the fact that it is not has implications for abortion, albeit not for voluntary medically assisted death.

For present purposes, though, I want to focus initially on two questions that need to be answered before proceeding further and then I will move on to a full consideration of the doctrine. First, there is a question about the values foundation envisaged by those who consider human life is sacred, or confers special moral standing. Second, there is a question about why human life is privileged as compared with other (non-human) life. After responding to these questions I will proceed to a more detailed consideration of the idea of the sanctity of human life and, in particular, to a consideration of whether, and in what circumstances, killing a human being can ever be morally justified.

The sanctity of human life has been advocated variously as a function of the *absolute* value of human life, or of the *infinite* value of human life, or of the *overriding* value of human life, or, most commonly, of the *intrinsic*, or, *inherent*, value of human life (or, some combination thereof). Those who eschew talk of 'value' in these contexts sometimes speak instead of 'respect for human life'.[5] Just as importantly, it has also been considered crucial to the idea of the sanctity of human life that all human lives are, in consequence of their sanctity, of *equal* value (whether the value of human life be understood as being absolute, infinite, overriding or intrinsic).[6] Various accounts of the sanctity of human life can thus be generated. What has to be determined is whether one of the variants more plausibly renders the idea than any of its competitors, and, if so, whether it can survive criticism, including the criticism that it is not the sanctity, but the quality, of human life, that matters.

I mentioned above that, according to proponents of the idea of the sanctity of human life, all human lives are of equal value. Given that it is a necessary condition for the sanctity of human life that all human lives have equal value, no human life is to be considered as having precedence in comparison with any other human life. Even if the claim that all

---

[4] The matter is not straightforward because not everyone is persuaded of the *humanity* of teratomas (monstrous or misshapen organisms) and anencephalics (in whom a congenital abnormality, involving a failure in the development of the cerebral hemispheres and overlying skull and scalp, exposes the brain stem and results in a lack of consciousness). I take it, however, that, as traditionally understood, all members of the species, including zygotes, embryos, foetuses, teratomas, anencephalics, and born individuals, enjoy the sanctity of human life.

[5] Cf. Benn (1973) and Frankena (1976).

[6] Frey (1996) rejects this element of the idea (and hence the idea itself) because he thinks human lives are not of equal quality and so cannot be equally valuable.

human lives are of equal value is defensible, it can, at best, be *a necessary condition* for the sanctity of human life that they are, since all human lives might be of equal but insignificant value. This is the case regardless of how the human lives in question are qualified. For example, consider the claim (often made in this context) that all *innocent* human lives have sanctity. The equal value of such lives still could not amount to anything more than a necessary condition for their sanctity. Moreover, the equal worth of human lives would not, of itself, preclude the possibility that several human lives in aggregate[7] might take precedence over a single human life.

The contention that all human lives are of equal worth generates a difficulty for all versions of the idea of the sanctity of human life, which can most easily be illustrated by reference to instances where killing one human in self-defence is necessary to save the life of another human. Famously, when Thomas Aquinas first enunciated a version of what has come to be known as the 'doctrine of double effect' to justify killing another human in self-defence, he resorted to distinguishing between foreseeing that the other would die in consequence of the self-defensive action (which he considered permissible) and intentionally killing the other (which he considered impermissible).[8] I will critically assess the doctrine of double effect (and thus the justifiability of Aquinas' manoeuvre) in Chapter 6 but, for the moment, I will simply register my agreement with him that killing in self-defence is, on occasion, morally permissible.[9] Whatever the value of Aquinas' suggestion, anyone who agrees that it is morally permissible in at least some circumstances for an agent to kill in self-defence, including, it should be noted, circumstances where the person against whom the agent defends himself is morally innocent,[10] must ask whether the permissibility of killing in self-defence is consistent with the sanctity of human life. If all human lives are of equal value, yet it is permissible on at least some occasions to kill in self-defence, then it will at least sometimes be permissible to violate the sanctity of human life, including that of innocent human

---

[7] If each human life were of *infinite* worth, claims about aggregation would be more problematic but I will argue against the infinite worth claim below. Taurek (1977) challenged the relevance of aggregation in contexts like the present one, though I do not find his argument convincing.

[8] *Summa Theologiae* 2a 2ae. 64, 7.

[9] Cf., for example, Boyle (1989). Boyle thinks that the option of upholding the elements in common morality based on the sanctity of human life is not taken sufficiently seriously.

[10] This is because the category of the innocent will include children, the psychiatrically ill, and those, more generally, who pose a threat for which they cannot be held responsible (e.g. because they are under duress at the time when they pose the threat).

life.[11] Notoriously, of course, state-sanctioned killing in the guise either of punishment or of war has traditionally been said by most defenders of the sanctity of human life to be permissible on the ground that the protection afforded by the doctrine does not extend to those who lack innocence. If the idea is understood in this restricted way there will be an issue about how to characterise those who are to be deemed innocent given my claim that there are several categories of person who are innocent but may still pose a lethal threat. The restricted version of the doctrine will still be subject to difficulties if killing in self-defence is permissible in the face of lethal threats from these innocents, to say nothing of instances in which it seems permissible to sacrifice the life of one human – or the lives of several humans – to save many others, or even intentionally to fail to save one human life in order to save another. In all such instances the doctrine lacks moral credibility. Since almost all proponents of the sanctity of human life are prepared to countenance such instances of killing, or sacrifice of human life, the idea cannot be saved simply by holding that it is only the innocent who may not be killed intentionally (or, let die intentionally). Nonetheless, in considering the further conditions thought to be jointly sufficient (along with the equality of all human lives) I will assume that the doctrine is to be understood in this more restrictive way.

I will now briefly answer the second of the questions I posed above, namely, the one concerning what it is about *human* life that makes it so special, and hence inviolable, when other sorts of lives are not. In the Judaeo-Christian tradition, the answer to the question of why human life is of special significance is that God has set humans apart from other created beings in virtue of establishing the *possibility*[12] of a personal relationship with them.[13] Contrary to the view of many commentators,[14] the idea of the sanctity of human life is not tied in Judaeo-Christian thought to

---

[11] The literature on the justifiability of killing in self-defence is vast, as befits its central importance in our moral thought. Among the more significant recent contributions to the debate are those by Thomson (1976) and (1991); Uniacke (1994); McMahan (2002); and Rodin (2002).

[12] The possibility may, of course, not be actualised. Much effort in Christian theology has been devoted to consideration of how this possibility may be actualised for those who, for example, die before they can enter such a relationship, or never know about its even being possible.

[13] The Christian theologian, Nigel Biggar, has recently expressed a similar point as follows. 'The special value of human life lies in the opportunity it affords to hear and respond to a call from God to make a unique contribution to the maintenance and promotion of created goods in the world' (2004: 55).

[14] Including such astute ones as McMahan (2002: 332). He rightly points out, though, that if the sanctity of human life has the relational quality I have suggested it has within the Judaeo-Christian tradition, then sanctity cannot be an *intrinsic* feature of human life. (It could, of course, still be a feature unique to humans, albeit not an intrinsic one.) This bears on the common view that human life is intrinsically valuable, as will be seen later.

humans having, or more strictly, being, souls. The contention that human beings are their souls became a widely held Christian belief only when Christianity began to develop as a tradition distinct from Judaism and then chiefly as a result of the influence of Hellenistic thought.[15] It is true that the Catholic Church holds that 'ensoulment' is the basis for person-hood but the justification it offers is neither empirical nor philosophical – it is moral. The doctrine is best characterised as an affirmation of the sanc-tity of human life and so need not be given separate consideration. In some other religious traditions (for example, Jainism[16]), and in some belief systems (for example, that of Albert Schweitzer[17]), *living beings, as such*, rather than just human beings, are supposed to be sacred or inviolable. Regardless of whether there is anything problematic about the notion that only human life has sanctity, the vitalist notion that *all* life has sanctity is clearly unsustainable if it entails that life must be protected at whatever cost, for the cost would be widespread death by starvation or disease. That is why Schweitzer, who sought to avoid the unnecessary destruction of the lives of insects by refraining from working with a lighted candle, was prepared to take life for certain purposes, including eating and fighting infections – as long as this was done with a due sense of seriousness – and why extreme animal liberationists, like vegans, also reject vitalism.

Those, like James Rachels,[18] who contend that neither the idea of the sanctity of *human* life (with its religious origins) nor that of vitalism is defensible, think that the focus on why human life has special significance, even if it does not have it exclusively, must be on the protection of 'biogra-phical' lives (to use his term), namely, lives that are lived in a self-conscious (or, self-aware) way. This is because it cannot be of any consequence to the being whose life is to be protected that it be protected, unless the being is aware of living it. If this is correct,[19] it implies that the supposition that it is a necessary condition for the sanctity of human life that all human lives be considered of equal value is (once again) open to challenge. This is because not all human lives are lives in the biographical sense. Moreover,

---

[15] Cf. Cullmann (1958).
[16] The Jains believe that it is violence inflicted on souls that impedes each individual entity's spiritual development, but they do not believe humans alone have souls. See Dundas (1992).
[17] See, for example, his discussion (1946: ch. 21) of the 'principle of reverence for life'.
[18] Rachels (1983: 33ff).
[19] I think that it is, at least, on the right track. But, even if it is, it does not follow (as Rachels was well aware) that only humans are capable of leading lives in the biographical sense, or that non-biographical life has no value. See Kleinig (1991). It should be noted, though, that those who think that it is sufficient for a life to warrant protection that it yields pleasant experiences and, so, that self-consciousness is unnecessary, will, nonetheless, have difficulty reconciling such a view with many of our practices, in particular, those involving the killing of non-human animals for food.

since at least some non-human lives would appear to be lives in the biographical sense (for example, those of the primates), it will be indefensible, in the absence of further argument, to regard only those *humans* who lead self-conscious lives as having inviolable lives. I do not wish to preclude its being claimed that the *traditional* idea of the sanctity of human life cannot be understood, or defended, apart from its theological or metaphysical moorings (regardless of whether an alternative foundation for the sanctity of life can be found in the idea of leading a self-conscious life). Nor do I wish to preclude its being claimed that it is because God has provided for the possibility of a relationship with human beings that human life has sanctity. Finally, I do not wish to preclude the further claim that it is *only* with humans that God has provided for the possibility of such a personal relationship. However, those who reject theological attempts to underpin the traditional idea of the sanctity of human life[20] are likely to insist that, because there can be reasonable disagreement about such theological underpinnings, the traditional idea cannot define public policy in a society that is not specifically committed to their truth. Be that as it may, in those societies where a notion of the sanctity of life is currently honoured in medical and legal contexts it is the sanctity of *human* life that is always meant. Hence, for present purposes, it is the sanctity of human life that must be reckoned with regardless of whether it can be separated from its theological underpinnings (or, indeed, from alternative metaphysical ones since many who have no religious beliefs remain convinced of the special significance of human life).

II

As previously pointed out, the idea of the sanctity of human life has been understood in a variety of ways by its supporters, so, before anything can be decided about its continued usefulness, it is necessary first to decide whether the foundational values on which it is built are sound. Earlier, I distinguished four accounts of the value of human life that have been put forward in justification of its inviolable status, namely, that it is of absolute value, that it is of infinite value, that it is of overriding value, and that it is of intrinsic value. I will consider these consecutively. A recurring critical theme will be that none of them can be rendered consistent with the conviction that killing another human being is sometimes morally permissible, short of adopting extreme pacifism, which rejects killing even to stave off a

---

[20] In recent philosophical work on the topic such a rejection has been very common. See, for instance, Rachels (1983); Kuhse (1987: 16–21); Singer (1994) and (1995); and McMahan (2002).

lethal threat. Since such a position lacks credibility my conclusion will be that there is no plausible way of defending the idea of the sanctity of human life.

Anyone who claims that it is foundational for the sanctity of human life that human life is of absolute value[21] is clearly committed to thinking that each human life is of equal value. However, such a person need not be committed to thinking that human life is the only thing of absolute value. Whatever else is encompassed in the idea of human life having absolute value, it seems clear that it must involve an absolute prohibition on the intentional killing of a human being *and* an absolute prohibition on intentionally failing to prolong the life of a human being whenever such a life can be prolonged.[22]

It is worthy of mention that when Aquinas argued that killing in self-defence was licit this was tied to the fact that the aggressor lacked innocence. On his account what was absolutely forbidden was the intentional killing of an innocent human being. But those committed to the absolute value of human life, and hence the absolute wrongness of ending it, must reject killing in self-defence as well as intentional killing, despite presumably being obligated, if attacked, vigorously to defend their own absolutely valuable lives. The moral issues raised by killing in self-defence are those that are central to the defensibility of pacifism. Because I do not have the space to give detailed separate consideration to the morality of pacifism, I am simply going to assume that it is permissible to kill in self-defence because I consider the extreme pacifist position to be implausible. It is implausible to think a competent moral agent, who has reason to live, should by default have to suffer the loss of his life in circumstances where it is impossible to avoid death through retreating but possible to avoid it by killing an aggressor bent on killing him. The same is true for an agent who intervenes to defend the lives of others who are victims of lethal aggression.[23]

---

[21] Some critics of the idea of the sanctity of life, such as Helga Kuhse and Peter Singer, have, on occasion, taken this to be the traditional understanding of the idea. See Kuhse (1987: 84) and Singer (1994: 192). This is a mistake and one that has been seized upon by their critics (e.g. Keown (2002: ch. 4)). Though Singer has contended on several occasions (e.g. 1994: 4) that those of his opponents who believe in the sanctity of human life think of it as an absolute value, he sometimes refers to its being based on a belief in the intrinsic value of human life.

[22] I am concerned here only with pointing out what it would be wrong to do. There will, of course, be acts and omissions leading to the loss of human life, which are not *intentional* violations of the prohibitions I have mentioned, but which, nonetheless, raise issues of *responsibility* rather than of wrongdoing (e.g. those involving negligent behaviour). I shall not discuss these latter matters here – not because they are unimportant, but because they would take me too far afield.

[23] Ryan (1983) argues that even if this judgment is correct it is not as easy to substantiate as many critics of pacifism have claimed.

Obviously, individuals whose extreme pacifist principles lead them to believe that fidelity to their principles matters more than their own or others' deaths would disagree. But if, as I am assuming, it is permissible to kill in self-defence, their position cannot be mandatory for others, including those who consider themselves pacifists but insist only on making strategic use of non-violent forms of resistance to thwart violence. These latter are not prepared to court certain death on principle.[24]

I now return to the implications of thinking that human life is of absolute value. Supporters of this position are committed to believing that it is never permissible intentionally to refrain from saving someone's life, even if that is required to avoid a greater number of deaths. They also have to reject the notion that medical treatment that is futile may be withdrawn or withheld.[25] Even if sceptical worries about whether it is ever possible to know that an aggressor can *only* be disarmed by being killed, or about whether the sacrifice of some human lives *will* lead to more human lives being saved, or about whether it is possible to know that a certain form of medical treatment *is* futile are set to one side, it should be clear that those who place absolute value on human life set the bar of morality very high. My illustrative examples were chosen to show that they set it far too high in holding that there is no amount of good that might be achieved, and no amount of bad that might be averted, that could make it right to kill an innocent human being.

It is, no doubt, true that most of us of would find it psychologically difficult to convince ourselves that we were entitled to kill another person who, for example, just happened to constitute a life-saving resource (for example, in a situation where, unless I kill a person, I will starve to death, or die of a lack of oxygen, or be killed by that person in his attempt to avoid starvation or suffocation).[26] But, even if this fact about ourselves gives us pause, it does not establish a general moral obligation to refrain from killing. As has already been pointed out, no such obligation exists in relation to acting in

[24] The context provides an opportunity to note that actions to provoke martyrdom were condemned by early Christian thinkers, including, most famously, Augustine. For a fascinating account of this and related issues see Amundsen (1996: ch. 4, 'Suicide and Early Christianity').

[25] The Catholic thinkers represented in Gormally (1994), who endorse the sanctity of human life, explicitly reject this suggestion on the ground that prolongation of life as such is no part of the purpose of medicine. See p. 134f. They contend that it is because critics of the idea of the sanctity of human life fail to understand this point that they misrepresent it, but they should equally hold those who think human life is of absolute value to be guilty of misrepresentation.

[26] I set to one side (as not relevant to the present discussion) the objection made famous by Bernard Williams that, in certain circumstances, it will be *my* killing of another that will lead to a loss of integrity. See his 'A Critique of Utilitarianism' in Smart and Williams (1973: 108–118). The objection will, however, be taken up in Chapter 7 when I consider professional integrity in more detail.

self-defence and that, strictly, is what an absolutist about the value of human life has to establish. Likewise, an absolutist must show that it is incumbent upon us morally to go on doing *whatever we can* to keep someone alive even when this has become medically futile. So, even if the absolutist's position is coherent, it is far from compelling. Finally, given that there are many who believe in the sanctity of human life who share my scepticism about human life being absolutely valuable, there is no reason to accept this first attempt at explicating the idea of the sanctity of human life, at least until it is certain that there is no more credible alternative.

III

If human life is not of absolute value, does it, perhaps, have infinite value? Those who think it does, deny that things of finite value, alone or in combination, can override the value of human life.[27] So, what would be required for something to be of infinite value? In the popular understanding, something has infinite value if it has unlimited value and this may seem to make it virtually indistinguishable from something having absolute value.[28] But that would be a mistaken inference. Someone who believes human life is of infinite value is not entitled to conclude that the killing of a human being (innocent or otherwise) is always wrong just because the being killed is of infinite value. This for the reason that killing one human being to save the life of another human being (for example, in a case of self-defence) will involve protecting one infinite value at the expense of another. If killing in self-defence is permissible (as it seems reasonable to suppose), there can be no absolute barrier to the taking of a human life regardless of whether it is of infinite value.

The popular understanding of infinity is, of course, not the only one. In a more technical conception, like that employed in mathematics, a thing's being infinite does not entail that it cannot be outstripped by another infinity (for example, when one infinity is a proper subset of another infinity). A technical conception like this would seem unlikely to be the model that those who claim human life has infinite value have in mind. This is because it cannot guarantee

---

[27] A recent advocate of the infinite (or, as he usually puts it, 'the incalculable') value of human life is Dyck (2002: ch. 4).

[28] Some adherents of Judaism have advanced this claim. See, for example, the sources cited by Kuhse (1987: 12f). However, it has been more common within Judaism for the *paramountcy* of the value of human life to be stressed (and human life thus to be considered as of overriding worth). On the latter account, suicide is impermissible (even a mass suicide like that at the fall of Masada); however, martyrdom, where the emphasis is on upholding God's honour, is permissible. Even so, the case of King Saul's suicide on the battlefield (*1 Samuel* 31: 4) has proved troubling to those who propose such an account. For further discussion, see Zohar (1998).

that human life will not be outstripped by something else of greater infinite value when their point is that, except for another human life, nothing has a value comparable with that of a human life (and that, in effect, makes their claim indistinguishable from the claim that human life is of overriding value). This suggests that it is probably the popular sense of infinity that those who claim human life has infinite value have had in mind. The difficulties facing that idea have already been canvassed.

IV

The third claim about the value of human life that I promised to assess is that human life is inviolable because it is of overriding value or worth. According to this understanding of the sanctity of human life, human life is not absolutely or infinitely valuable, just more valuable than anything else. Hence, there is nothing (other than another human life) whose value is sufficiently great that its realisation would be worth the loss of a human life. It is compatible with this understanding that someone be permitted to kill a lethal aggressor in self-defence, if there is no other way to stop the aggression, and compatible as well that the lives of the few may sometimes be sacrificed for those of the many. However, it appears to be incompatible with it that one human being can be justified in killing *several* human beings to save the life of *one* other human being (in, for instance, self-defence, or war). And, if that is so, killing a human being will not, as such, be wrong. Instead, the wrongness of killing will be a function not only of variables like innocence and non-innocence, but also of the numbers killed. While this understanding of the idea of the sanctity of human life will be thought by many traditional supporters to be too tolerant of killing, it nonetheless has some resonance with a frequently voiced objection to the legalisation of voluntary medically assisted death.

Let me explain. As I have already observed, it is often said that the legalisation of voluntary medically assisted death must be prevented in order to protect the lives of the vulnerable. In particular, it is said that if it were to become permissible to help people die who, without doubt, are able autonomously to choose to die, this would inevitably lead to the killing of many who are incapable of choosing autonomously to seek such assistance but whose life circumstances are nevertheless just like those who are capable of choosing autonomously to be helped to die. It would be wrong, in other words, to respect the autonomous choices of the few because of the risk this would pose to many others of losing their lives despite lacking the competence to make an autonomous choice to die. Even supporters of a more permissive understanding of the idea of the sanctity of human life would be opposed to the legalisation of medically assisted death if it would put in jeopardy many other lives. So, a more permissive understanding of the idea of the sanctity of human life would still not make the legalisation of voluntary medically assisted death tolerable.

Does this third account of the values foundation of the sanctity of human life avoid the serious objections raised against the two previous accounts? The answer has to be that it does not. While it clearly fares better in relation to some of the objections I made to human life being thought of as having absolute or infinite value, it implausibly prohibits someone acting in self-defence when he would have to kill multiple attackers, and rules out waging a just war whenever deaths on the belligerent side are likely to be the greater. But, more importantly for present purposes, it has to be asked: why should human life as such be considered to be of more value than anything else? Why think that the value of the life of someone in, for example, a persistent vegetative state is such as to override all other considerations of value? Why think that a terminally ill patient who competently judges that his life has become intolerable, or that the life available to him is no longer worthwhile, must value his life more than he values his autonomy?

Those, like me, who are unconvinced that human life is of overriding value do not find it hard to answer such questions because, for us, human life has *instrumental* value, in that it enables us to choose, and do, the things we consider worth having and doing. It is, of course, compatible with human life being instrumentally valuable that it also be intrinsically valuable. While I do not happen to believe that human life is intrinsically valuable – chiefly because I fail to see what it is about the life of a human being who is brain dead, or in a permanent vegetative state, that makes his life valuable for its own sake – the possibility that human life is both intrinsically and instrumentally valuable is not one that I reject out of hand. Moreover, historically, the most prominent understandings of the sanctity of human life have been formulated in terms of its having intrinsic value. Accordingly, I turn next to a consideration of the fourth and final of the putative bases for the sanctity of human life, namely, that it has intrinsic value.

v

For something to be intrinsically valuable it must be valuable for its own sake, rather than for any of the things that it may produce, or to which it may lead.[29] If human life is intrinsically valuable it will be valuable for its own sake, or, as such. If a human life has value as such, and not just derivatively, then to accede to the wish of a person to end his life will be objectionable because it will lead to the loss of something intrinsically valuable. Hence, the claim that human life is intrinsically valuable has an obvious bearing on the moral justifiability of medically assisted death.

There are two main grounds on which objections may be raised against the claim that human life is inviolable in virtue of its being intrinsically valuable. First, that there is no way of justifying the claim that human life is intrinsically valuable. Second, that even if there is a way of justifying this claim, there is no reason to think that the intrinsic value of a human life outweighs all other values (either other intrinsic values or instrumental values). I will consider these grounds in turn.

Suppose, for the sake of argument, that human life is intrinsically valuable. If so, it will be the non-evaluative features constitutive of human life that confer this value. To put the same point another way, the value of human life will be dependent upon[30] the non-evaluative features or properties that are intrinsic to human life. As was noted earlier, various properties have been proposed. For instance, I mentioned the claim made by some religious believers that humans alone have, or, more strictly, are, souls. I have already indicated why there is little support (including theological support) for the existence of souls, and, more importantly, why any reliance on a theological position as a foundation for social policy founders in societies that lack a shared commitment to the theological position. Some of the other properties mentioned previously can be ruled out as unsuitable because they are relational properties rather than properties intrinsic to being a human. This applies equally, for example, to the claim that what underpins the intrinsic value of human life is that humans, and only humans, are able to enter into a relationship with God, and to the non-religious suggestion that the source of the intrinsic value of human lives is that, as a species, humans have a more highly developed consciousness than any other species. Similarly, Ronald Dworkin's proposal[31] – that we

---

[29] For important discussions of the concept of intrinsic value see, e.g., Moore (1903) and (1922); Korsgaard (1983); Lemos (1994); and Zimmerman (2001).

[30] Many philosophers prefer the expression 'supervenient upon'.

[31] See Dworkin (1993: 73f, 84). For discussion of Dworkin's account see Rakowski (1994); McMahan (2002: 330ff, 464ff); and Biggar (2004: 23f, 47ff). Although he is a Christian, John Finnis does not appeal to religious grounds when he claims (1995: 33f) that it is in virtue of its intrinsic value that a human life may never intentionally be terminated (even if the person whose life it is craves death). However, John Keown (2002: 40) does. He says that 'human life is created in the image of God and is, therefore, possessed of an intrinsic dignity which entitles it to protection from unjust attack'.

derive our intrinsic value from the creative investment that, first, others, and, then, we, make in our lives – is implausible as a foundation for the supposed intrinsic value of human life. It is not clear, for instance, why such investment should be thought to produce something of *intrinsic* value. Certainly, the more that is invested in a human life the greater the loss, in at least one intelligible sense, when that life is ended, but that does not establish that the life has intrinsic value. Furthermore, even allowing that the loss is to be considered a loss of intrinsic value, the idea of investment in a living thing hardly applies uniquely to humans, so Dworkin's account fails to show why only human life is sanctified. Finally, Dworkin's proposal is incompatible with each human life having equal value (given the differential investments made in human lives), and so strays too far from the traditional understanding of the sanctity of human life to constitute a plausible account of it, or to be acceptable to its proponents.

There is one further proposal, however, which warrants careful attention, namely, one made by David Velleman.[32] He aims to provide a non-religious account of the sanctity of the lives of *persons* (that is, following Kant, beings with rational natures).[33] According to Velleman, the dignity or worth that a person has in virtue of his rational nature is to be distinguished from the value his life has for him. Human worth or dignity is *an interest-independent value*. Once a person exists, he has a dignity or worth that is incommensurable with the value that his interests have for him. For Velleman, a person's good can only matter if he matters for his own sake. This difference in kind means that there is no single metric available in which both the value that inheres *in* a person and the value his interests have *for* him can be measured. Rather, concern for the latter is conditional on concern for the former. From this Velleman concludes that the value that inheres in a person cannot be traded off against the value of a person's interests.[34] However, even supposing that the two values in question are incommensurable, it does not follow that all trade-offs between them are precluded. Even though incommensurable values cannot be accommodated on a single scale, it is only when the values in question are lexically ordered that trade-offs between them can be precluded. It is not entirely clear whether Velleman would wish to make this further supposition but (if I understand

---

[32] Velleman (1999a). For discussion, see Kamm (1999: 595ff) and McMahan (2002: 473–485).

[33] McMahan (2002: 476) contends that *sanctity* and *worth* are distinct notions because if a life has sanctity then necessarily there is a reason to preserve it, whereas if it has worth all that is required is the according of due respect. Be that as it may, I will construe Velleman's account as he intends it, namely, as an account of the (supposed) *sanctity* of human life.

[34] In this respect Velleman follows Anderson (1993).

his metaphorical language correctly) he might, given that he says 'The value of [a] means to an end cannot overshadow or be overshadowed by the value of the end, because it already is only a shadow of that value, in the sense of being dependent upon it. Similarly, the value of what's good for a person is only a shadow of the value inhering in the person, and cannot overshadow or be overshadowed by it.'[35] So, on Velleman's account, to destroy the intrinsic value that inheres in a person in order to promote interest-dependent values would be to violate Kant's maxim that a person must never be treated as a means only but always at the same time as an end in himself.[36] The upshot is that he sets his face against attempts to justify suicide (including physician-assisted suicide) and voluntary euthanasia that are based on the person not getting enough out of life. In other words, he opposes these practices *insofar as they are motivated solely by a desire to promote the interests of the person assisted to die.*

The qualification is important because Velleman does not wish to rule out all assisted dying, even though he professes not to know how to frame a public policy or law that would pick out just those instances where (voluntary) medically assisted death would be morally justified. Medically assisted death is, he thinks, 'morally justified to spare the patient from degradation'.[37] So, if a patient's life is degraded to such an extent that his rational nature is threatened,[38] including when that results from unbearable suffering, it is not disrespectful to cut it short. I take him to mean that it would not be disrespectful to cut short such a life, *provided no evidence exists of a contrary wish*, for otherwise he would have to endorse the cutting short of someone's degraded life despite his explicit directive to the contrary. It is striking that he says as well that 'anyone who is ready for assistance in dying is usually past the point where he can bear full responsibility for the decision, no matter how he may participate in it'.[39] This is striking because it suggests that even though an advance directive would be relevant evidence, a contemporaneous request to be helped to die probably would not. However, Velleman's empirical claim is dubious since there

---

[35] Velleman (1999a: 613).

[36] Jean Hampton makes a similar claim in 'Forgiveness, Resentment and Hatred' in Murphy and Hampton (1988: 46). Thomas E. Hill, Jr., by contrast, proposes a reading of Kant wherein it is possible to show respect for one's own person in committing suicide (or in being assisted to die). See Hill (1991). Even though I am not concerned with Kantian scholarship – Velleman's position is of interest regardless of whether it is Kant's – it is worth pointing out that Kant contended in his *Lectures on Ethics* (1780) that it would be better to choose death than voluntarily to submit to life as a galley slave, so his opposition to suicide was not absolute.

[37] (1999a: 626).   [38] (1999a: 618, 625).

[39] (1999a: 626). Cf., as well, his remark (also on p. 626) that such a person will be in 'the twilight of his autonomy'.

is little justification for thinking that the rational natures of, for example, sufferers from certain terminal cancers, or victims of motor neurone disease, will typically be under threat because of their medical conditions (in contrast with what is likely to be true of those in, say, advanced stages of dementia).

The more important point on which to focus, however, is Velleman's claim that it is only when a person's life has come to be so degraded as to threaten his rational nature that he can be given assistance to die. Given his claim about the incommensurability of the value of a person and the value of a person's interests, the case he thinks of as the exception presumably can only arise if the values at stake are restricted to the interest-dependent values. For then the person's value will drop out of the picture entirely in the event that he is no longer rational but merely remains in existence. In such a circumstance, interest-dependent values will be permitted to prevail. Nonetheless, Velleman elsewhere contends that 'to say that any candidate for assistance in dying must be diminished as a person is not to say that he cannot be a person at all'.[40] This makes his position perplexing because it suggests (contrary to what he maintains elsewhere) that interest-dependent values may be respected in the administration of medically assisted death and thus that sometimes, at least, they may matter. In his response to Kamm he acknowledges the problem and clarifies his position by indicating that 'when a person's dignity serves as grounds for his death, then his interests may *also* be taken into account, without any disrespect to his dignity'.[41] So, with that clarification, I turn to the main point of disagreement I have with his position.

Why should it be agreed, as he insists it must be, that assisting people to die who think they are not getting enough out of life, entails a lack of respect for them, or a rejection of their dignity? Those, like me, who are unpersuaded that interest-dependent values are incommensurable with people's worth or dignity are equally unpersuaded that assistance with dying entails a lack of respect for, or a rejection of the dignity of, a person. It certainly seems to be possible to recognise a person as an end in himself while agreeing to his request for assistance with dying (whether by withdrawing or withholding life support, placing him in pharmacological oblivion and not providing artificial food and fluids, or by administering a lethal injection). Moreover, honouring a relevant advance directive of a no longer competent person by helping him die, clearly shows respect for his dignity because it recognises a choice he made when rational. Finally, it is hard to see how

[40] (1999a: 626).   [41] (1999a: 622, note 17, italics in the original).

it can be any different when a competent person is able concurrently to request assistance with dying. It simply begs the question to claim that to be capable of making such a request a person must be leading a life worth living. But that is precisely what Velleman appears to claim since he believes that if a patient is in an intolerable condition his capacities must be impaired and, so, that whenever a patient is capable of rational judgment he cannot be in a genuinely intolerable condition and must, therefore, go on living to ensure that his intrinsically valuable life is not destroyed just to promote his interest in avoiding further suffering. Acceptance of Velleman's position would rule out not only the more controversial forms of medically assisted death, like physician-assisted suicide and voluntary euthanasia, but also refusals by competent patients of life-sustaining medical treatment (because, for him, such refusals are tantamount to suicide). Accordingly, I contend that his argument against voluntary medically assisted dying in such instances is not compelling. What, though, of instances involving sufferers from conditions like motor neurone disease, who request help to die because their lives have become intolerably burdensome? If Velleman's contentions were compelling there would be reason to deny these patients their autonomous choices on the ground that to accede to their requests would undermine their standing as persons. I do not find this claim compelling. In particular, I reject the implication that someone suffering, from, for example, motor neurone disease, should have his autonomous request to end an existence he finds unbearable disallowed, and be expected, instead, to continue suffering so as to preserve the worth of his person.

It might be said, in response, that Velleman's argument turns on a different understanding from mine – namely, that the request be made by a self-determining agent – of what it is for a request for such assistance to be autonomous. Perhaps, for Velleman, following Kant, if such a request is to be autonomous it must amount to acting freely on principles that all can adopt, that is, to acting only on universalisable maxims, and that unless it is, it can only be 'mere, sheer choice' (as the existentialists would have it), lacking in reason and coherence.[42] If, for Velleman's argument to work, autonomy must be understood in this way, I here only have space to indicate that I do not believe that a moralised understanding of autonomy, like Kant's, is more plausible than mine, nor (obviously) that the existentialist understanding of autonomy is the only serious alternative to a Kantian understanding.[43]

---

[42] Cf. O'Neill (2000: 38–44) and Keown (2002: 227–230).
[43] See Young (1986) and Dworkin (1988).

Suppose that Velleman's contention about the incommensurability of a person's good and his worth is set to one side. Suppose further, for the sake of argument, and contrary to all that I have been arguing for, that human life is intrinsically valuable. Does it follow that its value outweighs all other values? I do not believe that it does, as should be clear from my response to Velleman, but also because, as Sidgwick[44] helpfully suggested more than a century ago, the most credible way to think of the intrinsically valuable is as what is desirable (or, as I would prefer to put it, valuable), *other things being equal*. On Sidgwick's account, what is intrinsically valuable is not the same as what is valuable *all things considered*. To maintain in existence something that is intrinsically valuable will, therefore, not be the best course of action, all things considered, whenever maintaining it in existence results in more significant disvalue of other kinds. Hence, those who appeal to the sanctity of human life to oppose the legalisation of medically assisted death cannot rest content with trying to show, let alone merely asserting, the intrinsic value of human life. They must answer satisfactorily the question whether there are any other values capable of outweighing the intrinsic value of human life.

Opponents of the legalisation of medically assisted death often insist that no matter how bad a competent individual considers his life to be, he must be kept alive, even against his will, because of the intrinsic value of his life. If they wish, on the one hand, to claim that no other kind of value can be commensurate with (and, so, be capable of being weighed against) the intrinsic value of his life, they are, in effect, claiming that his life is of absolute value with all the attendant problems for such a claim that I have already pointed out.[45] If, on the other hand, they are willing to weigh other values against the intrinsic value of human life, as they must if they are prepared to countenance killing in self-defence or in war, or to sacrifice the lives of a few to save those of many, then they must bear the burden of proof to show why a competent terminally ill patient whose life could be prolonged, but who requests assistance to die, should not be assisted to die. The burden of proof is theirs because they must show why some values, but not others, can outweigh the intrinsic value of a human life. They must, in particular, show why the intrinsic value of a person's life has to outweigh the disvalue of his life to himself should he judge it to be no longer worth living.

---

[44] Sidgwick (1907: Bk. 1, Ch. 9, section 3).

[45] Because Velleman's focus is on rational persons, not human beings as such, he allows, as was noted above, that medically assisted death may sometimes be morally justifiable; he cannot, therefore, be an absolutist.

John Keown is one believer in the intrinsic value of human life who has made some remarks of direct relevance to this issue. According to him, even though human life is a basic good, 'it is not the highest good, a good to which all the other basic goods must be sacrificed in order to ensure its preservation'.[46] Thus, the sanctity of human life does not require the preservation of human life at all costs (or, to put the point as others might, human life is not of overriding value). However, elsewhere he makes clear his belief that it cannot ever be right for someone to judge that his life is no longer worth living.[47] In other words, even though the intrinsic value of a human life can be outweighed by other intrinsic values, it cannot be outweighed by the value autonomy has for the patient (even though the best understanding of autonomy is that it, too, is of intrinsic value). Given this, it is hardly surprising that when Keown confronts the crucial matter of whether a patient's autonomous choice to die is capable of outweighing the intrinsic value of his human life he falls back on what he refers to as the 'fundamental' value of human life – in contradistinction to his earlier claim that its value was merely 'basic', and in opposition to his acknowledgment that the intrinsic value of human life can be outweighed by other intrinsic values. Keown, therefore, fails to give supporters of the legalisation of medically assisted death, who believe a competent individual may appropriately judge his life no longer worth living, a compelling reason to alter their standpoint.

Jeff McMahan[48] has suggested that someone who upholds the sanctity of human life in virtue of its being intrinsically valuable might contend that the life of a human being may not be ended intentionally *as long as the human in question is morally innocent*. This is undoubtedly consistent with traditional practice, which has licensed at least some instances of killing in self-defence and in war, though it still would not permit the sacrifice of the lives of a few to save those of many, nor permit refraining from saving a few in order to save many. Moreover, a critic of the proposition that the sanctity of human life derives from the intrinsic value of human life is entitled to ask how it is that someone's lack of moral innocence, indeed, *only* his lack of moral innocence, can set aside the intrinsic value of his life. As was made clear earlier, it has always been a key element in the idea of

---

[46] (2002: 41).

[47] (2002: 55, 227ff). Unfortunately, it is hard to get a line on what other intrinsic values Keown thinks might outweigh the value of human life since he only mentions two other intrinsically valuable goods, namely, friendship and knowledge (2002: 41).

[48] (2002: 467).

the sanctity of human life that all human lives are of equal value.[49] But that means intentional killing in self-defence to forestall an unjustified attack by a lethal aggressor (the most obvious circumstance in which someone who is not morally innocent may permissibly be killed) can only be made consistent with the traditional idea by decommissioning one of its key elements. Moreover, the notion of 'moral innocence' being invoked here, which was developed specifically to license the use of force by the state (in contexts like that of the waging of war) is a contested notion, so it is far from obvious that it should be determinative in relation to medically assisted death for those who competently judge that they would be better off dead.

I have argued that the most promising ways to understand the idea of the sanctity of human life fail to pass muster. In consequence, I believe the onus is on its supporters to put forward an account that does not fall foul of the sorts of criticisms I have made. The unifying thread running through my criticisms has been that there can be moral justification on occasion for not protecting or preserving the life of a human being. Hence, it can be granted that when other things are equal human life ought to be protected or preserved, but it has to be added that other things will not always be equal. I have suggested that other things are not equal when an aggressor threatens the life of another human being; nor are they equal when the only way to save many human lives is to sacrifice the lives of a few other humans. Most importantly for present purposes, nor are they equal when a human being who competently judges that he would be better off dead because his life has become irreversibly intolerable, but is unable to end his life without medical assistance, requests such assistance.

In the remainder of this chapter I will argue that, for purposes of deciding whether to legalise voluntary medically assisted dying, human life should be considered inviolable when it is qualitatively significant, namely, when it is at or above a specifiable threshold, rather than inviolable because of its sanctity. I will focus mainly on the circumstance where a still competent

---

[49] On McMahan's account, the fundamental moral equality of *persons* (rather than of *human beings*) demands a commitment to the 'equal wrongness thesis', namely, the thesis that the wrongness of killing a person does not vary with considerations like the person's age, intelligence, social worth and so on. His commitment to this thesis is compatible, as he sees it, with his belief that the wrongness of killing persons varies with the killer's mode of agency, the victim's culpability, the number of persons killed, and so forth (2002: 235ff, 467ff). He advances a two-tiered account of morality, according to which *a morality of respect* is appropriate to competent persons (wherein the morality of killing a person is governed by respect for them as a person), and *a morality of interests*, which is appropriate to those who are not persons. He believes this distinction is compatible with the equal wrongness thesis because acts of killing persons are equally wrong if other things are equal. By contrast, acts of killing non-persons are to be evaluated by reference to their interests (2002: 470–474).

individual's life has become so intolerable to him (because of suffering, or loss of dignity, or dependence on mechanical and other supports) that he wants to be helped to die. Similar issues arise where an individual has competently issued an advance directive that deals with how he wishes to be treated in the event that he suffers a permanent loss of competence. The issues are somewhat different when a substituted judgment has to be made, or when there is no way of knowing what a particular patient would wish to have done (as in the case, say, of a young child), and we are faced with circumstances where the patient's life can never again reach the threshold of acceptable quality. But even in these circumstances the issues are not so different as to require the focus to be moved away from the quality of the patient's life.

There are instances where an individual is competent, or has competently issued a relevant advance directive, but his life lacks the quality he wants it to have. There are also instances where a judgment may have to be made about whether an individual's life retains sufficient quality, or holds the promise of regaining sufficient quality, for it to be worth keeping him alive. In other words, an individual's life can be lacking in sufficient quality as assessed either by him, as a competent individual, or by his proxy. I take it that this is relatively uncontroversial for, as already noted, many believers in the sanctity of human life do not think that life-prolonging medical treatment must be continued if that would be medically futile. This, in itself, is an acknowledgment that, when continuing treatment will not restore or maintain an acceptable quality of life for a patient, it is not necessary to prolong his life (albeit just how his life may be brought to an end is morally and legally contentious). However, some of the implications this has are far from uncontroversial. It is, for instance, an implication that human lives do not all have the same *quality* (though this is not to say that they do not have equal *worth*); it is a further implication that some human lives lack the quality needed to make them worth living any longer.

I have stressed that it is essential to the traditional understanding of the sanctity of human life that all human lives are held to be of equal worth or value (or, as some would say, are equally to be respected). Supporters, as well as some critics, of the idea of the sanctity of human life often appear to conflate judgments of the *worth* of a human life with judgments of the *quality* of a human life. But, if all human lives are of equal worth, judgments of the former sort are not subject to variation, whereas those of the latter are, given the uncontroversial point that the quality of human lives varies. It is quite consistent to maintain that each human life is of equal worth, and so is deserving of equal respect, *but* that some human lives, from the perspective of those living them, are not worth living because they are of unacceptably diminished quality. Those who are not persuaded that the traditional idea of the sanctity of human life is defensible are at liberty to contend that (in the context of care for the dying) human life should be considered inviolable as long as its quality is at or above the threshold for a life to be worthwhile to its possessor.

Just where such a threshold should be set is a matter of dispute but the following considerations seem to bear directly on the quality of a dying person's life (supposing it to be in irreversible decline) and hence to be relevant to setting the threshold: how imminent death is for the person; whether he is having to endure pain and suffering that he is finding hard to bear; whether he is able to communicate with others or, at the very least, remain aware of them; and how much autonomy he is able to exercise – in particular, whether he can make competent decisions, and whether he is dependent on, for example, machines or pharmaceutical products for the maintenance of a tolerable existence. The list is not intended to be either definitive or complete but merely indicative of the sorts of considerations that are relevant to someone's assessment of the quality of his life (or to its assessment by others on his behalf). Discussions of what should be included in lists of this sort have often been bedevilled by disputes about the quite separate issue of whether the items to be included should be based wholly on subjective considerations, wholly on objective ones, or on some combination of the two. Those who think the quality of a person's life is to be determined solely by reference to his preferences (and, so, that he is the best judge of what is in his interests) think subjective considerations should determine the quality of a person's life. However, since preferences may be uninformed their satisfaction does not guarantee that life will be of the desired, let alone of an acceptable, quality. Even when preferences are formed after all relevant information has been taken into account their satisfaction is no guarantee of a qualitatively satisfactory life. This is because informed agents may suffer weakness of will, or be irrational about certain matters, or make mistakes in reasoning. These difficulties for wholly subjective accounts of the quality of life have led many to the view that the quality of a life should be judged by reference to considerations that are independent of preferences and so, in that sense, are objective. This, of course, carries with it a risk that people's autonomously formed preferences may be paternalistically overridden. The autonomously formed preferences of competent individuals, including those of the dying, must surely, however, have a role in the determination of the quality of an individual's life and that is why it is plausible to believe that a wholly objective set of considerations will not furnish a suitable account of the quality of a human life anymore than a wholly subjective set. Instead, a mixed set seems to be needed. The brief list I mentioned above was devised with that in mind.[50]

Proponents of the legalisation of voluntary medically assisted death contend that merely remaining alive when all quality of life has been lost need not be regarded as of supreme importance for humans. Since medical assistance with dying shows no disrespect for human life it should be made legally possible for a competent human who judges that the quality of his life is no longer acceptable to be assisted to die, if that is his choice. This would obviously necessitate the removal of existing legal barriers to the facilitation of such a choice. In the case of someone who is not competent to make such a choice, and who has not, while competent, issued a relevant advance directive, any decision to end his life (whether by ceasing to offer mechanical and other life-sustaining support, or via voluntary medically assisted death) must be based on the judgment that he would be better off dead, that is, that the quality of his life has fallen below the threshold deemed appropriate. In the former sort of case, the competent individual determines whether the quality of his life has so diminished that remaining alive is no longer of importance to him. In the latter, the judgment must be made on the basis of whether further treatment will be futile. Once it is clear that remaining alive is not of absolute value, is not of infinite value, is not of overriding value, and is not valuable for its own sake (or, even if it is, that its value does not outweigh all other relevant values), it is reasonable to reject the claim that it is impermissible to offer medical assistance with dying because to do so would violate the sanctity of human life.

---

[50] There is an extensive literature on these matters. Among the more important general discussions are Parfit (1984: Appendix I, 'What Makes Someone's Life Go Best?'); Griffin (1986: chs. 1–3); Brock (1993b: 95–132) to which Griffin replies (1993: 133–139); and Crisp (1994: 171–183). Many consequentialists claim that QALYs – 'quality adjusted life years' – provide a measure of both life expectancy and quality of life that enables decisions to be made about which health care activities are beneficial. See, for example, Harris (1987); Lockwood (1988); Williams (1996); and McKie, *et al.* (1998). As with consequentialist proposals more generally, the use of QALYs is open to criticism on the ground that they fail to be substantively (as against merely procedurally) fair in virtue of their exclusive concentration on maximisation of value.

CHAPTER 6

Killing versus letting die, the doctrine of double effect, and palliative care for the dying

Traditional morality considers harming others to be of great moral significance and, in consequence, incorporates constraints on certain ways of harming others. Within the tradition it has been claimed that, other things being equal, those instances of harming that result from an agent *doing* something are morally worse than those that result from an agent *allowing* something similarly harmful to occur. In this chapter I will, first, consider whether there is a morally significant distinction between doing and allowing, particularly in the context of end-of-life medical care wherein it manifests as the distinction between killing a patient and allowing a patient to die. Much of the criticism of the moral significance of this distinction has come from consequentialists, for whom minimising harm is obligatory, but it has also been criticised by those traditionalists who think a more refined approach is needed to effectively prohibit only a narrower band of harmful behaviour.[1] Many of these latter critics think what needs to be constrained is harm that is done *intentionally*,[2] rather than harm that is *merely foreseen* to flow from otherwise justifiable behaviour. So, my second concern in this chapter will be to consider the moral significance of the 'doctrine of double effect', particularly as it bears on end-of-life palliative care. According to this doctrine, it is sometimes morally permissible unintentionally to occasion harm (including, bringing about death), despite the harm being foreseen, provided there is a sufficiently grave

---

[1] A prominent reason for this has been that on those occasions when it appears morally justifiable for a person to do something harmful, in order to avoid an even greater harm, it would be disingenuous to describe the person as merely allowing the harm to eventuate. Thus, for example, if S were to divert a runaway trolley laden with coal from a track on which six miners are working who cannot be warned of the impending danger, to another where one miner, who likewise cannot be warned, is working, many would consider S's action in diverting the trolley to be morally permissible.

[2] I use the term here in what philosophers have labelled the *narrow* sense – the sense in which the actions an agent does intentionally are characterised by reference to what she is *aiming at*. By contrast, the *wide* sense of 'intention' requires only that an agent be *aware* that she is doing a particular action (as against doing it unintentionally). Bennett (1995: 211ff) is often credited with drawing the distinction between the narrow and wide understandings.

reason, whereas to intend the harm as a means, even with equally grave reason, is prohibited. (As will emerge later, the precise focus of the doctrine is on harm that is intended as a *means* to a certain goal as against harm that is intended as a goal in itself.)

I

The distinctions between doing and allowing something harmful, and between killing a patient and allowing him to die, have played prominent roles in debates about what constitutes permissible behaviour in the care of the dying. In a number of religious traditions, in medical practice, and in the law in most jurisdictions, these distinctions have been taken to establish parameters for managing, for example, the care of the dying. In particular, those who conceive of morality exclusively, or, at least, predominantly, within a traditional (deontological) framework, claim that *doing* something harmful is *intrinsically* morally wrong – that is, is morally wrong in itself, regardless of any good consequences it may produce. By contrast, when something similarly harmful is *allowed* to happen, a lesser intrinsic wrong is thought to be involved.[3]

Those who operate within such a framework do not, of course, think that allowing something harmful to occur is of no moral significance, only that doing something harmful is intrinsically worse than allowing it to happen. Allowing something harmful to occur that I could have prevented does not relieve me of responsibility for that harm just because I did not initiate it. Thus, for example, if someone dies as a result of my inaction it does not follow that, because I did nothing, I am absolved of responsibility for his death, or that no blame attaches to me. Hence, even if I cannot be said to have killed him, I may still be held responsible for having allowed him to die, and be blamed for my role in his death. Allowing harm to occur remains a matter of moral importance. Moreover, those who think acts of killing are intrinsically worse can agree that a killing *typically* has extrinsic features that are lacking in an instance of letting die – malice, violation of the victim's rights, violence, and so on – and that the presence of these features generally makes killing far more morally reprehensible. What they insist, however, is that even in medical settings, where such extrinsic features are not normally present, it is intrinsically worse to do something harmful than to allow something harmful to occur.

---

[3] Among the more impressive recent philosophical attempts to support such a conclusion are Donagan (1977); Foot (1994); and Quinn (1989a).

By contrast, those who conceive of morality exclusively within a consequentialist framework consider that, where other things (like motive, intention, and the effort or sacrifice required to achieve a certain outcome) are equal, it is outcomes that determine what is morally good or bad. They reject the claim that bringing about a certain outcome by doing something involves an intrinsically worse wrongdoing by comparison with allowing the same outcome to occur.

Given that, for present purposes, the issue is whether it is intrinsically morally worse to kill a dying patient at his request than to allow him to die at his request, I will assume, for the sake of argument, the legal permissibility of assisting someone to die by either means. Whilst this is true in a small number of jurisdictions, as was explained in Chapter 1, it is, of course, not generally the case. I make the assumption here simply to ensure that questions of the legality of assisting someone to die do not distract from the (mainly philosophical) issues I wish to take up. The following example will serve to illustrate the supposed difference between an instance of letting die and an instance of killing in a medical context. Suppose a ventilator-dependent patient, who is being fed and hydrated artificially, deteriorates into a persistent vegetative state. Suppose further that, while competent, the patient had requested that he be assisted to die should he enter a persistent vegetative state. A number of options will be open to the attending doctor. The doctor could, for example, simply withdraw the patient's artificial nutrition and hydration and allow him to die (which, as previously indicated, usually occurs because of electrolyte imbalance, but may also result from dehydration, which, in turn, may lead to vulnerability to infection and pneumonia); or, she could remove his ventilator; or, she could maintain his life-support arrangements. If she were to withdraw artificial nutrition, or remove the ventilator, would she be honouring her patient's request to be assisted to die? Those who insist that whether she kills him, or merely allows him to die, depends on the intention with which she acts, are apt to contend, if she withdraws the nutrition, or the oxygen, that she has allowed him to die. By contrast, if she were to give him a lethal injection of potassium chloride they would contend that she must have intended to bring about his death (and so must have killed him).

Allow me to suppose, once again for the sake of argument, that there is a clear distinction between these two sorts of response to the patient's situation. Even with that concession in place, it remains far from clear that it is the doctor's intention alone that determines whether she has allowed the patient to die, or has killed him. Even if, in the above case, she did not intend the withdrawal of nutrition, hydration or oxygen to bring about the patient's death, it is obvious that in other closely related circumstances it would be accurate to say that she did intend to let him die (and to have done so because she thought it clear, from his request not to have his life pro-longed in such circumstances, that, were he capable of doing so, he would judge his life to have no significance for him). Suppose, for example, that any of the following occurs: the ventilator is accidentally disconnected; the electrical power supply is interrupted; or, there is a loss of gas pressure that causes the ventilator to malfunction. In any of these circumstances the doctor would rightly be said to have intended to allow her patient to die if she refrained from having the ventilator reconnected, or from having the power supply restored, or from having the gas pressure returned to an appropriate level. Hence, it cannot just be the doctor's intention that deter-mines whether her behaviour is to count as a killing or a letting die. It is possible to kill someone unintentionally, and it is possible intentionally to let someone die. So, the issue of whether a killing is intrinsically morally worse than a letting die cannot be decided by reference to the agent's intentions alone.[4] If the important and controversial issues that turn on the distinction between killing and letting die are to be settled, it will, therefore, be necessary, first, to consider how best to draw the distinc-tion, and, then, second, to determine whether the distinction thus drawn has the moral significance that has been attributed to it, particularly in the context of the care of the dying. The latter task has to be undertaken because it might turn out that there is a clear distinction between killing and letting die, but that it nonetheless signifies nothing of moral importance.

II

Attempts at distinguishing killing from letting die in medical contexts have often taken the form of describing what is *said to be* a killing and setting it side-by-side with an instance similar in all relevant aspects except that it is *said to be* a letting die. In describing such pairs it is presupposed that agree-ment can be reached that the motives, intentions and outcomes in the sepa-rate instances are identical and that the effort involved in letting a patient die (for example, via the withdrawal or withholding of life-sustaining medical measures) is indistinguishable from the effort required to kill

---

[4] This does not commit me to the claim that an agent's having a certain intention is never the chief factor in moral wrongdoing. I will have more to say about the role of intention later in the chapter when I consider the doctrine of double effect.

(for example, via the administration of a lethal injection). Those who hold that the distinction between killing and letting die has intrinsic moral significance contend that the moral judgment to be made about such a killing differs from the moral judgment to be made about such a letting die.[5] Those who are opposed to according intrinsic moral significance to the distinction have replied that when the instances are carefully enough described so as to ensure that they share all of their properties in common, except for those that differentiate a killing from a letting die, the instances will prove to be morally equivalent, that is, neither will be morally worse than the other.[6] This use of what some (e.g. Kagan (1988)) call a 'contrast argument', and others (e.g. Rachels (1986)) call a 'bare difference argument', is intended to show that, since there is no moral difference as between the respective behaviours, the bare difference (that one form of behaviour is a killing and the other a letting die), can have no moral significance.[7]

One difficulty with proceeding in this way is that it is presumptuous to suppose (as those who adopt this strategy do) that disputes about what is to count as an instance of killing and what is to count as an instance of letting die can always be decisively resolved. Another difficulty with arguments like the one above is that they controversially assume that if a factor is intrinsically morally significant in one circumstance it will be significant wherever it is present.[8] I shall not here consider the second of these difficulties because it would take us too far afield to do so, but I will endeavour instead to determine, first, whether killing and letting die can always

---

[5] See, for example: Casey (1980); Dinello (1994); Trammell (1994); Quinn (1989a); McMahan (1993) and (2002); Kamm (1996) and (2000: 208–219). It should be noted that McMahan thinks that even though we can distinguish killing from letting die, it is difficult to believe that the way in which an agent is instrumental in an outcome can be more important than the outcome itself.

[6] See Russell (1980); Rachels (1986) and (1994); Bennett (1994) and (1995); Tooley (1994); and Kagan (1989) and (1998).

[7] Graham Oddie attempts to develop an argument that does not rely on the bare difference strategy to show that killing is not morally worse than letting die in Oddie (1997). Elsewhere (1998), however, he, too, resorts to a bare difference strategy.

[8] This possibility is discussed by Kagan (1988) and (1998: 98f), as well as by Norcross (2003). They each point out that those who claim a distinction is morally relevant in one circumstance, but not in another, must bear the burden of proof to show why that is so. Kagan contends (1988: 14) that contrast arguments make 'the additive assumption', namely, the assumption that the status of an act depends on the 'net balance or sum, which is the result of adding up the separate positive and negative effects of the individual factors'. He then argues, first, that there is no plausible reason to think that contrast arguments are sound if the additive assumption is false, and, second, that there are good reasons to believe the assumption is false. Thus, he thinks there is no way of avoiding having to consider whether in any particular circumstance the factors involved interact to alter the particular effects and so to preclude their simply being aggregated in the way advocates of contrast arguments suppose they can. For a critical response see Malm (1992).

be clearly distinguished, and, second, whether a bare difference argument can be successfully employed in the context of medically assisted dying.

Intuitively, to be let die, a patient must already be dying from an underlying medical condition, so that he will be likely to die if the medical help keeping him alive is withdrawn or withheld. Nonetheless, there are at least two reasons why this is not a sufficient account of what it is to be let die. To begin with, a doctor who withdraws or withholds[9] life-support must be entitled to do so if what is done, or omitted, is to count as an instance of letting die rather than as a killing.[10] If a doctor were, say, to withdraw life-support from a patient currently reliant on it, who is expected eventually to make a good recovery, in order to make the relevant equipment available to one of her close relatives, then, supposing the relative not to have a stronger medical claim to the equipment, the withdrawal (if it resulted in death) would constitute a killing, not an instance of letting die. Removing the life-support would involve breaking the implicit commitment to the patient to provide ongoing care. (However, this is not to assert that under no circumstances may life-prolonging equipment be transferred from one needy patient to another.) Merely introducing this first additional condition does not as such enable the distinction to be drawn satisfactorily. It is necessary to add as well that the patient should not be in the process of dying because of anything the doctor has previously done or failed to do.[11] If, for example, a patient is dying because previous actions by his doctor put his life in jeopardy, the withdrawal, by that doctor, of life-sustaining measures would amount to killing the patient (because it would 'complete the causation' to use a phrase coined by Eric Mack[12]). To sum up: a doctor[13] lets her patient die, but does not kill him, if he would die (from his underlying medical condition) were the medical help that is keeping him alive to be withdrawn or withheld, provided always that the doctor is entitled to withdraw or withhold that medical help

---

[9] I do not deny that there will sometimes be epistemic issues in determining which non-interventions amount to letting someone die. But, in the context of the care of the dying, I think such difficulties represent less of a problem than they may do elsewhere. For further discussion of this issue see e.g. McMahan (1998: 412f).

[10] Cf. Thomson (1999: 504).   [11] Cf. Kamm (1996: 28ff) and McMahan (2002: 380f).

[12] (1980: 240).

[13] Typically, of course, a patient is not cared for by just one doctor, even though there may be one doctor who has notional charge of his case; so, strictly, it would be more accurate to speak of 'doctors'. Some think doing so would also avoid the objection that if doctor A provides a patient with life-support, which is subsequently withdrawn by doctor B, then B may be regarded as having killed the patient rather than having let him die (since it was not B who came to his aid). Certainly, if a person other than a doctor withdraws the life-support, or the life-support is withdrawn by a doctor who is not entitled to do so, this amounts to a killing. See further McMahan (2002: 380).

and the patient's underlying medical condition is not a result of something
the doctor has previously done or omitted to do.

It is worth drawing attention to a couple of points that emerge from this
way of drawing the distinction. First, to let someone die is not merely to
forbear from all action, or to expend no effort. At the very least, it involves
knowingly bringing about the victim's death because action that could have
been taken to keep the victim alive is (knowingly) not taken. Not taking
such action may, in fact, require strenuous psychological or physical
effort. Second, since it has not been necessary to mention the agent's intention in defining either killing or letting die, there can be no basis for claiming, as has so often been done, that in killing, but not in letting die, there
must be an intention to bring about death. In the UK case of *Airedale
NHS Trust v. Bland*,[14] which I have previously mentioned, the Law
Lords who ruled that withdrawing the life-support system keeping
Anthony Bland alive was lawful relied in part on their belief that withdrawal
of life-sustaining systems and procedures should be regarded as an omission
rather than an act. Only thus, it was argued, could the discontinuance of
life-sustaining treatment be regarded as lawful because, if such discontinuance were to be construed as an intentional act, it would violate the
principle that it is the intention to kill which constitutes the *mens rea* of
murder. Alas, as has already emerged, the belief on which they so heavily
relied is false. Hence, the position they took is clearly philosophically
indefensible, whatever its merits as a rationale for protecting medical
professionals who act in what they judge to be the best interests of
their patients.

III

Now that I have indicated how to distinguish between killing and letting die
in the context of the care of the dying, I can turn to the more important
matter of whether the distinction has moral significance. As previously mentioned, debate about the moral significance of the distinction has largely
been about whether there can be instances of killing a patient and of
letting a patient die that are morally indistinguishable. More formally, the
issue is whether an instance in which a patient is killed and an instance
in which a patient is let die can have all of their properties (including
moral properties) in common. If either includes a property (or properties)
not found in the other, and if there is moral significance in the presence of

[14] [1993] 1 All ER 821.

that property (or those properties), killing and letting die cannot be morally equivalent. If, on the other hand, the two instances share all of their properties they will be morally equivalent forms of behaviour.

Since my task is to determine whether the distinction between them has moral significance, it cannot be *presupposed* that killing is harder to justify than letting die. It would simply be question-begging to assert that it is having the property of being an original cause of death,[15] which, as already mentioned, is part of the traditional understanding of a killing but not of letting die, that makes an act of killing morally worse than an act of letting die (on the ground that the latter, by definition, does not have that property).

With this in mind, various consequentialists, like James Rachels,[16] have contended that once clearly morally relevant variables like motive, effort (or, sacrifice), and intention are equalised in instances of killing and letting die, it is obvious that they are morally equivalent (given that the outcome, death, is the same in each case). Hence, in instances where these morally relevant variables are, in fact, equalised (or, neutralised), letting die will not be morally superior to killing, but, rather, on a par with it, for once these variables are taken out of the picture, no morally significant difference will be attributable to the distinction between killing and letting die. Accordingly, there will be instances where killing is as morally justifiable as letting die. This so-called 'equivalence thesis' is central to the first of the two main arguments that have been advanced by consequentialists to show that the distinction between killing and letting die has no intrinsic moral significance, and thus that it is not always worse morally to kill as against to let die. There is a second argument to the same conclusion, namely one to the effect that there can be instances where to let someone die is actually morally worse (not morally better) than to kill them. It will become clear in a moment that this second argument cannot be dealt with in isolation from the first so I shall consider it briefly before discussing the first argument in greater detail.

Consider the following example as an illustration of what proponents of the second argument have in mind. Suppose that a patient, who is suffering both terminal bone cancer and severe emphysema, is being plagued by pain

---

[15] Kamm (1996: 22). For her, an agent is an original cause of death if she acts so as to bring about an event that causes a death, but not if she removes a defence against death (as, for example, when A removes B's protective asbestos covering and B is consumed by an approaching fire). The removal of the defence is a *new* event and so cannot constitute an *original* cause of death.

[16] See (1986: Chs. 7–8) and (1994).

that has proved impossible fully to control, is finding his situation intolerably burdensome, and further medical intervention is viewed as physiologically futile. Suppose, further, that he has, at most, only days to live. Suppose that he remains competent and presses his case to be helped to die rather than endure further suffering. Suppose, finally, that he refuses an offer of terminal sedation because he is adamant that he does not want to die in such a condition. Proponents of the second argument contend that, contrary to the conviction of those who believe that it would be impermissible to kill such a patient, it would, in fact, be morally worse not to assist the patient to die. Only by granting such assist-ance can he be enabled to avoid needless suffering and be given the respect to which he is entitled as a competent patient.[17] Those who believe that facilitating a medically assisted death is morally impermissible will respond that the patient may only have his suffering relieved by means that do not involve intentionally bringing about his death. Regardless of whether this is a satisfactory way to resolve the problem of the patient's intractable suffering it obviously fails to address the issue of his competent refusal of such a strategy. Supporters of the argument believe that it is only those who assume that killing is morally worse than letting die who will think it justified to deny the patient his competent request for medical assistance with dying. But, equally, those who believe that killing is morally worse than letting die think that their opponents' argument gains its force entirely from the underlying assumption that only conse-quences matter morally. There will be no hope of resolving the stand-off unless it is possible independently to determine whether killing is always morally worse than letting die. In other words, the success or otherwise of the second argument depends on the success or otherwise of the first.

I turn, therefore, to a more detailed consideration of the argument that there is no intrinsic moral significance to the distinction between killing and letting die. As mentioned above, in his well-known defence of the moral equivalence of killing and letting die, James Rachels utilised a 'bare difference argument'.[18] He outlined two instances in which a person dies that he contended were exactly alike, except for the bare difference that one involved killing while the other involved letting die, and then argued that this bare difference, *in itself*, had no moral significance. Here is his well-known pair of instances.

1. Smith stands to gain a large inheritance if anything should happen to his six-year-old cousin. One evening, while the child is taking a bath, Smith

---

[17] The example is a modification of one described in Menzel (1979).   [18] (1986: chs. 7–8).

sneaks into the bathroom and drowns him, and then arranges things so that it looks like an accident. No one is the wiser, and Smith gets his inheritance.

2. Jones also stands to gain if anything should happen to his six-year-old cousin. Like Smith, Jones sneaks in planning to drown his cousin in his bath. However, just as he enters the bathroom Jones sees the child slip, hit his head, and fall face-down in the water. Jones is delighted; he stands by, ready to push the child's head back under if necessary, but it is not necessary. After only a little thrashing about, the child 'accidentally' drowns as Jones watches and does nothing. No one is the wiser, and Jones gets his inheritance.

Rachels acknowledges that there are important respects in which these imaginary instances involving Smith and Jones are quite unlike those in which dying patients who request medically assisted death have their request facilitated. For example, doctors who administer voluntary euthanasia will only rarely, if ever, be motivated by avarice in the way Smith and Jones are, and patients seeking medically assisted death who have concluded that their lives no longer have value for them are differently placed compared with the unfortunate cousins of Smith and Jones. Nonetheless, he believes these points do not gainsay the fact that his central claim can be applied straightforwardly to instances in which a competent patient requests medically assisted death, so that whether he is killed or let die makes no difference *in itself* to the moral justifiability of fulfilling his request.

Various critics have disputed Rachels' claim about the moral equivalence of the behaviour of the respective adults in his examples by disputing the generalisability of his claim. Some have offered what they take to be counter-examples to his position. Consider, for example, the following supposed analogy: even though a person has no moral obligation to sacrifice his wealth to save the life of another person, it would be morally wrong to kill someone in order to save the same sum of money. But this is not decisive against Rachels since he could claim that the alleged counter-example depends on not having equalised all of the features involved (for example, the effort to be expended in each instance). It might also be said (more promisingly) that it is because Jones has the intention to kill his cousin that the two cases have to be thought of as involving similar wickedness. It was not necessary, of course, for Jones to kill him, but had his cousin not simply been able to be left to die presumably Jones would have intervened and drowned him. Thus, it is because Jones intended to kill that there appears to be no morally significant difference between his behaviour and Smith's.

Perhaps the most impressive attempt to uncover a flaw in Rachels' bare difference argument has been made by Frances Myrna Kamm. It is of interest that she is neither a consequentialist nor a traditionalist, even though, like traditionalists, she thinks the moral significance of the distinction between killing and letting die ultimately rests on the distinction between doing and allowing. Despite this, she believes that it is not the case that the distinction *always* picks out a morally significant difference. Hence, she contends that: there are instances within health care in which killing is morally permissible, for example, when a person competently requests help to die because that is best for him; there are instances in which letting someone die is morally wrong, as when someone who has a duty to aid commences aid and then withdraws it; and, there are instances in which letting someone die is morally worse than killing, as, for example, when it leads to needless suffering. Nonetheless, she argues that killing and letting die are not *as such* morally on a par.[19] I do not have the space to consider her labyrinthine arguments against what she dubs 'the equalisation thesis', but instead I will consider some related remarks she makes when she adopts the tactic of working with the argumentative strategy of those who endorse the equalisation thesis in order to show that the conclusions they have drawn cannot be justified. I think her remarks are instructive.

Kamm thinks that, even when cases have been properly equalised, various tests to determine whether such instances of killing and letting die turn out to be morally on a par show that they are not.[20] The tests she proposes concern, first, any further effort that is morally required of someone who has attempted, unsuccessfully, to kill another or to let him die, *after* a failed attempt. This she calls the *post-efforts test*. Second, she proposes a *pre-efforts test*, that is, a test for what efforts a person would be required to expend (or, what losses the person would be required to suffer) to avoid killing someone or to avoid letting him die. Third, she puts forward what she calls a *choice test*. It asks which of a killing and a letting die should be avoided if it is not possible to avoid both. Finally, she outlines a *good motive test*. Suppose a benevolent (paternalistic) motive for a killing and for a letting die. Kamm claims that requiring aid from an agent who

---

[19] (1996: chs. 1–4). She offers two main arguments. First, she argues (1996: 49f) that, by its very definition, letting die has at least one property in favour of its moral permissibility that killing lacks (viz., that the victim loses his life only as a result of the agent's actions). Second, she argues (1996: 58) that while it is permissible to let someone die rather than make a certain effort or sacrifice, it is harder to justify avoiding these same efforts by killing someone who will lose more than he would have gotten causally by those efforts. For critical responses see Kagan (1989: 116–121); Rakowski (1998); and Norcross (2003: 452f).

[20] (1996: ch. 4).

refuses to give it is less easily justified than preventing an agent bent on killing from killing. It is her claim that it is a killer, not someone who refuses to aid, who interferes with what a person would have retained independently of the deadly imposition on him, and that explains why we can legitimately enforce a prohibition on the killer's behaviour, but not the other way round.

In the context of caring for dying patients, neither the third nor the fourth test decisively shows that letting die has the moral advantage over killing. More details about an individual's circumstances would be needed before there could be any determination of what those tests showed. Certainly, it is not difficult to think of circumstances where a choice to kill could be made with equal justification as a choice to let die, and circumstances can easily be imagined where a paternalistic killing would be no worse, and possibly even better, morally, than a letting die. The former could include instances of medically assisted death (as Kamm recognises[21]), while the latter could include instances of non-voluntary euthanasia (for example, of infants who are suffering intolerably and are without hope of ever enjoying worthwhile lives).

The first two tests, however, do pose a challenge to attempts to equalise the moral significance of killing and letting die in all circumstances, because it is plausible to think that where two forms of behaviour are equally wrong the maximum loss we may impose on an agent to prevent her engaging in either form of behaviour ought to be the same. Yet it is not considered permissible to kill someone to prevent her letting another die, even though it is sometimes permissible to kill someone to prevent her from killing. Interventions in such instances are not aimed at imposing comparable losses on the killer and on the one who lets die. Kamm has undoubtedly identified an important consideration. Consider again Rachels' pair of cases involving Smith and Jones. Would the post-efforts morally required of Smith, if he failed to kill his cousin, be the same as for Jones should his attempt to let his nephew die be unsuccessful? Kamm plausibly suggests that they would not – if the cases have been genuinely equalised it follows, *pace* Rachels and various other consequentialists, that killing *is* morally worse than letting die, at least in such instances. Much the same holds for the pre-efforts test. The efforts that may be required of someone (or, the sacrifice that may legitimately be asked of her) to avoid a killing are plausibly greater than for a letting die. That being so it is reasonable to explain the

---

[21] (1996: 194ff) and (1998).

difference by reference to the greater moral significance that attaches to avoiding killing someone than to avoiding letting someone die.

Despite her belief that the difference between a killing and a letting die is *sometimes* morally significant, Kamm, it will be recalled, also claims that, in at least some instances of terminal illness, killing is not just morally permissible but morally preferable to letting die. There is no inconsistency in her taking the position she does on the moral significance of the distinction between killing and letting die *and* endorsing the argument previously outlined to the conclusion that, in, for example, end-of-life cases, allowing someone to die may actually be morally worse (not morally better) than killing him. As she realises, context can make a significant difference.[22]

Earlier, I contended that it is of significance in end-of-life matters, not least for classificatory purposes, whether the dead person would have died anyway, whether the person who prevents the provision of aid is entitled to do so, and whether that person was instrumental in the dead person being in mortal peril. Once these details are filled in, and an instance has been appropriately classified, there is then a separate and, I believe, more important, issue about the propriety of the behaviour. An instance of letting die, for example, may be more or less morally condemnable than, or equally as morally condemnable as, a killing, *depending on the context* (*vide* the second of the two arguments about the moral significance of killing versus letting die that I previously set out). In so-called 'easy rescue' cases,[23] for example, it is clear how the context may make someone's behaviour in letting another die quite reprehensible. To let someone die who would be easy to save rightly evokes moral condemnation, perhaps just as great condemnation as had the victim been killed. By contrast, to kill someone who would die an excruciating death if let die, rightly evokes moral praise except among those who are already convinced that all instances of killing are morally worse than all instances of letting die. These latter reject the importance of context in determining the propriety of certain behaviour. But to ignore context is to make a serious mistake. The mistake is decidedly serious when the context is the care of the dying because, in such a context, if it is in a person's interest to die, and he competently requests to die, it will be better that he be killed, or assisted to die, than that he be let die, if letting him die will prolong his distress. Given such

---

[22] (1996: 82f) and McMahan (2002: 386f).
[23] Cf. Peter Singer's well-known example of a child who is lying face down in a shallow pool of water and will die unless a passing adult is prepared to wade into the pool and muddy her clothing while effecting a rescue – see Singer (1972) and Unger (1996).

a context, it is reasonable to believe that killing is not morally worse than letting die; indeed, it is morally preferable.

I V

I argued in the previous section that the reliance placed on the distinction between killing and letting die in medical practice cannot be justified. Just as much reliance has been placed on the doctrine of double effect. In the remainder of this chapter I shall show that it, too, cannot be relied upon in the way it traditionally has been.

According to the Catholic Church, as well as various medical authorities, it is always wrong intentionally to cause the death of an innocent human being. Nonetheless, the doctrine of double effect, to which they subscribe, allows that it is sometimes morally permissible unintentionally to occasion harm (including death) despite the harm being foreseen, provided there is a sufficiently grave reason for doing so, whereas to intend the harm as a means, even with equally grave reason, is prohibited. Thus, for example, the entry in *The New Catholic Encyclopedia*[24] states the doctrine as requiring that:

1. The act itself must be morally good or at least morally indifferent.
2. The agent may not positively will the bad effect but may permit it. (If he could attain the good effect without the bad effect he should do so. The bad effect is sometimes said to be indirectly voluntary.)
3. The good effect must be produced directly by the action, at least as immediately (in the order of causality, though not necessarily in the order of time) as the bad effect. In other words the good effect must be produced directly by the action, not by the bad effect. Otherwise the agent would be using a bad means to a good end, which is never allowed.
4. The good effect must be sufficiently desirable to compensate for the allowing of the bad effect.

In an earlier formulation, Joseph Mangan[25] explicitly required that the bad effect not be intended and offered a subtly different rationale for the proportionality requirement. According to him, a person may licitly perform an action that he foresees will produce a good effect and a bad effect provided that four conditions are simultaneously verified:

1. that the action in itself from its very object be good or at least indifferent;
2. that the good effect and not the evil effect be intended;
3. that the good effect be not produced by means of the evil effect;
4. that there be a proportionately grave reason for permitting the evil effect.

---

[24] Connell (1967).   [25] Mangan (1949).

In a more recent formulation Joseph Boyle[26] has claimed that it is permissible to bring about harms that it would be absolutely impermissible to bring about intentionally, provided:

1. the harms are not intended but are brought about as side-effects;
2. there are sufficiently serious moral reasons for doing what brings about the harms.

Similar principles are reflected in pronouncements from representative medical organisations about what constitutes permissible care of the dying. Here are a few typical examples:

American Medical Association: The administration of a drug necessary to ease the pain of a patient who is terminally ill and suffering excruciating pain may be appropriate medical treatment even though the effect of the drug may shorten life. . . . The ethical distinction between providing palliative care that may have fatal side-effects and providing euthanasia is subtle because in both cases the action that causes death is performed with the purpose of relieving suffering.[27]

Australian Medical Association: The Australian Medical Association believes that doctors should not be involved in interventions that have as their primary goal the ending of a person's life. The Australian Medical Association endorses the right of a patient to refuse treatment and the right of a severely and terminally ill patient to have relief of pain and suffering, even when such therapy may shorten that patient's life.[28]

British Medical Association: The British Medical Association sees an important difference between intentional killing and the withdrawal of treatment in a way that will foreseeably result in the patient's death.[29]

World Medical Association: Physician assisted suicide, like euthanasia, is unethical and must be condemned by the medical profession. Where the assistance of the physician is intentionally and deliberately directed at enabling an individual to end his or her own life, the physician acts unethically. However, the right to decline medical treatment is a basic right of the patient and the physician does not act unethically even if respecting such a wish results in the death of a patient.[30]

According to these various pronouncements, euthanasia (whether voluntary or non-voluntary) is to be prohibited because it involves intentional killing. Physician-assisted suicide is regarded in a similar light. Yet it is

[26] Boyle (1991: 476).   [27] American Medical Association (1992: 2231).
[28] Australian Medical Association (2002).   [29] British Medical Association (2006).
[30] World Medical Association (1992).

permissible to administer pain relief, or withdraw life-prolonging treatment, as long as it is only foreseen (rather than intended) that doing so will lead to the patient's death. These pronouncements seem to be underpinned by the doctrine of double effect, but, if that is considered too strong, then, at the very least, they reflect an acceptance of the central principle in that doctrine, namely, that a distinction can be drawn between the intentional use of a harmful means to achieve an important purpose and the incidental bringing about of a harmful side-effect (or, second effect) in the process of achieving a similar, important purpose. Voluntary medically assisted death is regarded not only as ethically unacceptable but medically unnecessary. Actively assisting a dying patient to die is held not only to be unethical but unnecessary when there are, for example, legally accepted methods of providing palliative care to enable the patient to have an easy death.

An adequate response to these claims requires that I first bring greater precision to the statement of the doctrine of double effect. Consider, for example, the reference in Mangan's formulation of the fourth condition to a 'proportionately grave reason'. This leaves vague just when it would be permissible to bring about a harmful, but unintended, second effect. Despite its vagueness, there is a significant advantage in this formulation as compared with one in terms of a proportionately good effect, namely, one where the good effect suitably outweighs the harmful effect.[31] Any formulation of the doctrine suggesting that the value of the good end to be achieved must be weighed against the harmful side-effect in order to establish the permissibility of bringing about the side-effect would fail to distinguish it sufficiently from consequentialist moral reasoning.[32] Moreover, if it were permissible for an agent, who foresees that there will be side-effects, merely to ensure a proportionality between the good achieved and the harm occasioned, there would be no obligation to cause the least incidental harm feasible in the circumstances, an obligation that is a feature of the traditional understanding of the doctrine of double effect. On the traditional understanding of the doctrine, a doctor, for example, is not permitted to use a form of pain relief that will prove lethal if there is an equally effective means available that will not result in death. Hence, if a doctor gives a lethal dose of morphine when a lesser dose would serve, the doctrine affords no protection, even if she did not intend to bring about the death of her patient. (It has become customary

---

[31] Connell (1967).
[32] See Anscombe (1982); Boyle (1991); Bennett (1995: 197); Botros (1999); and McIntyre (2001: 221ff).

in Catholic teaching, and in medical circles, to regard as intended not only the good that is aimed at, but also the means used to achieve that good. So, to bring about the death of an innocent human being as a means to achieving some good effect is considered a violation of the teaching that it is always wrong intentionally to bring about the death of an innocent human being.)

A second point to note concerning the precise meaning of the doctrine is that it is distinct from the claim that an agent who foresees that harm will result from what she does, but nonetheless does not intend that harmful outcome, is thereby relieved of responsibility for her actions. There are those who contend that, as long as these requirements are satisfied, an agent is not responsible for harm that is unintentionally brought about, even when it is foreseen that the harm will eventuate, whereas an agent is responsible for what is intentionally brought about, since that is a matter of choice.[33] But the doctrine has traditionally been (and, I believe, should be) formulated so as to set out conditions for those means that it is morally permissible for an agent to use. Hence, it should not be construed as the position that an agent is relieved of responsibility for what she does as long as she merely foresees, but does not intend, that harm will result. Accordingly, in what follows, I will take the doctrine to be concerned with the permissibility of occasioning incidental harm as against intended harm.

Though the origins of the doctrine of double effect are frequently traced to some remarks of Thomas Aquinas about why it is legitimate to kill in self-defence,[34] the positions of the various medical bodies I cited show that, regardless of its origins, the doctrine is not merely of theological and philosophical interest. Some[35] think that it has had both desirable and undesirable effects on clinical practice, especially in relation to palliative care. Allow me to elaborate.

It is sometimes necessary to administer increasingly large doses of analgesics to help dying patients with pain relief. The administration of these large doses will on occasion lead to respiratory depression and the speeding up of patients' deaths. (Of course, there can be other side-effects such as incontinence and drowsiness, but in what follows they will be ignored since they are not relevant to my present concerns.) Many palliative care

---

[33] See Dworkin (1987).
[34] *Summa Theologiae*, 2a 2ae. 64, 7. Bennett (1995: 200, notes 13 and 14) does not think that what Aquinas says there commits him to the doctrine of double effect *as it has come to be formulated in the last two hundred years*.
[35] Cf. Quill, Dresser, and Brock (1997).

specialists believe that patients can tolerate increasingly large but titrated doses of opioids like morphine, and so believe that it is not the opioids as such, but whether the drug is new to the patient, the size of the initial dose, and the steepness of the rate of escalation of subsequent increases, that influences whether there will be any respiratory effects and any hastening of death.[36] Nonetheless, though there is still some controversy about these matters, it is widely accepted that at the very end, at least, death can be, and usually is, hastened. Those who apply the doctrine of double effect to such cases contend that the intention of those administering the analgesics is the relief of pain even if they foresee the (unintended) hastening of the patient's death. The relief of pain is considered to be a sufficiently grave reason for administering the analgesics (despite the knowledge that a second effect, namely, the death of the patient, will be produced), and to be proportionate in the circumstances. If this is accepted, the doctrine of double effect can then be regarded as having the desirable effect of giving reassurance to physicians concerned about the moral permissibility of relieving pain even when, in the process, they will hasten death. Others, however, consider it has the undesirable effect of reinforcing the idea that it is not morally permissible to bring about death as a means of relieving pain.[37]

The doctrine of double effect has also had significant influence on the law.[38] As already noted, the doctrine declares it to be morally permissible in certain circumstances for physicians to administer analgesics that may prove lethal. In many jurisdictions, physicians are legally permitted to administer potentially lethal drugs provided a proportionality requirement is satisfied that is akin to the one contained in some formulations of the doctrine of double effect (albeit not the one most faithful to the way the doctrine has traditionally been understood), namely, such drugs may be administered provided only that they will relieve serious suffering and there is no equally efficacious alternative with fewer side-effects. It is not unreasonable to find here the influence of the doctrine. In Chapter 1 I mentioned the trial in the United Kingdom of Dr Cox who injected a patient suffering from severe rheumatic pain with potassium chloride.

---

[36] DuBose and Berde (1997).   [37] Cf. Quill, Dresser and Brock (1997).

[38] Cf., among British cases, *R v. Adams* [1957] Crim. LR 365; *R v. Lodwig* [1990] (Unreported) *The Times* 16 March, 1990; *R v. Cox* [1992] BMLR 38 and *In the Matter of Ann Lindsell v. Simon Holmes* [1997] (Unreported) *The Guardian* 29 October, 1997. *Adams* and *Cox* are discussed, along with other relevant material, by Price (1997). *Adams*, *Cox* and *Lindsell* are discussed in Keown (2002: ch. 2). See, too, Finnis (1991).

In that trial the presiding judge (Justice Ognall) directed the jury in the following terms:

. . . if [Dr Cox] injected [Ms Boyes] with potassium chloride with the primary purpose of killing her, of hastening her death, he is guilty of [murder] . . . If a doctor genuinely believes that a certain course is beneficial to his patient, either therapeutically or analgesically, then even though he recognises that that course carries with it a risk to life, he is fully entitled, nonetheless, to pursue it. If in those circumstances the patient dies, nobody could possibly suggest that in that situation the doctor was guilty of murder or attempted murder.[39]

Dr Cox was convicted of attempted murder but only a suspended sentence was imposed. The judge's direction echoes the remarks of Justice Devlin in the earlier trial of Dr Bodkin Adams for murder. Devlin there remarked in passing that 'the doctor is entitled to relieve pain and suffering even if the measures he takes may incidentally shorten life'.

In another case mentioned in Chapter 1, that of *Airedale National Health Service Trust v. Bland*,[40] where the issue was whether nutrition and hydration supplied via tubes could be withdrawn, Lord Goff stated that:

The established rule [is] that a doctor may, when caring for a patient who, for example, is dying of cancer, lawfully administer painkilling drugs despite the fact that he knows that an incidental effect of that application will be to abbreviate the patient's life. Such a decision may properly be made as part of the care of the living patient, in his best interests; and, on this basis, the treatment will be lawful. [41]

Notwithstanding these judicial remarks, it has to be remembered that it is a principle of the criminal law in many jurisdictions that an agent who acts in such a way as to cause death, *either* intentionally *or* in the knowledge that death will probably ensue, is liable for that death.[42] Otlowski has summarised the situation in the common law jurisdictions

---

[39] *R v. Cox* [1992] 12 BMLR 38 at 39. Mason, *et al.* (2002: 490ff) point out that a subsequent pronouncement by the Law Lords in *R v. Woollin* [1999] 1 AC 82 means that a consequence can be said to be intentional if an agent is 'virtually certain' that it will occur. This pronouncement caused Justice Walker in the Court of Appeal in *Re A (Children) (Conjoined twins: surgical separation)* [2001] Fam 147 some concern because he could see that it introduced a complication for those like him who wished to rely on the doctrine of double effect in ruling that conjoined twins could be surgically separated despite it being foreseen that this would lead to the death of the weaker twin. Nonetheless, he stated that he could readily see how the doctrine of double effect could be reconciled with *Woollin*!

[40] [1993] 1 All ER 821.   [41] [1993] 1 All ER 821 at 868.

[42] Otlowski (1997: 15f, 31f, 170ff).

as follows: '. . . upon a strict interpretation of the criminal law, doctors are potentially liable for murder if they administer palliative drugs in the knowledge that death will probably result even though their intention is to alleviate the patient's condition'.[43] So, the widespread practice of administering palliative drugs in the knowledge that they may at least sometimes hasten death is clearly legally fraught. Nonetheless, it is also clear that it is part of public policy in common law jurisdictions that the practice is acceptable and, therefore, that doctors may engage in the practice without fear of legal repercussions. The doctrine of double effect (underpinned ultimately by the idea that acts are morally worse than omissions) has undoubtedly been a major influence on medical law. Its influence can perhaps most easily be seen by juxtaposing the fact that a competent patient may refuse life-prolonging treatment, including when he knows this will result in his death (and is, therefore, tantamount to committing suicide), with the fact that his physician is nevertheless not permitted intentionally to help him die in the event that he competently requests assistance.

As foreshadowed, I will argue in what follows that the significant influence the doctrine has had, and continues to have, on clinical medical beliefs and practices concerning the care of the terminally ill, and on the law relating to such matters, is unwarranted.

V

Much is made of the intentions of medical personnel when appeal is made to the doctrine of double effect in connection with the withholding or withdrawing of life-preserving medical treatment. Where such medical treatment is held to be *extraordinary*, or, more commonly these days, *disproportionately burdensome*[44] to the patient (as compared with any benefit the patient may obtain), it is said to be permissible to withhold it, or withdraw it if it has already been instituted.

I agree with the sentiment that it is permissible to relieve dying patients of painful or burdensome existences even if doing so hastens their deaths. There is no conflict between advocating voluntary forms of medically assisted death and acknowledging the value of good palliative care. Conflict

---

[43] (1997: 170).

[44] Because the distinction between so-called 'ordinary' and 'extraordinary' medical treatment lacks precision (given rapid changes in medical technology) and is, anyway, of unclear moral relevance unless (as, I believe, is now the position taken within Catholic moral theology) it is supposed to register the point that from a patient's perspective only some treatments will produce benefits proportionate to the burdens they impose, it is better to drop any reference to the distinction in favour of a reference to the (proportionately) burdensome nature of particular medical treatments.

only arises when the latter is supported to the exclusion of the former. Nevertheless, I want to show how highly problematic is the doctrine of double effect and hence how unhelpful it is as a source of guidance – medical, moral or legal – for determining what help may be afforded the dying. To this end I will argue that there are serious doubts about its defensibility, particularly in the context of palliative care. These doubts arise because: first, there is difficulty in drawing a distinction between what is merely foreseen and what is intended, independently of judging which acts are morally permissible; second, even if a more relaxed view is taken on whether a distinction can usefully be drawn between a death being intended and its being foreseen but unintended, such a distinction cannot sustain the moral differentiation of acts (or, omissions) that may permissibly bring about death, and those that do so impermissibly; third, in at least some cases of medically assisted death, the doctrine is irrelevant anyway since the person assisted to die is not harmed but benefited. I will argue for each of these claims in turn. (Even though I will couch much of the discussion in terms of the illustrative example given above concerning the relief of pain, the criticisms I will make do not depend on the details of the particular example.)

Consider again the palliative care example. According to the doctrine of double effect, there is a world of moral difference between administering pain-relieving drugs to relieve pain even though it is foreseen (known) that death will eventuate, and administering pain-relieving drugs in such a way as to bring about death (and thereby provide pain relief). I do not think it is obvious that there is this world of moral difference. It is possible to suppose that: the causal process resulting in death is identical; what the two physicians do is identical; each physician would act in the same way in the event that increasing the dosage of the drugs failed to relieve the patient's pain, namely, each would continue to increase the dosage until the pain was relieved, including, if necessary, until death occurred; each physician acts from the same motive (to relieve suffering); and, each physician will have the same emotional reaction to the eventual death of her patient, namely, regret that the pain could not be relieved without death ensuing. Given these considerations, where is the allegedly great moral difference in the behaviour of the respective physicians to be located?

Supporters of the doctrine of double effect contend that the difference lies in the intentions of the physicians (and thus that the moral significance of the means each employs differs). Because the doctrine of double effect is concerned with the permissibility of well-intentioned agents occasioning incidental harm in the course of seeking to achieve good ends, as well as with the prohibition of instrumental harming, it in effect aligns the latter with the wrongfulness of acting with malicious intent.[45] This suggests it is the distinction between incidental harming and instrumental harming that is central to the evaluative role that the doctrine is supposed to play. How, though, are we to tell an intended means from a foreseen but merely incidental side-effect?

It is clear, to begin with, that the matter cannot be decided by reference to how language is used since in some usages an intention is unhelpfully taken to include all consequences of an action that are foreseen as certain or highly probable.[46] It is better, as Jonathan Bennett has urged, to consider the concept of intention as explanatory in character (rather than moral). Thus, for example, a doctor's intentions in acting are 'defined by which of [her] beliefs about consequences explain [her] acting in that way'.[47] Understanding intentions in this way helps avoid begging the question about the morality of certain actions. This is significant because the matters raised by the doctrine of double effect cannot just be decided by first determining which acts of causing harm are morally permissible and which not (with the permissible ones then being judged to have been merely incidental).

Even more importantly, employing the concept in this way sits well with a narrow understanding of the idea of an intended means (as distinct from a broader understanding). According to the narrow understanding, an effect (like a death), as specified by a certain description, is intended as a means 'only if the agent is motivated to bring it about because he believes it will be instrumental, *under that description*, in achieving his desired end'.[48] By contrast, on the broader understanding, when an act of killing is intended as a means, the killer acts 'with the intention of affecting an individual in a way that [the killer] believes will either be causally sufficient for [the individual's] death or have a high probability of causing his death'.[49] The force of the doctrine of double effect is drastically restricted when the narrow understanding of an intended means is employed because it entails that it is only in instances where the agent is motivated by a desire to cause

---

[45] McIntyre (2001: 226–229).

[46] See, for example, the accounts of consequentialists like Sidgwick (1907: 202) and Kuhse (1987: 151ff).

[47] (1995: 201). In this he takes himself to be following the lead of Anscombe (1957: 41f). The two senses of the term 'intention' highlighted by Bennett are, as previously mentioned, nowadays referred to by philosophers as the wide and the narrow senses. Earlier I explained the difference in terms of what an agent *aims at* (narrow sense) as contrasted with what an agent is *aware of bringing about* (wide sense). My focus is on the narrow sense.

[48] McMahan (2002: 410).   [49] (2002: 410).

harm that the action can be classified as a case of intending to do harm (for example, as wrongful killing). Thus, suppose a doctor intends to give a patient a lethal dose of morphine and thinks of herself as *giving him morphine to relieve his suffering*. What is being supposed is that because she does not think of her patient's death as a means to the achievement of her desired goal she does not intend it to be a means to that goal. Clearly, such a conclusion is at odds with the traditional prohibition on intentional killing and that suggests that it must be the broader sense of 'intended as a means' that is presupposed in the traditional prohibition. Effectively the same point can also be expressed as a response to those supporters of the doctrine of double effect who have proposed what they have called 'the test of failure'. The test involves asking the following question: 'If the foreseen bad effect – the patient's death – had, against all expectations, failed to occur, would the doctor have failed to achieve what she intended?'. Unfortunately for such supporters, the test counter-intuitively implies that only actions chosen for their harmfulness are to be counted as instances of intentional harm. Thus, a doctor who intends to give a patient a lethal dose of a drug in order to end his suffering (as, for example, Dr Cox was judged to have done) could not be said to have intended the patient's death were he somehow to have his pain relieved but survive the dose.[50]

Just as the use of language cannot provide determinate answers about what is intended versus what is merely foreseen, neither can it be supposed that, if we were able to carry out a mental inventory of, for instance, each of the physicians in my earlier example, their respective mental states would be found to have different contents.[51] Our ordinary notions of means, ends, and intentions simply prove to be unhelpful when they are tested in instances like these because they are so imprecise.

Finally, there is no accepted, philosophically rigorous account of these notions to which it is possible to appeal to resolve the issues raised by the doctrine of double effect. Even accounts of the distinction that many of its defenders seem disposed to accept do not show that the intentions of the two physicians in the earlier example must differ. Consider a view often espoused by proponents of the doctrine, namely, that what an agent intends is what the agent is *committed to bringing about*. On such a view, it is certainly possible to make sense of the purposes, desires and actions of a doctor who seeks to relieve her dying patient's pain, foreseeing

---

50 Cf. McIntyre (2001: 234).
51 The detailed reasons do not matter here, but see Davis (1984: 118ff), where she shows that supporters of the doctrine cannot take such a line without falling into inconsistency given the range of ways in which they wish to apply the doctrine. See also Quinn (1989b).

all the while that death will follow, but without intending the patient's death. The test for discerning the presence of intentions, according to this view, is what a doctor who intends a particular outcome will *continue to do* if the outcome does not eventuate. Those who propose such a test say that a doctor who, for example, does not intend death, but merely foresees that it will occur, will continue to administer opioids only up to the point where pain relief is achieved (a point somewhere before respiration is affected and death is brought about). They claim that a doctor who intends death will, by contrast, continue to escalate the dosage beyond the point where pain relief is achieved. Unfortunately for the proponents of this view, the test establishes nothing of the kind. A physician in the imagined circumstance may simply be unwilling to break the law if increasing the dosage would require that she do so. Accordingly, it is not always possible to divine a physician's intention from what she does. Moreover, the test fails to distinguish between instances in which an agent acts (or, omits to act) *because* a harmful event will occur, and those in which the agent acts (or, omits to act) *in order that* the harmful event will occur.[52]

So, to reiterate the main point I have been making: there is no sound philosophical basis for the claim that the intentions of my two imaginary physicians must differ in the example given earlier. Hence, it has not been established that the doctrine of double effect shows that it is permissible for the one physician to administer analgesics because she merely foresees that this will lead to her dying patient's death, but impermissible for the other to relieve her dying patient's pain by bringing about his death. A further, quite separate point that needs to be made in this context is that when, as is increasingly happening, dying patients are sedated to the point where they become comatose – which, as previously mentioned, is known as 'terminal sedation' – and artificial nutrition and hydration are then withheld, nothing could be clearer than that the death of the patient is intended. Unless a physician is acting in direct response to a competent advance request made by her patient, what else could her goal be?[53]

Still, some will, no doubt, refuse to concede that there are the uncertainties surrounding central elements of the doctrine of double effect that I have alleged. Notwithstanding what I have argued to date, they will, therefore, be unmoved and will wish to insist that commonsense remains

---

[52] Cf. Kamm (1996: 196f) and (2000) and the reply by Harris (2000).
[53] Winkler (1995: 323), Brock (1993c) and (1999: 534f). For a discussion of the legal situation by a supporter of the doctrine of double effect see Finnis (1993: 332).

on the side of the doctrine, whatever its philosophical difficulties. Hence, in the next phase of my critique of the bearing of the doctrine on the care of the dying, I will assume, for the sake of argument, and contrary to what I have hitherto argued, that the doctrine is philosophically defensible. I will argue that, even on that charitable assumption, it does not have the moral significance often attributed to it (and so should not continue to have the medical, moral and legal influence that it has had hitherto).[54] However, before doing so I want to comment briefly on two important matters concerning the doctrine which are germane to any assessment of it, albeit only of indirect relevance to the issues on which I am concentrating.

First, some locate the source of the moral difference between cases where death is merely foreseen, and those where death is brought about to ensure relief from pain, in the certainty of death in the latter as compared with the former. It is true that how likely it is that a certain event will occur is sometimes of moral relevance. However, that truth can be no comfort to adherents of the doctrine of double effect because it accords moral significance to intentions not probabilities.[55] And, as should be obvious from the previous discussion, there are clearly imaginable circumstances where there will be no difference at all in the probability of death occurring when it is foreseen but unintended as compared with when it is unquestionably intended.

Second, I draw attention in passing to a point that is often overlooked in discussions of the doctrine that focus largely on intentions, namely, that the usual formulations of the doctrine do not require that a patient be consulted before, for example, pain relief may permissibly be administered. Where the pain relief will have the secondary effect of causing death this can, therefore, occur without the patient's consent. Surely, though, the consent of the patient (supposing it can be obtained) remains morally relevant regardless of whether death is a side-effect.[56] Advocates of the doctrine should, I believe, insist that the doctrine only come into play after consent has been obtained (whenever it is obtainable). Nothing in the doctrine precludes this, but it is striking that most of its defenders ignore the relevance of patient consent and so give the impression that they have no objection to the doctrine being applied paternalistically.

---

[54] Bratman (1987) gives an account of intentions that he thinks clarifies the commonsense distinction between intending an outcome and merely foreseeing that there will be a certain side-effect, even though he doubts that the distinction can bear the moral weight placed on it by defenders of the doctrine of double effect.

[55] Anscombe (1982: 24).   [56] Kamm (1991: 578f).

I now return to the matter of the moral significance of the doctrine of double effect. The permissibility of giving pain relief when it is foreseen that death will ensue is said to be dependent on there being a grave enough reason so to act. The doctrine, in other words, applies when death is a lesser evil compared with allowing pain to continue unrelieved. As has been noted many times, competent patients are permitted to refuse life-prolonging treatment when they judge continued life to be worse than death (regardless of whether others judge their situation differently). Why is it, then, that, according to those influenced by the doctrine of double effect (including the various medical and legal authorities cited earlier), it is not permitted intentionally to bring about death when death, as far as the patient is concerned, is the lesser evil, or, to put the same claim another way, the greater good?[57] The doctrine's defenders are apt to maintain that it is because intentionally bringing about the death of a dying patient is intrinsically and absolutely wrong, that is, wrong in itself, and wrong regardless of whether it is better for the patient. However, this defence is a failure.

To see why, consider Elizabeth Anscombe's[58] argument in support of the central importance of the doctrine based on what she controversially referred to as '*the* Christian ethic'. According to her account of it, no one can be required to do something that is absolutely wrong in order to prevent a foreseeable harm. Her contention was that if an agent were answerable for the foreseen consequences of an action, as much as for the action itself, then these absolute prohibitions would break down. The doctrine, however, establishes that '. . . you are no murderer, if [someone's] death was neither your aim nor your chosen means, and if you had to act in the way that led to it or else do something absolutely forbidden'.[59] Thus, for her, the absolute prohibitions contained in the ethic are the bedrock from which supporters of the ethic can repel the idea that 'anything can be justified' (by consequentialist considerations) – without the doctrine of double effect the absolute prohibition against killing the innocent would break down.

Alison McIntyre[60] has, however, plausibly suggested that where an agent has reason not to take the prospect of a certain kind of consequence into account when deliberating about which course of action to adopt, the

---

[57] See Buchanan (1996: 30f).
[58] (1970: 50f). In her (1958) she gives a list of absolutely forbidden acts including killing the innocent for any purpose, vicarious punishment, treachery, idolatry, sodomy, adultery, and making a false profession of faith.
[59] (1970: 50).   [60] (2001: 238ff).

agent is engaged in 'screening off' that consideration. Accordingly, what is screened off should not figure in the deliberation. When consequences are screened off in this way not only are they not to be taken into account, their exclusion affects what should count as a reason for action. Thus, she suggests, it is not the doctrine of double effect that 'explains why the merely foreseen consequence is something for which the agent is not responsible',[61] it is the fact that an absolutist cannot have a reason to act in a way that is absolutely forbidden (and therefore screens off the consequences that would follow from acting in that way), rather than that certain consequences are merely foreseen, that accounts for the consequences being left out of account. Hence, if intentionally killing an innocent is absolutely forbidden, it is not the doctrine of double effect that explains why an agent should not be held responsible for the foreseen death of an innocent if the alternative is to kill him intentionally.

I have contended that the doctrine of double effect cannot bear the moral weight so often placed on it. I shall now show that, in at least some instances of medically assisted death, namely, those instances where the person assisted to die is *benefited* rather than *harmed*, the doctrine is morally irrelevant. The doctrine is, of course, concerned with side-effects that involve the occasioning of harm. When a dying person wishes to be assisted to die because he competently judges that death will not be harmful for him, but, rather, will be a benefit (or, perhaps, more cautiously, a comparative good or benefit), the doctrine of double effect is irrelevant. Such a patient may judge that shortening his life will not cause him to miss out on any of the good things life normally makes possible (because these are now beyond his reach) and will spare him from having to suffer bad experiences that he would otherwise have to undergo.

Defenders of the doctrine cannot reasonably respond by asserting that death is *always an evil*, or that it is *always a greater evil than the continuation of intolerable pain and suffering or being unacceptably dependent upon others*, for these claims are precisely the ones that have to be established. Nor can it just be asserted that death constitutes a greater harm for a person than does suffering pain, or being unacceptably dependent upon others, if his life is intentionally ended by a lethal injection of painkilling drugs, but a lesser harm for him when death is only a foreseen effect of such an injection. This would obviously beg the question. Finally, it is an issue of great significance for many that the choices of competent dying persons be respected, including their requests for medical assistance with dying. (Hence the

---

[61] (2001: 240).

importance of the point I made in passing about ensuring the doctrine is not given precedence over a competent patient's choice by being implemented without reference to his choice.) Supporters of the doctrine of double effect will undoubtedly jib at this and contend that it is consistent with the doctrine to respect the wishes of dying patients not to have their lives prolonged unnecessarily, but quite another matter to assist them to die.

This reaction might be construed as no more than a reiteration of the idea that intentionally bringing about the death of an innocent human is illicit. If so, it would require painstakingly going back over territory already traversed and I do not propose to do that. There is, however, another way of understanding the reaction. It might be seen, instead, as a way of proclaiming the moral importance of the distinction between allowing some state of affairs to come about, and doing something to bring it about. As was seen to be the case with the distinction between killing and letting die, formulations of the doctrine of double effect also generally presuppose the moral importance of such a distinction.[62] But even though the distinction between doing and allowing has moral significance in some contexts, it does not decisively sort out what is morally permissible from what is not. First, it is sometimes morally more objectionable to allow something to occur rather than actively to bring it about. That being so, the requests of competent patients who prefer to be helped to die, rather than simply being allowed to die, should be honoured. This is clearly at odds with what supporters of the doctrine of double effect believe. Second, making the doctrine depend on the distinction between doing and allowing would imply that the latter distinction offers a more fundamental explanation of why allowing harmful side-effects to occur is morally permissible, whereas intending to do harm as a means to something good is not. If so, the doctrine of double effect could have only secondary importance, contrary to the belief of its supporters. Third, it is clear that to support the distinction between doing and allowing is not to support the doctrine of double effect even though there are formulations of the latter that presuppose the former.[63] This is because the distinction between doing and allowing does not capture the idea so central to the doctrine of double effect that, other things being equal, agents are prohibited

---

[62] See, for example, Mangan (1949) and Connell (1967). Quinn (1991) argues that the real bite in the doctrine of double effect is in the contention that more negative moral significance attaches to the intentional harming of another (since that involves *using* that other person) than to cases where it is foreseen that the person harmed will be harmed only incidentally in the carrying out of the agent's purposes.

[63] Bennett (1995: 214).

from *intentionally* inflicting harm on innocent human beings. It does not capture this concern because a state of affairs can equally be brought about intentionally by allowing as by doing (a point clearly recognised in most statutes dealing with homicide).

In sum, it is clear that various medical bodies have either based their official pronouncements about what constitutes permissible palliative care on the doctrine of double effect, or been strongly influenced by it, and that medical law has also been influenced by the doctrine. I have objected to the doctrine on three main grounds in an effort to combat the significant influence it has had, especially in the field of palliative care. First, I argued that a sound basis for distinguishing between what is morally permissible and what is morally impermissible (for example in the provision of palliative care for the terminally ill) cannot be provided by attempting to distinguish between what an agent intends to do and what she foresees will happen. Second, I argued that the doctrine does not establish a moral foundation for absolutely prohibiting the killing of, for example, a dying patient. But the defender of the doctrine of double effect claims that an absolute prohibition applies even to instances where a competent dying patient judges death to be for the best (or, alternatively, to be his least worst option). Third, I argued that where a person judges that he would be better off dead, the doctrine of double effect is actually irrelevant to decisions about how he should be treated. But many cases of voluntary euthanasia and physician-assisted suicide are properly characterised in just this way. Thus, for all that the doctrine has been relied upon by various medical, legal and religious authorities to ground their opposition to the legalising of medically assisted death, it is, in such instances, irrelevant to the issue.

CHAPTER 7

Professional integrity and voluntary medically assisted death

Health care professionals (like professionals in other fields) sometimes say both that there are particular actions that they *cannot* in good conscience undertake to perform, and actions that they *must* undertake if they are to maintain their professional integrity. Physician-assisted suicide and active voluntary euthanasia have often been cited by health care professionals, and their professional organisations, as actions that would violate professional integrity. Some individuals go further and insist that because participation in voluntary medically assisted death is professionally unacceptable to them, that even to transfer someone in their care to another health care professional who has no qualms about facilitating a request for medically assisted death would be inconsistent with their personal and professional integrity.

Medical critics of the legalisation of voluntary medically assisted death often appeal to considerations like these in order to challenge its compatibility with professional integrity. In this chapter I will consider whether physicians may justifiably appeal to professional integrity as a ground for refusing to participate in physician-assisted suicide and voluntary euthanasia (and thus to oppose their legalisation). To do that will require, first, that I set out, albeit briefly, an account of professional integrity. Next, I shall argue that responding to a request for medically assisted death is compatible with what professional integrity demands in medicine. (From this nothing follows, of course, about whether a particular doctor ought to offer such aid.) In the ensuing sections I will investigate both the moral case for the claim that professional integrity should be protected and the ways in which legal provision has been made for its protection in instances where to uphold it would threaten the interests of patients. In the process some of the limits to the scope of professional integrity will be clarified.

I

In general, integrity requires, at the very least, consistency of values, standards or principles. It is an idea that finds application in a variety of contexts: artistic, intellectual, personal and moral, as well as professional. To help achieve a better understanding of the nature of professional integrity I will briefly consider personal and moral integrity, because they are foundational for professional integrity. Consider personal integrity: to have personal integrity is to hold steadfastly to a consistent set of values, standards or principles that have been deliberately and successfully integrated into a person's sense of self. Personal integrity thus requires both *consistency* and *cohesiveness*.[1] Consistency alone is not enough because it is possible for an individual to act thoroughly consistently while undermining her most significant convictions. To behave in this manner is to lack the behavioural cohesion required for personal integrity. However, a person who acts in accordance with her declared values, standards or principles (which may, but do not have to, include moral values, standards or principles) has personal integrity.[2] It is for this reason that the requirements that have to be satisfied for someone to possess moral integrity are even more stringent than they are for someone to possess personal integrity.

Professional integrity differs from each of personal and moral integrity in that its focus is not on the personal, or even the moral, nature of the values, standards or principles that the professional is committed to, but on the relationship between those values, standards or principles and the fulfilment of a particular professional role. Since the focus is on how the responsibilities of a particular profession are to be fulfilled, it is the values and principles relevant to the profession that are the centre of attention. (Nonetheless, I will have occasion later to observe that professional values and principles must ultimately be subject to important moral constraints.)

To the extent that the responsibilities that are attached to a particular professional role arise out of the values and principles that are distinctive of the relevant profession, those values and principles (including, but not merely, *moral* values and principles) have to be taken into account in any assessment of professional conduct. So, though it is possible for a person to display personal integrity while leading a very idiosyncratic existence,

---

[1] McFall (1987: 7–11) suggests that to have integrity an agent must not only subscribe to a consistent set of principles or commitments, and be prepared to stick with them in the face of challenge or temptation, but that the commitments or principles must warrant recognition by others as having *a certain importance* (even though those others may disagree with them). See, too, Calhoun (1995). Less complimentary sentiments about integrity are to be found in Rorty (1999).

[2] Blustein (1991: 121ff).

to behave with professional integrity requires conformity with the hallmark commitments of the relevant profession. This is a major reason why professional integrity is distinct from personal and moral integrity, albeit not necessarily more important than them.

No doubt there are members of some professions who will insist that identification with their professional commitments must be total, in the sense that their moral and professional lives have to form a seamless web. But this cannot amount to a demand that all members of such professions ought to uphold those commitments *no matter what they entail.* Consider a geographically isolated doctor who is faced with an epidemic of a highly infectious and deadly disease (as in the outbreak a few years ago of severe acute respiratory syndrome, or, SARS) in circumstances where infection control is likely to be increasingly compromised. Suppose that she considers she has a moral obligation to her children to evacuate them by personally accompanying them out of the infected area, and that she can do so without spreading the disease. Let us assume that in order to get them out of danger she must drive a considerable distance to a safe haven and that, in consequence, she will be unable to provide medical care for the seriously ill people she will have to forsake during the time it takes to make the return journey. A number of seriously ill people will, therefore, suffer more than they would were she to stay and care for them. Even though caring for the victims of disease and illness is a hallmark commitment of medical practice it is not at all obvious that a doctor must put aside all thought for the interests of her family, or must put their lives at risk. Suppose another doctor, who is placed in a similar circumstance, claims that because, for her, there is a seamless connection between her moral and professional values, she must care for her patients and cannot, therefore, evacuate her family. It may be admirable of her to stay at her post, but that is no reason to think others are *required* to emulate her. Professional integrity should not be identified with a total commitment to the hallmark requirements of a profession, *regardless of the circumstances, or the consequences.*[3]

I have stressed the role of the hallmark commitments of a profession for an adequate understanding of professional integrity. It has not, however, been my intention to suggest that agreement can always be reached, let alone can easily be reached, about the nature of those commitments. In some professions only inchoate attempts have been made to specify with any precision or completeness the details of the obligations of the

---

[3] For discussion of related issues see Zuger and Miles (1987).

members of the profession. For instance, it is only fairly recently within the academy that any systematic attention has been given to the issue of the propriety of sexual relationships between faculty and students. The medical profession, by contrast, has long insisted on proscribing sexual relationships between medical practitioners and their patients. Moreover, as professions change in the light of new demands, or of increases in their capacity, what was once agreed may come to be contested. This has certainly been the case in recent decades in the various health care professions, especially medicine, in large part because of the new possibilities that have been opened up by increases in medical knowledge and innovations in medical technology, but also because of changes in our understanding of the nature of the relationship between a health care provider and her patient or client. A case in point is the provision of appropriate information by health care professionals to competent patients to facilitate the legal requirement for such patients to give voluntary, informed consent to treatment.

It is, at least in part, because of efforts to include physician-assisted suicide and voluntary euthanasia within the legitimate bounds of health care that disputes about the values and principles distinctive of the practice of medicine have been put under the spotlight. Thus, when voluntary medically assisted death came to be permitted in The Netherlands, and when physician-assisted suicide was legalised in the Northern Territory of Australia and the State of Oregon in the United States, medical practitioners were in each instance explicitly given the option of refusing to participate if they conscientiously objected to doing so. In like fashion, Lord Joffe's *Assisted Dying for the Terminally Ill Bill*, whose introduction in 2005 into the UK House of Lords was mentioned in Chapter 1, includes a whole section on conscientious objection and the protection to be afforded not only to practitioners but also to hospices, hospitals, nursing homes, and clinics. If medical practitioners were *merely* servants of their patients, or of the organisations employing them to care for patients, there would be no point in their having the shield of conscientious objection to enable them to avoid doing as requested by their patients (or health care provider organisations).[4] That they are afforded this option (subject to certain qualifications to be noted later concerning referrals and transfers), and that their professional organisations vigorously defend the importance of the option,[5] is best explained by reference to values,

---

[4] Cf. Blustein (1993: 290ff) and Davis (2004).
[5] Cf. Miller and Brody (1995: 10) and Wicclair (2000).

standards and principles that those who insist on the availability of the option see as distinctive of medical practice.

When a medical professional refuses, on conscientious grounds, to perform a particular action, she contends that what is at stake is her professional integrity, not just her personal or moral integrity. Where an action is clearly and straightforwardly immoral[6] there is, strictly, no need to appeal to professional considerations to rule it out. But competent patients sometimes ask physicians to do things (like performing surgery or prescribing drugs) that are not medically indicated. Even if it is neither illegal nor clearly immoral to perform such actions, performing them will be at odds with the requirements of professionalism, that is, with the physician's professional values and principles. In such instances professional integrity should hold sway. Alas, however, medical practice is not always so straightforward; hence, the scope properly to be given to professional integrity will have to be worked out in light of harder cases (including those involving requests by competent patients for medically assisted death).

According to a number of recent writers, there are values and norms that are internal to the practice of medicine. Some, including Leon Kass, Edmund Pellegrino and David Thomasma, have relied on an essentialist account of the nature and ends of medicine to ground their views on what is morally permissible within medicine,[7] whereas others, like Franklin Miller and Howard Brody, claim that while medicine does have an internal morality it is one that evolves in accordance with social change, including changes in societal values.[8] (This remark brings into question the very idea of an internal morality, that is, a morality whose standards are set by practitioners, and hence derive wholly from within a practice, but rather than press the point here I will seek to assess Miller and Brody's claim on its own terms.[9]) While Miller and Brody do not see professional integrity as coextensive with the whole of medical ethics, they do see it as 'the internal morality of medicine'.[10] Whether medicine has an internal morality has direct relevance to decisions to offer medical assistance with dying. As has

---

[6] Note that I have made no reference to *illegal* actions because actions may be illegal (in certain benighted or immoral jurisdictions) even though the values and principles of a particular profession such as the medical profession positively require them.

[7] Kass (1989); Pellegrino and Thomasma (1988). Given the tone of a work to which he subsequently contributed, Thomasma may subsequently have revised his position. See Thomasma, *et al.* (1998). Pellegrino has independently written about these matters in (1999) and (2001b). Another widely cited paper of relevance is Gaylin, *et al.* (1988).

[8] See (1995) and (2001).   [9] Cf. Beauchamp (2001).

[10] (1995: 12). Other ethical considerations in medicine that they mention include respect for patient autonomy, social utility, and justice.

already been seen, efforts to provide for lawful physician assistance with dying have been prominent in disputes about the values and norms internal to the practice of medicine because there are many who consider medically assisted death to be a violation of those values and norms. Professional medical associations typically (albeit with notable exceptions like the Royal Dutch Medical Association)[11] hold that for a doctor actively to assist a patient to die, or to kill a patient, even at the patient's request, is to do something diametrically opposed to the internal morality of medicine, not just something that is presently illegal. However, there are many medical professionals who consider that helping patients who request assistance with dying may, under certain specified conditions, be the best means of exemplifying those values and principles in medicine that are concerned with the relief of suffering, the amelioration of the effects of serious disabilities, and the avoidance of unnecessary or futile medical interventions.

As regards the essentialists, I shall focus on Leon Kass, a prominent critic of physician-aid-in-dying, who thinks medical professionals should have nothing to do with helping competent patients to die, and claims that for physicians to give such aid would run counter to the *essential* purpose of medicine, namely, that of healing.[12] This narrow, essentialist understanding of medicine should be rejected. To begin with, medical care is not always directed toward the purpose of healing, as even a cursory inspection of the goals of medicine mentioned at the end of the previous paragraph, or in areas of medicine outside the clinical realm, like preventative care, public health and health promotion, would show.[13] Even the goals of palliative care, an aspect of medicine of central relevance for this book, are not obviously concerned with healing, as that term is generally understood.[14]

---

[11] See, for example, American Medical Association Council on Ethical and Judicial Affairs (1998); Australian Medical Association (2002); and British Medical Association (2006).

[12] For helpful discussion of Pellegrino's views see Beauchamp (2001: 601–604) and Veatch (2001).

[13] Varelius (2006) distinguishes, more sharply than is necessary, the notion of the goals of medicine from that of whether medicine has an internal morality. He lists seven (of what he regards as) *objective* goals of medicine: avoidance of premature death; preservation of life; prevention of disease and injury; promotion and maintenance of health; relief of pain and suffering; avoidance of harm; and, promotion of well-being. However, he believes that this way of thinking about the goals of medicine cannot be considered in isolation from a *subjective* take on them that emphasises whether particular medical practices benefit or harm patients. Accordingly, he thinks it is only possible to determine whether voluntary medically assisted death is consistent with the goals of medicine after identifying the most plausible theory of prudential value and the nature of harm. I have already given my reasons for thinking voluntary medically assisted death may be a benefit and will reiterate that point of view below.

[14] The same holds for various other aspects of medicine, many of which have nothing to do with the care of the dying, such as: diagnostic work in circumstances where there are no known remedies for conditions that are, nonetheless, diagnosable; much of obstetrics and gynaecology; assistance with contraception; vasectomies and tubal ligations; cosmetic surgery; and so on.

More importantly, unless Kass is to be allowed to beg the crucial question, it is appropriate to ask why assisting patients to die in a manner, and at a time, of their autonomous choosing should be seen as being at odds with the goals of medicine. Since Kass agrees that a physician should not continue medically futile treatment, his answer, when all is said and done, is that because medical morality recognises a morally significant difference between acts and omissions, there has to be a prohibition on actively helping patients to die on request. In the previous Chapter I challenged the moral significance of the distinction between acts and omissions precisely in those contexts where it is supposed to show both the permissibility of not treating when it is known that not treating will lead to death, and the impermissibility of actively assisting in the bringing about of death.[15] So, quite apart from the narrow conception of medicine on which it relies, the case put forward by Kass, at least as I have thus far detailed it, is already shaky in attributing more moral significance to the distinction between acts and omissions in such contexts than it can be given.

There is, however, a further reason to resist the position Kass advocates. Along with many other medical professionals,[16] Kass thinks the injunction in the Hippocratic Oath not to do anything harmful to a patient constitutes a fundamental constraint on the practice of medicine. Because he thinks it is always harmful to assist a patient to die, he concludes that physician-aid-in-dying is contrary to the internal morality of medical care. I will show that this is not the case.[17]

Death frequently is harmful, but it does not have to be.[18] Indeed, death can, on occasion, be in a person's best interests. Kass thinks that this is impossible because, as far as he is concerned, '[t]o intend and act for someone's good requires his continued existence to receive the benefit'.[19] This is a mistake. We can, for instance, clearly act now with the intention of benefiting future generations, and achieve our goal, even though those future generations do not yet exist.[20] Furthermore, to eliminate something that would be bad for someone benefits that person. So, if a dying patient requests help with dying because his continued existence would constitute an intolerable burden for him, he is benefited by a physician assisting him to die.[21] Since this claim is critical to the present dispute I will briefly elaborate on why death can sometimes be beneficial.

[15] Effective challenges have previously been made by others. See Kagan (1989) and Kamm (1996).
[16] Baumrin (1998).   [17] Miles (2004) argues for a similar position.
[18] Bradley (2004).   [19] (1989: 40).   [20] Lockwood (1988).
[21] Compare my (1976: 273) and Miller and Brody (1995: 13f).

A common philosophical way of tackling the question of what it is that makes our lives valuable has been to ask (somewhat indirectly) what it is about death that is bad.[22] Most philosophers have concluded that when death is bad it is because of the possible future goods of which it deprives us. However, until this conclusion has been supplemented with answers to the many further questions it raises, it is too cryptic to be very useful. Much of the philosophical debate has been about how to refine the view so as to answer the various further questions to which it gives rise. For present purposes, though, I need only concentrate on the most obvious of those questions, namely that concerning the extent of the possible future goods of which we are supposed to be deprived by death, since it might seem that, no matter when it occurs, death always deprives us of an infinite number of possible future goods. If so, does it follow from the claim that what makes death bad is that it results in the deprivation of possible future goods that it makes no difference when we die? Put another way: if it is true that we will be deprived of an infinite number of possible future goods no matter when we die, how can the time of our death be of any consequence to us (since our loss will be the same whenever death occurs)?

If this reasoning were sound, it would raise an obvious question about the usefulness of the claim that what makes death bad is that it results in the deprivation of possible future goods. However, the reasoning is not sound, because the possible future goods of which death deprives us should not be represented as being infinite, but, rather, as limited to what we actually, or, perhaps, probably, would have had access to had we not died. Thus, death is bad for us when the goods we realistically would have had access to (or, in all probability, would have been able to have access to) can be considered of positive value to us, or, as it will sometimes be more idiomatic to say, for us. Contrariwise, death is good for us when no (or, perhaps, few) goods of positive value would have been accessible to us had we continued to live.[23]

Still, it may be said, the practice of medicine requires physicians to be guided by relevant medical indications in deciding on the best course of treatment to follow. My response is simply that there is nothing internal to the practice of medicine that dictates that it is acceptable to refrain from prolonging a patient's life, but unacceptable to give a dying patient the

[22] Among the more important contributions have been Nagel (1970); Feinberg (1984: 79–93); Feldman (1991) and (1992); McMahan (1988) and (2002: ch. 2); and Bradley (2004). Fischer (1993) is a collection of many of the important papers on the topic. I will explore the issue of the value of a human life more fully in Chapter 11.

[23] Cf. McMahan (1988) and (2002: ch.2).

assistance he seeks in order to be able to die more expeditiously. A patient's best interests can be served by either practice. Kass, like many other medical professionals, has no difficulty with the idea that it is permissible not to prolong the life of a dying person if that becomes futile (regardless of the person's explicit consent). Nor do he and other opponents of physician-aid-in-dying have trouble squaring their professional standards with the practice of inducing unconsciousness via 'terminal sedation', or 'pharmacological oblivion', even when this hastens death. If these ways of allowing a patient to die do not constitute an abandonment of the patient, neither does physician-aid-in-dying. Yet it is only the latter that is ever described in such a way (and, hence, alleged to be professionally unacceptable).

Some medical professionals may be persuaded by the preceding argument but still think that it leaves out an important consideration, namely, that it is an aspect of professionalism to use the *agreed* professional standards to work out how to behave whenever there is *uncertainty*. If there is uncertainty, professional integrity requires them to go with their best judgment (after taking account of the views of other professionals), and their best judgment is that medically assisted death should be prohibited. Those who reason in this way clearly cannot be reasoning just in terms of the values of the medical profession, since one of their premises is that *there are not known to be any professional standards that are decisive for the matter at hand*. Most likely, those who think in this way are importing other values (for example, religious or cultural values) to fill out their vision of the values for which they think the medical profession *ought* to stand. If this is right, what is bearing the weight here is the broader moral vision (the religious or cultural values) and not the idea of professional integrity. Be that as it may, voluntary medically assisted death has already been made legal in several jurisdictions without requiring doctors to violate their convictions.

As previously mentioned, Miller and Brody reject essentialist accounts of medical morality in favour of an account that acknowledges the influence of social factors on the goals and ends of medical practice. They do not believe that the goals and ends of medicine are timelessly true. Instead, new goals may emerge within the scope of medicine, and traditional goals may be interpreted anew in the light of changed social circumstances, because medical morality cannot be entirely insulated from values that are external to medicine. There has been so much social change since, for example, the formulation of the Hippocratic Oath, that medicine has had to re-conceive itself. It now incorporates the relief of suffering as well as healing, and hence should accommodate physician-assisted suicide. It is not necessary to embrace Miller and Brody's starting position to reach a similar conclusion to theirs. Nonetheless, it is of interest that a more nuanced view of medical morality (than is espoused by essentialists) gives no comfort whatsoever to medical opponents of medically assisted death.

I conclude that no reason has been found for thinking that participation by physicians in either physician-assisted suicide or voluntary euthanasia is incompatible with the goals of medicine, or its internal morality, or with professional integrity. Advocates of voluntary medically assisted death cannot, however, rest content with such a limited conclusion. So, let me recap my argument to date before I attempt to embellish this conclusion. I claimed, first, that to behave with professional integrity requires conformity with the hallmark commitments of the relevant profession and, second, that doctors may assist competent dying patients to die without forsaking the hallmark commitments of medical care. This still leaves unanswered whether, and, if so, how, professional integrity and patient autonomy relate to each other. What should happen, for instance, in the event that a doctor refuses to accede to a request by a competent patient for medical assistance with dying because she believes it to be incompatible with professional integrity? Although many think patient autonomy should have priority, courts in several jurisdictions have given regard to the protection of the integrity of physicians in circumstances similar to those described. So, in the next section, I will seek to establish the moral basis for protecting professional integrity, and, then, in the following section, I will consider how the claim has been handled in law. Once that has been accomplished I will be in a position to suggest how to adjudicate conflicts between patient autonomy and professional integrity, especially in relation to end-of-life care.

II

It has seemed to some[24] that the moral basis for professional integrity, and the reason why we should afford it protection, is that professional autonomy has comparable importance to a professional as patient autonomy has to a patient. From this perspective what is needed is a system that accommodates the value of both patient autonomy and professional autonomy. At first glance this is an attractive idea. Many professionals, and their professional associations, take the view that a professional should respond to a request for professional help unless there is a conscientious

[24] Daar (1993: 1259–1274).

reason for refusing to do so. This suggests that the professional is, as a result, afforded greater autonomy in matters of conscience than she otherwise would be. However, there are at least two reasons for resisting the suggestion that professional integrity turns on professional autonomy.[25] First, to respect the autonomy of a professional is not the same thing as respecting that person's professional integrity. As I have already shown, professional integrity has to do with adhering to principles that constitute the hallmark commitments of a particular profession. To cite professional integrity as a reason for not doing something is thus to ask for protection against having to violate conscientiously held principles, or commitments, considered crucial to professional practice. This is a long way from an appeal to the right to practise autonomously, because the considerations relevant to the maintenance of professional integrity are much narrower than for the exercise of practitioner autonomy. Second, an autonomous practitioner practises in accordance with her own conception of medical practice, whereas a practitioner who invokes the standards of a profession effectively imposes a constraint on her autonomy, for, otherwise, what would count as professional integrity would be decided by each practitioner acting in accordance with her own lights. When a competent patient refuses to agree to a particular form of treatment (as, for instance, when a Jehovah's Witness refuses a blood transfusion that would save his life) his doctor is precluded from practising as she wishes. She may respect such a refusal only because she has pledged to abide by the established standards of professional practice, and greatly regret not being able to follow her own judgment. (Nothing I have said should be taken to imply that practitioner autonomy *as such* is incompatible with professional integrity. My point is more restricted; it is that divergences between them show that they cannot be one and the same.)

On several occasions to date, mention has been made of a connection between professional integrity and the consciences of professionals. It will come as no surprise that some have suggested that conscience is the moral basis for professional integrity. But this suggestion proves no more convincing than the one just considered. Even allowing for differences in the ways that conscience is conceived,[26] the conscience of an individual is

---

[25] Cf. Wicclair (2000: 212f).

[26] See Hill (1998) for a very helpful discussion of some of the ways that conscience has been conceived. Hill favours a Kantian conception, according to which conscience is 'an involuntary response to the recognition that what we have done, are doing, or are about to do is contrary to the moral judgments that we have made' (p. 34). An account having a certain amount in common with Hill's is Velleman (1999).

not a reliable enough foundation for professional integrity. The conscience of an individual is an unreliable foundation because the judgments it delivers are prone to error, and because the wide variety of influences that form the consciences of individuals include some that are neither morally admirable nor morally defensible.[27] Consider a medical practitioner who has no difficulty in reconciling her conscience with the needless prescription of drugs to a troublesome patient because that avoids her having to engage in a difficult consultation. The conscience of such a practitioner clearly furnishes no foundation for professional integrity. (Plenty of other examples could be given to illustrate the point: doctors who prescribe a particular drug because the manufacturer offers them inducements; doctors who are blasé about obtaining informed consent from patients for experimental treatments; and so on.) Accordingly, it is quite ill-judged to consider appeals to conscience to be decisive in the way that appeals to professional integrity are often regarded as being decisive (regardless of whether they *ought* to be).

Nonetheless, it might be urged (following a suggestion by Jeffrey Blustein[28]) that to expect, or require, someone to act against the dictates of her conscience is to fail to respect her desire for inner harmony or integrity. Suppose this is right. It still does not give us sufficient reason to make respect for individual conscience the moral basis for professional integrity given the points made above about the unreliability of appeals to conscience. (I should add that Blustein does not think that appeals to conscience ought always to prevail over other considerations and, instead, considers that compromise may sometimes be reached without loss of personal integrity.[29])

A second and related reason for not taking individual conscience as the moral underpinning for professional integrity connects with a point made earlier, namely, that standards of professional conduct should be governed by what is required to honour the hallmark commitments of a profession. Accordingly, it is medicine's commitments, and the means considered acceptable to their achievement, that set the moral framework for the medical profession, not the consciences of individual practitioners (a point of some importance given that the conscientious judgments of sincere and honest practitioners are not only unreliable but can, and do, differ over, for example, the acceptability of voluntary

---

[27] Cf. Bennett (1974), whose views are criticised by Glover (1975) and by Harris (1980: 117–123).
[28] (1993: 294ff). Cf. Childress (1979).   [29] (1993: 300ff). Cf. Kuflik (1979).

medically assisted death as a means to the achievement of the goals of medicine).

Can anything more positive be said about the moral basis for professional integrity in medicine? Mark Wicclair has suggested that 'an appeal to conscience has significant moral weight only if the core values on which it is based correspond to one or more core values in medicine'.[30] I think this proposal is on the right track provided the 'core values' referred to are consistent with moral knowledge. Since that knowledge is apt to expand, it is compatible with his proposal that our appreciation of what professional integrity permits, or requires, may change over time. Given my earlier point that the hallmark commitments of medicine ought to be seen as subject to change because of frequent developments in medical knowledge and associated technology, this flexibility is to be welcomed.[31] Moreover, the proposal has the merit of being generalisable to other professions. I think this is a merit because it suggests, plausibly, that professional integrity is not something radically different in each of the professions, even allowing for variations in core values.

III

Professional associations trumpet the importance of affording protection to individual professionals who consider that their integrity as professionals would be violated or compromised if they had to carry out certain tasks. But where appeal is made to professional integrity to avoid carrying out a particular task, it is conceivable that the person requesting the professional service will be put at risk of being disadvantaged. The point cannot be put more strongly than this because many professions have endeavoured to introduce arrangements that minimise disadvantage, or even eliminate it. Thus, for example, in the United States, if a lawyer wishes to withdraw from a case, on the ground that continuing with the client's case would violate or compromise her professional integrity, she may do so regardless of whether this will have an adverse effect on her client. Moreover, she may withdraw at any time for other reasons provided only that this does

---

[30] (2000: 217; see also 221–227).

[31] Daar (1993: 1259–1280) gives a useful history of the evolution within United States law of the assertion of professional conscience. These issues have not been as well considered elsewhere but Kennedy and Grubb (1994); Skene (1998); and Mason, *et al.* (2002), all consider material of relevance to other jurisdictions.

not adversely affect her client.[32] Because a lawyer has to petition the court for permission to withdraw, it becomes the responsibility of the legal system (via the court) to find an alternative legal representative for the client. The court is made responsible for finding an alternative representative presumably to ensure, as far as possible, the integrity of the legal process. In the absence of such a requirement there would be a risk of the person being unrepresented, and, so, being put at an enormous disadvantage (thereby increasing the likelihood of an injustice occurring).[33]

Apart from this concern to ensure the integrity of the legal process, there appears to be another consideration at work, one that has a parallel in the practice of medicine. In not being required to find a suitable replacement, the withdrawing lawyer is having her professional conscience further protected. To the extent that her withdrawal enables her to avoid doing something she considers repugnant, or so ill-advised that it would reflect on her professional integrity, not requiring her to continue her involvement effectively keeps her at arm's length from a process she considers would contaminate her. There is a precise parallel in the circumstance where a physician seeks to withdraw from caring for a patient for reasons of professional integrity. Ought the physician be required to organise a transfer of the patient to another physician who would be willing to care for the patient? There are those who believe that the way lawyers are able to call upon institutional help with the transfer of clients yields the model that should be adopted within medicine. Unfortunately, though there is much to be admired in the way the legal profession handles the issue of client transfer, it is not possible to emulate the legal practice in every medical setting. First, doctors sometimes provide care in a patient's home. In these instances there is no institution comparable to the court – hospitals and health maintenance organisations cannot serve – to

---

[32] In Australia and New Zealand (following British practice) a retainer may only be terminated for 'just cause' and, even then, the client must not be disadvantaged. Hence reasonable care is required to avoid foreseeable harm to a client, including allowing reasonable time to retain a substitute practitioner. See Dal Pont (2001: 62ff). For an account of the American Bar Association's approach to lawyer withdrawal see Daar (1993). Interestingly, Daar sees the approach as founded on respect for the professional autonomy of lawyers. For reasons given earlier when discussing the moral basis for professional integrity, I do not consider her position satisfactory. Freedman (1988) challenges the practice in the United States of lawyers withdrawing from cases in which they would have to stay silent about information provided in confidence by a client if they are to avoid giving away the client's guilt. He holds that there is no reason based on the demands of professional integrity for them to withdraw and, indeed, that the adversarial system demands otherwise.

[33] Because of this concern for the proper administration of justice, the court can order a lawyer to continue to represent her client (even if she has good cause for terminating her representation) if permitting the withdrawal would preclude the client's being adequately represented. See, for example, *Bordreau v. Carlisle* [1989] 549 So. 2d 1073, 1074 Fla. Dist. Ct. App.

administer a referral or transfer. Second, it is more likely in the medical context than in the legal that a relationship will have developed over a prolonged period. Third, as I will shortly show, if care is being given in, for instance, a hospital, it may have a policy against participation in the relevant medical procedures or practices, or there may be no suitable alternative facility to which the patient can be transferred. In the former case it may seem harsh to require the practitioners in such an institution to cooperate in referring or transferring such a patient. Yet morality surely demands that the patient receive appropriate assistance. It is to the handling of this sort of circumstance that I will now turn. In the process I will set out some limits to the application of the idea of professional integrity in medical contexts (including requests for medically assisted death).

Courts have been reluctant to require doctors to continue to provide care if their objection is based on conscience or professional integrity.[34] To coerce doctors into acting against their professional commitments (or, for that matter, moral or religious commitments) would represent an enormous imposition on them.[35] However, it would be curious, to say the least, to claim that a competent patient's right to refuse treatment should depend on being able to find a doctor who is willing to comply with his refusal. Courts have recognised that patients ought not be disadvantaged just because of their choice of doctor (even when the professional relationship between doctor and patient is a long-standing one), and have sought to protect the interests of patients in ways compatible with not forcing doctors to violate their professional integrity. Thus, while a doctor may withdraw her provision of care for a patient, as long as she gives proper notice, courts have generally ordered doctors to continue care until arrangements can be made to refer or transfer the patient to an acceptable alternative doctor or facility. The courts would seem, sensibly enough, to have presumed that action against conscience is more burdensome than action to assist a transfer.

---

[34] Daar (1993: 1264ff).

[35] In British law there is a well-established principle that a court will not order a doctor to administer treatment she is unwilling to provide. The principle has recently been reaffirmed in two separate cases involving parents of severely disabled children who disputed the judgments of attending doctors about options for treatment. In *Re C* (A minor) (Medical Treatment) [1998] the dispute was about whether, if C suffered a respiratory arrest, positive pressure ventilation should be restarted. Sir Stephen Brown P declined the parents' request to order C's doctors to do so. In *An NHS Trust v. MB and Anor* [2006] EWHC (Fam) 507 Justice Holman reaffirmed the principle even though he went on to rule that the attending doctors should not deliberately withdraw ventilation. I consider his written judgment to lack internal coherence but he states clearly that he based his final ruling on his belief that MB's life was still of positive value to MB and that ventilation should be maintained solely for that reason.

Though, at first glance, this may seem to be a resolution that is both legally and morally defensible, further reflection reveals that a number of serious issues remain unresolved. First, this way of resolving matters is silent about how to proceed when there is no suitable alternative medical professional available. This may happen for reasons to do with expertise, or because of geographical isolation, or in an emergency. Moreover, the resolution will be of no help if a medical professional considers that to refer a patient to another practitioner, or to facilitate a transfer, would make her party to a morally objectionable outcome and, so, cause a loss of professional integrity.[36] This latter sort of difficulty has arisen both when physicians have considered that it would be medically futile to continue treating even though patients or their surrogates insist on continued treatment, and when patients have requested physician assistance with dying. I shall consider these points in turn.

Where there is literally no medical professional available with the expertise to help a patient, other than the one who wishes to withdraw, it would seem reasonable for a court to insist that the medical professional not be permitted to withdraw her expertise.[37] Fortunately, such circumstances are only rarely likely to eventuate, so they can, for all practical purposes, be set aside. Cases involving geographical isolation or emergency are, however, far more likely. When it is not possible through prior planning to overcome the problem occasioned for a doctor by her patient's geographical isolation, the patient's interests should prevail given that the patient is in the more vulnerable situation (in virtue of having a more restricted range of acceptable choices). In practice, the opportunity for prior planning will generally exist and this should ensure that few problems of this sort arise. For example, suppose a geographically isolated patient wishes to have a medical procedure performed that his medical care-giver considers medically futile, and is thus conscientiously opposed to performing. Prior planning should be able to obviate the problem. Of course, if even referring a patient seeking such a procedure to another provider would

---

[36] Cf. Bayles (1979); Blustein (1993: 306ff); Daar (1993: 1269ff); Wear, et al. (1994: 148f); Wicclair (2000: 221ff); and Davis (2004: 86f).

[37] It is interesting to see how the American Medical Association's *Code of Medical Ethics* has been altered in relation to such matters over the last half century. In 1957, Section V of the code required that 'A physician may choose whom he will serve. In an emergency, however, he should render service to the best of his ability. Having undertaken the care of a patient, he may not neglect him; and unless he has been discharged he may discontinue his services only after giving adequate notice.' The comparable clause in the 2001 formulation of the Code, Section VI, requires that 'A physician shall, in the provision of appropriate patient care, except in emergencies, be free to choose whom to serve, with whom to associate, and the environment in which to provide medical care.'

violate the conscience of the patient's doctor, the problem cannot be so easily resolved. I will consider this sort of case in a moment. When the patient's geographical isolation is compounded by medical emergency, a medical practitioner who feels that her professional integrity would be subverted in having to provide treatment should nonetheless provide it (because she would have to endure much less in acting against her professional convictions than would her patient if he were to be left untreated). Once more, however, only very rarely would doctors be faced with such a dilemma, particularly in the context of the care of the dying. Hence, I will set it aside.

Those who consider that even to refer or transfer a patient to another care-giver would run counter to the requirements of professional integrity do, however, face a problem, and it is a problem that looms large in the care of the dying. In cases involving a request by a competent dying patient for the termination of life-prolonging treatment, the patient's right to refuse treatment should ensure that such treatment is ceased. But there are, at least, three other circumstances in which issues of professional integrity may come into play: first, when the patient is no longer competent and the doctor judges continued treatment to be medically futile, but this judgment is disputed by the patient's family or proxy; second, when a competent patient refuses food and fluids and attending medical staff believe that to go along with the refusal would make them complicit in something tantamount to suicide, which they consider immoral; and, third, when a competent patient seeks a medically assisted death but his attending doctor is opposed to it (supposing, of course, that this occurs in a jurisdiction where it is legally permitted to render such assistance[38]).

Before giving direct consideration to these three circumstances it will help if I first set out the various positions that have been proposed by professionals who have wished at times not to continue to provide medical care, or to provide only care of a kind not sought by, or unacceptable to, their patients. It is important to distinguish these various positions since only some of them pose a difficulty for reconciling patient referrals or transfers with a medical professional's concern to maintain professional integrity. If an appeal to professional integrity is to be given weight it is necessary to know which particular position the appellant has in mind. Jeffrey Blustein (1993) has provided a very helpful analysis of some of the possible positions

---

[38] Where voluntary euthanasia and physician-assisted suicide are not illegal (as in The Netherlands, the State of Oregon and Belgium) there is, as I have previously noted, provision for conscientious objectors to avoid participation.

and what follows owes much to his account. I will set out six distinguishable positions. In the first four, the interests of professionals *and* their patients can, I believe, be accommodated. On any of these positions there should be no difficulty with the referral or transfer of a patient to another willing and appropriate professional. In the fifth, it may also seem possible to accommodate the interests of both professionals and their patients. I will suggest, though, that the accommodation is likely to involve the former in behaving hypocritically and so comes with a high moral price tag for those committed to professional integrity. The final position to be adumbrated will indicate why there cannot be an unqualified (or, absolute) right of referral or transfer.

First, it is possible for a particular medical professional to be faced with a conflict of professional interests or duties in relation to a request by a patient (or, proxy) to provide, or continue with, a specific form of treatment. In such instances it is proper for the professional to seek to withdraw from caring for the patient if there is no other way of avoiding the conflict of interests. Consider a case (of a kind that has come to light recently in a number of countries) where a sportsman complains that a team doctor approved his return to the sporting contest despite an injury and that this has had repercussions for his subsequent sporting career, or, more commonly, his health subsequent to his sporting career. Let us suppose (as has been true in some of the cases that have come before the courts) that the doctor in question is a part-owner of the team, though similar issues may also arise for a doctor who is either a director or an employee. Assume that the doctor is committed to improving the chances of success of the team by having its best players on the field for the maximum time. In such circumstances the doctor would be better advised not to act as the team doctor. The conflict of interests such a doctor would face over the management of player injuries would engender a risk of professional responsibilities being breached. The best way to protect the doctor's professional integrity would be to hand management of the players' medical care to someone else. Similarly, in the context of the care of the dying, a doctor with a financial interest in a particular facility would be well advised to avoid any suggestion of conflict (arising from, say, recommendations for maintaining life-prolonging treatment) either by handing over management of relevant cases to other professionals, or by transferring particular patients to a different facility.

Second, a professional may be uncertain of the rightness or wrongness of offering a particular form of care (or, of withdrawing or withholding it) and, in consequence, may feel uncomfortable about offering (or, withdrawing or withholding) the form of care. Such a professional might well desire to step aside from a case because she is doubtful that remaining in charge is compatible with maintaining her professional integrity. Yet she could acknowledge that other respected professionals may not share her discomfort and so she may see her discomfort about continuing to care for the patient as an inadequate basis for refusing to refer or transfer the patient elsewhere.

Third, a professional suffering a similar discomfort to that just mentioned might believe that respect for the integrity of fellow professionals who do not share her discomfort entails a preparedness on her part to refer or transfer her patient to one of them. Here the basis for her action would not be her uncertainty about whether there is a right course of action but her respect for the integrity of her colleagues.

Fourth, many consider it is not the business of public institutions, like public hospitals, to enforce specific moral or religious values in a pluralistic society. (Among those who share this conviction some, nonetheless, are willing to concede that a private institution with a well-publicised stance on a moral or religious issue may insist on that stance for all who voluntarily come within its orbit.) Those who adopt such a standpoint in relation to the responsibilities of public institutions will have no difficulty in both supporting the professional conscience of a particular practitioner and making provision for patients to be referred, or transferred.

Fifth, some hold that while their own consciences do not permit them to accede to certain requests made by patients, because that would require them to act morally impermissibly (in a deontological sense), or contrary to the virtues,[39] they recognise that there will be others willing to fulfil those requests and so, for consequentialist reasons, they are prepared to refer or transfer patients in such circumstances.[40] I said earlier that such a position might well be regarded as a hypocritical one. To the extent that such a professional's understanding of integrity is based on deontological convictions, or virtue ethics, it seems inconsistent to allow consequentialist considerations to override those convictions. Of course, someone may believe (as, for example, an ethical pluralist does) that deontological and virtue considerations can work in harness with consequentialist

---

[39] Modern virtue theorists, as is well-known, claim that virtue ethics represent an alternative to both deontological and consequentialist approaches to morality. I remain unconvinced by their claim but there is no need to adjudicate on it for present purposes. For a virtue ethic-based approach to issues of professional ethics see, for example, Oakley and Cocking (2001).

[40] Though they themselves have no difficulty reconciling physician professional integrity with patient transfer, Quill, *et al.* (1992) recommend this approach to those who do. Their recommendation is criticised by Wildes (1993).

considerations. But that is not the position described above. Accordingly, it seems to me that anyone who withdraws from a caring role to maintain her professional integrity, on deontological or virtue-based grounds, would be acting hypocritically were she to refer, or transfer, a patient elsewhere for consequentialist reasons. This would amount to condoning what she is convinced is an impersonal wrong.[41]

Sixth, some take the position that their concern to act with professional integrity is not a concern about impersonal wrongdoing but a concern with ensuring that *they* do nothing wrong. While it is precisely this concern that is at the heart of debates about the justifiability of agent-centred restrictions on action,[42] there is a risk that this very concern can appear precious because it will often cut no ice at all to maintain that it makes all the moral difference whether, on the one hand, *I* do a certain act, or, on the other, facilitate, or allow, *another* party to do it even though I could have intervened to prevent it. Those who adopt the attitude that what matters is that *they* do not do a certain thing are morally bound to consider how serious the wrong would be were they to do it. To refuse, for example, to care for a patient on the ground that doing so would be a violation of professional integrity lacks credibility unless the wrong involved is thought to be very serious. Given the potential for hazard to the patient in such a course of action, a doctor must be clear that refusing to help is not just a form of self-righteousness. There are important reasons (to do with the psychological and emotional impact of requiring them to do what they are convinced involves a serious evil) for upholding the right of doctors not to have to participate in a particular procedure when they are convinced that doing so would make them complicit in an evil. Equally, those who have such a conviction have an obligation to make this known well in advance of the issue arising so as to ensure that patients are not denied the opportunity to make autonomous choices.

Where a professional considers that to refer, or transfer, a patient to someone else's care would be incompatible with her understanding of the internal morality of medicine, and therefore with her commitment to act in accord with that internal morality, such a professional surely ought to refuse to make the referral, or transfer.[43] I have, of course, argued that there is no incompatibility between the internal morality of medicine and

---

[41] See further Glover (1975).
[42] See, for example, Williams' contribution to Smart and Williams (1973) and Darwall (1986: 300f).
[43] For one account of when a doctor would be entitled on moral grounds to refuse to transfer a patient see Davis (2004: 84ff).

voluntary medically assisted death. Even so, the present reality is that, in all but a few jurisdictions, medically assisted death by these means is illegal, so, in general, doctors do not have to face the prospect of having to refuse in conscience to refer, or transfer, a competent dying patient to someone willing to fulfil that patient's request for assistance with dying. But they can be put in a comparable position if they conscientiously refuse to continue treatment they consider futile (and, should they refuse to budge, may end up having to defend themselves in court).

There already have been some celebrated cases involving patients (or, their proxies) wanting treatment to be continued despite continued treatment being deemed medically futile. Among them, the previously mentioned case of Helga Wanglie is perhaps the best known. As will be recalled, the attending physicians judged her prospects to be poor and considered that the aggressive medical care she was being given was of no benefit. They urged her family to disconnect the respirator and other life-sustaining supports, but the family, and especially her husband, Oliver, strongly disagreed with the recommendation and wanted all treatment to be continued. Her family claimed that Mrs Wanglie had expressed the view (while competent) that she didn't want her life prematurely shortened. Eventually, the Minnesota District Court was petitioned to appoint a conservator for her with the responsibility of making recommendations to the court concerning her best interests.[44] The presiding judge found that Oliver Wanglie was the person best placed to be his wife's guardian, and found no difficulty in *compelling* the medical staff concerned to continue with life-prolonging care for Mrs Wanglie, despite their professional judgment to the contrary, and despite it clearly being the prevailing view among professional medical associations, and probably the majority of individual practitioners, that doctors are under no obligation to provide therapy they judge to be futile.[45]

I have already had occasion to observe that the courts have seen the interests of patients as having priority over those of doctors, but have sought, nevertheless, to find ways to accommodate both sets of interests. Consider how patients have fared when they (or their guardians) have sought to have life-prolonging treatment stopped. In *Conservatorship of Morrison v. Abramovice*[46] the patient's daughter requested removal of the feeding tube from her ninety year old mother who was in a persistent vegetative

[44] Cf. Miles (1991a) and (1991b).
[45] *In re Conservatorship of Wanglie* [1991] No.IX-91-283, Minn. Dist. Ct., Prob. Div., at 8.
[46] [1988] 253 Cal. Rptr. 530 Cal. Ct. App. For helpful discussion see Daar (1993: 1267f).

state. The hospital physician refused the daughter's request on grounds of 'personal moral objections'. The court held, in line with the well-established right of a competent patient to refuse medical treatment, including life-prolonging treatment, that the surrogate decision-maker, just like a competent patient, could reject the physician's view and, in this instance, lawfully authorise removal of the naso-gastric tube. The court went on to consider whether a physician must comply with a lawful request contrary to the physician's personal moral view. It commented that:

> The prevailing viewpoint among medical ethicists appears to be that a physician has the right to refuse on personal moral grounds to follow a conservator's direction to withhold life-sustaining treatment, but must be willing to transfer the patient to another physician who will follow the conservator's direction.[47]

Nonetheless, in other cases it has been made clear that while physicians ought to facilitate a transfer, when they cannot in conscience respond to a competent patient's (or proxy's) request, they cannot be compelled to take measures that would contravene their own view of the ethical duty they owe to their patient.[48] In practice, of course, it may not be a simple matter to transfer a patient. As Daar points out,[49] those caring for Helga Wanglie endeavoured to transfer her to another facility but none could be found that was prepared to accept her. She notes that the seemingly strong endorsement of transfer in the court's judgment in *Conservatorship of Morrison v. Abramovice* was made conditional on there being a willing, alternative care-giver.

Wherever possible, these matters should be resolved by the patient competently refusing further treatment (including via a previously devised directive), or by the patient's proxy giving a substituted judgment to that effect. However, when push comes to shove, it is likely that there will be instances in which the wishes of patients (perhaps especially as expressed by their proxies) will conflict with the wishes of professionals not to compromise their professional integrity, including instances where the conflict will not be resolvable simply by transferring the patient to the care of another professional. My claim has been that where the conflict cannot be resolved by way of a competent refusal of further treatment, or a competent request for further treatment, the conflict should be resolved in favour of the patient. That is what eventually happened in

---

[47] Cited in Daar (1993: 1267). (The quotation is from p. 534 of the court's judgment.)
[48] Cf. *Brophy v. New England Sinai Hospital* [1986] 497 N.E. 2d 62b6 Mass.
[49] (1993: 1270).

In re Jobes.[50] Nancy Jobes' husband sought a court order for the removal of a jejunostomy tube from his wife who was in a persistent vegetative state. The tube was providing Mrs Jobes with nutrition and hydration via an opening from the abdominal wall into the jejunum. The facility refused, citing 'moral grounds'. The trial court upheld Mr Jobes' authority to order the removal of the tube but held, as well, that the nursing home did not have to remove the tube. The tube was to stay in place until Mrs Jobes was transferred to another more compliant facility. On appeal, the New Jersey Supreme Court highlighted the difficulty in locating such a facility and found that if the nursing home was not required to remove the tube that this would frustrate the patient's right of self-determination (in virtue of frustrating the right to refuse medical treatment). Accordingly, it overturned the earlier decision.

IV

Let me summarise my argument. I have argued that professional integrity is a function chiefly of professionals behaving as required by the hallmark commitments of their particular professions. Those commitments (and the means considered acceptable to realising them) can be, and at times are, contested. But, even when they are, there will be certain commitments that will have to be fulfilled if professional integrity is to be preserved. While the matters in dispute are being fought over, and until a resolution has been reached, professionals may disagree among themselves without there being any question that they are all acting with integrity, provided only that the remaining commitments on which there is agreement are upheld. I have claimed that voluntary medically assisted death is an area where there is just such a dispute about the proper scope of the practice of medicine. I have further argued that not only is the practice of doctors giving assistance with dying to those of their competent patients who request it not contrary to the ideals and values of medical care, but that it actually fits well with what are widely recognised to be central ideals and values of medicine. Moreover, I have suggested that some of what is presently accepted as appropriate care of the dying is open to question in light of those values and ideals.

[50] [1987] 529 A.2d 434 N.J. In some jurisdictions there is an offence of *medical trespass* that makes it illegal for a doctor to treat a patient who is no longer competent if the patient had, while competent, refused such treatment. The refusal endures and any treatment to the contrary is medical trespass. See further Skene (1998: 224f) and Mason, *et al.* (2002: 432ff).

I further argued that several considerations commonly advanced as providing a sound moral basis for professional integrity, notably professional autonomy and individual conscience, fail to provide such a basis. My alternative suggestion was that the conscientious convictions of individual professionals should only be given weight for purposes of assessing professional integrity when they reflect the core values of the profession.

I argued, finally, that costly and distressing battles concerning clashes between the wishes of competent patients (which may be expressed via advance directives, or articulated by proxies) and the desires of attending professionals not to do anything that would violate their own integrity (in particular, continuing with futile treatment, or facilitating medically assisted death in those jurisdictions where it is legally permissible) can be avoided if, other things being equal, the claims of patients are given precedence, for then all that is required is a referral or a transfer. My contention has been that patients' wishes should be given precedence because their options are the more restricted.

CHAPTER 8

Competence and end-of-life decision making

In many jurisdictions there is a presumption that because competent adults[1] have a right to self-determination their choices should be respected. For that reason, their choices are afforded legal protection against unwanted interference by others as long as they occasion neither harm nor serious offence to others. However, when adults make choices, or signal that they intend to make choices, that raise concerns about their competence, matters are often viewed very differently. Thus, for example, when patients reject the recommendations of those in charge of their health care, their capacity to make decisions about their own health will often be challenged. This is especially apt to be the case in circumstances where life is at stake. In such circumstances some health care professionals are loath to accept a decision as competent unless it *can be shown to be rationally justified*. As far as these health care professionals are concerned, rejection of medical advice aimed at preserving life is evidence of irrationality. Nevertheless, in jurisdictions where respect is paid to individual self-determination, the law firmly supports a competent patient's right to refuse treatment, even though there is no agreed account of the requirements that have to be satisfied for someone to be regarded as competent.[2] The law does,

---

[1] The global presumption is reserved for adults. On certain specific issues (e.g. as to which parent in a divorce should be granted custody of them) children and early adolescents are often considered competent. In relation to health care decisions, children and early adolescents are generally presumed not to be competent (though this does not preclude their involvement in determining how they should be treated). For discussion of the issues, along with reasons for thinking that the generality of the presumption should be challenged because competence to take health care decisions increases with age, see Brock (1989: 200–211).

[2] Let me reinforce my claim with three representative illustrations. In the United Kingdom courts have held that the common law permits competent persons to refuse medical treatment even if this should result in death. See, for instance, *Re B (Adult refusal of medical treatment)* 2 All ER [2002] 449. Ms B was awarded notional damages in recognition of the fact that her health care-givers had technically committed assault in continuing to treat despite her explicit refusal of the treatment (being hooked up to a ventilator). In Canada, *Malette v. Shulman* [1990] 67 Dominion Law Reports (4th) 321 served to establish the right. In 1990 in the United States the passing of the *Patient Self-Determination Act* decisively entrenched the right.

however, permit doctors to override the decisions of patients deemed not to be competent.[3] This has particular significance for end-of-life care because those opposed to the legalisation of voluntary medically assisted death have often alleged that many who might wish to take advantage of its legalisation lack the necessary competence. In particular, they have alleged that the dying commonly suffer from depression and other causes of cognitive impairment, leading to loss of competence to make end-of-life decisions.

In this chapter I will, first, set out the requirements for competence, especially as regards those features that are particular to decision making in health care settings. I will start with relatively uncontroversial features of the idea of competence and then move on to consider some of the complexities to which decision making in a health care context is subject. In section II, I will outline the various capacities a patient must possess to be a competent decision maker. In section III, I will argue against the contention that competence is solely a cognitive matter. In section IV I will seek to show how my account can help with assessment of the decision making of psychiatric patients and those of uncertain competence. Finally, in the concluding section, I will show how my account of competence provides the resources to answer the objection that, were voluntary medically assisted death to be legalised, many dying persons could not be considered sufficiently competent to choose it.

I

There is general agreement about at least several of the features required for an agent to be competent.

First, although there are contexts in which we talk about competence to perform certain physical tasks,[4] the term has its central application in relation to the capacity for making decisions. In this chapter I will focus specifically on the requirements for people to be competent to make decisions about their health and lives.

Second, though we sometimes do make use of the idea of *general* or *global competence* to give expression to the judgment that an individual should be permitted to make decisions concerning all aspects of his life, it is widely

---

[3] Cf. Jackson (1994: 54ff).

[4] *Pace* Culver and Gert (1982: 53ff). I do not agree that competence 'involves mental or valuational rather than physical abilities' (p. 54). There is nothing odd about speaking of the competence of builders, dentists, surgeons, and so forth, to perform relevant physical tasks. Even if competence in such matters is not just physical dexterity, it is, at least in part, a function of physical abilities.

agreed that competence is specific to a particular task or decision.[5] No one is omnicompetent. I may, for instance, be competent to make decisions about the handling of my finances but not competent to decide whether my car requires a particular replacement part. The fact that competence is task-specific should not be found surprising if only because the criteria that have to be satisfied for someone to be competent over a range of tasks are so obviously varied. The meaning of the term remains the same across the range of tasks, but the criteria that have to be satisfied for someone to be competent will vary with those tasks and, thus, make competence a task-specific notion.

Third, competence is also generally agreed to be a threshold concept.[6] Though it is clearly the case that the decision making capacities of different individuals vary in degree, for legal and policy purposes people are considered *either* to be competent as regards a specific task *or* not competent. The role competence plays in the law, and in public affairs, virtually requires that it function along these lines because it is a way of giving recognition to the fact that autonomous individuals have the right to determine for themselves what they will do in, and with, their lives. Though some people undoubtedly are able to exercise their autonomy over a wider range of activities than others, it would run counter to the recognition of a right to self-determination to say that someone able to exercise his autonomy in a wider range of activities has a greater right to self-determination. By necessity, thresholds need to be established for various tasks. How, and where, particular thresholds are set will vary with what capacities policy makers consider individuals must be able to exercise in order to have the presumptive right to make particular decisions for themselves. In making a determination, they should consider, among other things: consistency with similar settings elsewhere; whether any threshold they decide upon is fair (for instance, in that it ensures that wrongful discrimination as between candidates is avoided); whether the threshold is capable of being met, subject to the provision of appropriate assistance. In a health care context, including that of terminal care, that will mean that, because competence is a central element in

---

[5] Culver and Gert (1982: 54f); Buchanan and Brock (1989: 18ff); and Beauchamp (1999: 50f). Buller (2001) objects to the characterisation of competency as task-specific.

[6] Cf. Wikler (1979); Buchanan and Brock (1989: 26ff); Cartwright (1994: 70ff); and Beauchamp (1999: 55f). Becky Cox White (1994) argues that it is misdirected to support an account of competence in terms of reaching a threshold. Instead, she proposes that competence be understood as a matter of degree. I am unpersuaded. If to be competent requires that competence be displayed to a particular degree, to establish the relevant degree is to establish the threshold. Moreover, it is not obvious that her suggested standard is more practical, less expedient, or less likely to lead to the rigging of assessments of competence.

whether a patient is capable of giving or withholding informed consent[7] for a particular form of treatment, or for refusing it, thresholds should be set so as to be sensitive to the task of obtaining informed consent.

This much, then, is agreed: an agent's decision making competence in relation to a particular matter is a function of his capacity to make decisions specifically about it which satisfy the relevant threshold requirements. But, even if this is correct for decision making in general, there are at least three features specific to clinical situations that have been thought to bear adversely on the ability of patients to make competent decisions about their health care.[8] First, in addition to the pathology of their underlying medical conditions, and any effects from drugs used to treat them, certain concomitants of illness and disease, like pain, stress, fear, and depression, may diminish or undermine the decision making capacities of sufferers. Second, some patients may be in a state of denial about their illness or disease and about the outlook for them, while others may fail to understand information given to them about what is wrong with them and the options for treatment (including, having no treatment at all). Many clinicians claim that patients affected in any of these ways should not be considered competent. Third, some clinicians contend that it is a clinical reality that patients do sometimes make unduly risky decisions about their medical care – decisions that would have disastrous outcomes if implemented – and, in consequence of making such rationally unjustifiable decisions, should not be considered competent (at least as far as their medical care is concerned).

The first two alleged clinical realities can be dealt with quite quickly. Whilst the competence of certain patients will be diminished to levels below the appropriate threshold because of the pathology of their diseases, the effects of their medication, their depression, their failure to understand the information required to make a competent decision, and so forth,[9] not everyone who is, for example, depressed, or in denial about being ill, or taking medication, is reduced to incompetence. Consider denial by way of example (though the same point could be made about at least some forms of depression, fear, being on medication, and so on). According to a reasonably plausible view about denial, it simply indicates an unreadiness

---

[7] Cf. Buchanan and Brock (1989: 28f). For more on the idea of informed consent see Faden and Beauchamp (1986); Appelbaum, *et al.* (1987); Brock (1987); Wear (1998); and Young (1998).

[8] Cf. Wear (1999).

[9] Wear (1999: 232ff) denies that there is sufficient documented evidence to support these claims. I do not know whether there are properly conducted studies to support them, but they seem intuitively plausible. Even so, the evidence from both The Netherlands and Oregon suggests that depression, for example, is not a significant risk factor among those who seek medically assisted death. See Ganzini (2004: 172ff) and Kimsma and van Leeuwen (2004: 226ff).

to make a decision at a particular time; if so, it signifies that more time is needed to facilitate a competent decision (and preclude an incompetent one). Thus, given the presumption that adults are competent, the first response of health care professionals should be to try to help overcome depression, to allay fear, to modify medication where that is possible, or to endeavour to enhance understanding of treatment options. In other words, attempts should be made to bolster the capacity of patients to make competent decisions. Sometimes, of course, such attempts will not be feasible, but, whenever they are, skilled professionals should give them a try in order to promote competent decision making on the part of their patients. Because end-of-life care generally affords strategic opportunities to test the presumption that adults are competent until shown otherwise, educational and therapeutic responses should be the first resort, circumstances permitting. I will have more to say about this later (in section III), but it is worth noting in passing that responding in these ways may, on occasion, enable a patient's fears and anxieties to be enlisted to help him gain a better grasp of a medical procedure.

A separate important point arises from the tendency to question whether dying patients can meet the threshold requirements for the decisions they must make when their circumstances make them so dependent on others. Elsewhere, in relation to major life decisions about choices of partners, whether to reproduce, whether to make expensive purchases, and so forth, far less concern is expressed about the ways in which emotions, stress, and lack of information may interfere with competent choices. What this suggests is that the third of the issues under consideration – the rational justifiability of decisions made by the dying – tends, in practice, to be more crucial than the two previously addressed. Though the stakes are high in, for example, choices about life partners, about reproducing, and about making expensive purchases, those choices are not regarded as properly subject to scrutiny by others, at least in part because those who make them are not typically regarded as vulnerable (in the way that the terminally ill are), but also because they are thought less likely to have irreversible effects than decisions about end-of-life matters. Given these two factors – the extent to which health care decisions, especially end-of-life decisions, tend to be subjected to greater scrutiny because of the dependent position of patients, and the higher threshold that competent agents have to satisfy whenever the ratio of risks to benefits becomes stringent – the competence of the terminally ill to make (rationally justifiable) decisions tends to be subject to greater challenge. It is, therefore, necessary to give close attention to whether, and, if so, how, risk bears on decision making competence.

Buchanan and Brock contend that 'the standard of competence ought to vary in part with the expected harms or benefits to the patient of acting in accordance with the patient's choice'.[10] This carries the implication (which they readily acknowledge) that a patient may be competent to consent to a particular treatment but not to refuse it, and, conversely, may be competent to refuse, but not to consent to, a particular treatment. Where a low risk procedure is proposed, a patient will need to be of undoubted competence if he wishes to refuse it, whereas, with a high risk procedure, a patient who wishes to refuse will need only to satisfy the minimum threshold standard of competence. This is because competence is properly assessed by reference to a process that balances respect for individual self-determination and protection of individual values, goals, and projects.

If competence were just a matter of someone's mental condition (being in a sound state of mind), it could be determined independently of the things being chosen, and so risks and benefits could be ignored.[11] But any number of examples suggest that this is not credible. Suppose that my car requires a roadworthy certificate, which can only be issued by an authorised mechanic, before I am legally permitted to drive it again. Suppose, further, that the mechanic advises that the brake linings need to be attended to before a certificate can be issued. I may be competent to accept that advice (given that I have good reason – based on certification, or testimony, or some other reliable means – to believe that the mechanic is a competent mechanic), and to give the go-ahead for the work to be done, but, because I lack sufficient technical expertise, I may not be competent to challenge the advice. Were I a highly qualified motor mechanic or engineer I might be able to debate the mechanic's finding and persuade him that the problem is not with the brake linings, but, since I am not, I lack the competence to challenge the assessment. Nonetheless, I am competent to approve the work that is necessary to obtain a roadworthiness certificate. It might be objected that the correctness of my call does not hinge on the magnitude of the risk, but rather on my lack of the knowledge (to be able competently to make the right call about the brake linings). My competence cannot, however, be denied simply because I lack sufficient relevant knowledge. My lack of knowledge renders me less than competent only when my being allowed to make ignorant decisions would have such

---

[10] (1989: 51).

[11] This appears to be the position of Wicclair (1991). For replies see Brock (1991) and Wilks (1997). Like Wicclair, Culver and Gert (1990) hold that if a person is competent to agree to a proposal, that person must also be competent to refuse the proposal, which, for all that it may seem an attractive principle, is inconsistent with a risk-related understanding of competence.

seriously bad consequences as to undermine the presumption in favour of my self-determination. The seriousness of the consequences has to be measured by their impact on my values, goals and projects.[12] A second example will help elucidate this point.

Suppose A is keen to build up his assets and so wishes to make an investment involving virtually all of his existing assets. He has heard that trading in 'derivatives'[13] represents a good opportunity to achieve his goal, especially if he leverages[14] his investment. Because leveraging an investment can trigger a multiplier effect it can lead to spectacular gains. At the same time, it dramatically increases the risks associated with an investment. For example, suppose that the derivative instrument that A wishes to utilise will be affected negatively if the prime interest rate rises before he is obliged to fulfil his contractual obligations under the instrument. Suppose, further, that the leveraged derivative calls for A to be liable for ten times the amount represented by the intervening rise in the prime rate (a figure not uncommon in practice). Because of this feature even a small rise in the prime rate would dramatically raise the risks to which A would be exposed. A significant rise in the prime rate might be catastrophic. So, given that A is a rank amateur in the field of derivatives, and lacks a sound understanding of the way that leveraging can impact upon an investor, he should not be considered competent to make and manage a substantial investment like the one described because he lacks the capacity to exercise his self-determination in a way that coheres with his stated goals. The coupling of his lack of relevant knowledge with the inherent riskiness of his choice threatens to undermine his chief reason for investing.

[12] Demarco (2002) has argued for an alternative view, namely, that in very risky circumstances the proper thing to do is not to raise the standard required to be considered competent but to require greater evidence of autonomy on the part of the person making the decision. His position seems motivated more by concerns about paternalism than by a desire to ensure an appropriate role for competence.

[13] A derivative is a contractual relationship established by two or more parties where payment is based on (or 'derived' from) some agreed benchmark. The function of a derivative is to shift risk, for example, exposure to movements in commodity prices, interest rates, foreign exchange rates, or share indices. Among the better known kinds of derivatives are 'options' (rights to buy or sell a security or other asset during a given period for a price specified in advance), 'futures' (rights to buy or sell an asset of a standard quality at a specified future date and price), and 'swaps' (simultaneous buying and selling of the same security or obligation such as an interest payment or a foreign currency payment).

[14] Leveraging is a technique used to minimise negative cash flows. In the present context it refers to the borrowing of significant debt capital by someone who has a minimal equity capital investment. When carried out successfully, leveraging preserves an investor's equity as opposed to requiring the investor to utilise it. Of course, borrowing money isn't the only way to apply leverage in a commercial setting. When a business rents space, or leases equipment, only as needed (rather than purchasing them), it is leveraging.

By contrast, A might be considered competent to buy small parcels of shares in the share market even though he may know only a little more about the share market than he does about leveraging derivatives. My claim is that in this latter circumstance his lack of knowledge does not render him incompetent. Some will think there must be differences between the cases because they consider paternalism would be justified to prevent A from entering into the leveraged investment but not the share market investment. But this is too swift. Even among those who are at odds over the grounds on which paternalism may be justified,[15] there is agreement that paternalism cannot be justified *just because* someone fails to make suitable choices. Consider our hesitation about intervening paternalistically to force an adult to improve the nutritional value of his diet, or his pattern of exercise, even if he is making unsuitable decisions about his food intake, the need for exercise, and, ultimately, his future health. The same holds for decisions about significant relationships, reproduction, major consumer purchases and, most importantly for present purposes, end-of-life decisions. So, even when imprudent decisions involve significant risk, it does not follow that those making them should be paternalistically prevented from doing so.

Lest there be any uncertainty about my point, let me be categorical in saying that it is not just the magnitude of the risks people are willing to take that is the measure of their competence to take decisions relevant to those risks. Individuals are sometimes prepared to risk life and limb to defend what they believe in, or to explore the hitherto unexplored, or to set new standards of accomplishment, or to risk their savings to start new ventures, or to pursue dreams, without there being any suggestion of a lack of competence on their part because of their preparedness to take such risks. Nothing I have said should be taken to imply that decisions to engage in these sorts of activities must be incompetent. Whether those who make such decisions are competent has to be judged, among other things, by how consistent the decisions are with the values, goals and projects of those who make them, not just by reference to the risks taken. Moreover, given that such decisions may be based on values, goals or projects that others do not share, the fact that those others find them uncongenial does not show them to be incompetent (as has previously

---

[15] Feinberg (1986: ch. 19) argues that paternalism is only appropriate when an action or decision is not autonomous. Even though I go further in believing that there can be justified instances of paternalism directed towards (occurrently) autonomous acts or decisions – see my (1986: ch. 6) – neither of us thinks paternalistic interventions should occur *whenever*, or, just because, someone makes choices that are incompetent.

been noted in connection with the choice of adult Jehovah's Witnesses to refuse life-saving blood transfusions).

It is time to relate the preceding discussion to the context of health care and, in particular, end-of-life decision making. Granted that competence is a task-specific idea, the spelling out of the implications of a particular decision will be relevant to a judgment about someone's competence to make it. As Wilks puts it: 'reckoning the risks and benefits involved in the options is part of what is required for understanding the task, and so is part of what is required for determining whether someone is competent to perform the task'.[16] Accordingly, someone may, for instance, be competent to decide on an appendectomy, but not to decide whether to undergo risky, highly experimental neurosurgery. Likewise, someone may be competent to refuse a proposed medical treatment but not to consent to it, or to consent to a proposed medical treatment but not to refuse it. Where medical procedures, which are not inherently risky, are *refused* – say, blood transfusions by adult Jehovah's Witnesses – a higher threshold of competence is demanded than when such a procedure is *agreed*. That they may surpass the required level of competence does not, however, gainsay the relevance of risk to the assessment of their competence.

II

Even supposing that the points made so far have all been found convincing, an account of the qualities or capacities necessary for someone to be competent still remains to be given. For instance, in virtue of what capacities are the Jehovah's Witnesses to whom I just referred to be judged competent? Judgments of specific competence are routinely made by medical professionals, but there are occasions when an informal clinical assessment is not appropriate. For that reason various tests have been devised to determine the competence or incompetence of patients when matters are not straightforward.[17] In such instances testing may take place within a directed clinical interview or may involve administration of a formal assessment tool.[18] Performance on these tests is supposed to help assess whether a patient is able to understand the nature of his situation and the

---

[16] (1997: 426). Cf. Buchanan and Brock (1989: 51–57) and Beauchamp (1999: 70ff).

[17] Cf., for example, Roth, *et al.* (1977); Lidz, *et al.* (1984); Appelbaum and Grisso (1988); and Grisso and Appelbaum (1998). For discussion of the sorts of tests that have been used, see White (1994: 54ff, 186f); Beauchamp (1999: 64ff); and Erde (1999: 239ff).

[18] Among the better known are The MacArthur Competence Assessment Tool (MacCAT) and the Aid to Capacity Evaluation (ACE). The former was designed for patients with complex psychiatric or neurological conditions, the latter for more general use in a clinical setting.

procedure(s) being proposed; whether he is able to understand information disclosed to him by those in charge of his medical care (for instance, about the procedure being proposed); whether he is able to give a reason (or reasons) for any decision that he makes; whether that reason is rational; whether it is based on an appropriate weighting of the risks and benefits of the proposed procedure; and, whether he is capable of communicating his decision.

It seems clear that regardless of the success or otherwise of these particular tests, the capacities they are intended to test – understanding, reasoning, deliberating, communicating and so forth – are central to what it is to be competent. Hardly surprisingly, they are also central to the legal concept that is most directly and closely related to competence, namely, informed voluntary consent. Nonetheless, there are several reasons why the kinds of tests used to assess the competence of patients cannot be decisive but, instead, are, at best, indicators of the need for further investigation. First, the tests are prone to produce inaccurate results because of the way that educational, linguistic and cultural variations can, and do, affect understanding among those to whom they are administered.[19] Second, since competence is specific to particular tasks and decisions, reliable testing has to be tied to specific tasks and decisions, whereas the tests that are typically relied upon are concerned with competence of a more general kind. Third, existing tests focus strongly on cognitive matters and so are apt to ignore the bearing of affective considerations on competence. I will say nothing further about this here but will return to it in the next section. Finally, and this is a point that I have already had occasion to mention, the tests take no account of what Buchanan and Brock have argued is a vital ingredient for someone to be a competent agent, namely, having 'a minimally consistent, stable [set of values that is] affirmed as his or her own'.[20] They suggest, entirely plausibly, that, without such a set of values, an agent will be unable to settle on a decision and carry it through. The values do not have to be fixed in concrete but they must be stable enough to provide a foundation both for a patient's decision and for the subsequent resolve to implement the decision once it has been made.

A competent decision maker will, of course, alter his decision if new evidence comes to hand that, for example, changes the ratio of risks to benefits. Hence, it might be thought that if a patient's values undergo significant

---

[19] Buchanan and Brock (1989: 71f) cite evidence of how false positive results can be generated by considerations like these, and of how false negative results can be obtained for the well-educated.
[20] (1989: 25).

alteration in the course of medical treatment, he may equally be expected to change his mind about the treatment regime. I see no reason to disagree, but the change of mind must result from a process that takes due account of the patient's competence to make such a change, for otherwise it will lack credibility. Were the change in values to result from bullying or hectoring (either by medical staff, or by family and friends), there would be reason to doubt the voluntariness of the decision and the change of mind about treatment. However, if a patient simply comes to realise that things he previously thought to be of great value no longer matter, and the realisation results from a reconsideration of what he finds important, rather than because he is, say, depressed about his illness, the change in his values will be straightforwardly intelligible and there will be no ground on which to challenge his competence to change his mind about treatment.

Even if there is reason to be sceptical about the sorts of *tests* that have been used to assess whether patients have the *capacities* needed to make competent decisions about their health care, the capacities themselves are not in doubt. It is clear that a competent health care decision maker must have at least the following capacities: the capacity to understand his health care situation; the capacity to understand the options open to him (including not only the various possible modes of treatment, but the possibility of not having any treatment at all); and the capacity to make an assessment of the risks and benefits associated with the various options for treatment, including non-treatment. In addition, he must have a minimally consistent and stable set of values to which he can appeal in exercising the various capacities just adumbrated. However, as previously flagged, consideration still needs to be given to whether, and how, emotional or affective factors may influence the exercise of these various capacities and the expression of these values. The next section will be devoted to these issues.

III

Is decision making competence wholly a cognitive matter? When I previously referred briefly to the sorts of tests that have been employed in hospitals and other health care institutions to help determine patient competence, I mentioned that one of the tests concerned the rational justifiability of the reasons given by patients for their decisions. This has typically been understood in an intellectualist way, yet, if, as I also previously indicated, it is a clinical reality that patients who are making decisions about their treatment are often depressed, or fearful, or under stress, or in a state of denial, to ignore emotional or affective considerations and their bearing on the competence of patients to make decisions would appear to be very foolish. Is it possible to account for the role emotion plays in our lives, especially in regard to its impact on our ability to make competent health care decisions?

It has been traditional to emphasise the negative impact of emotions on competence. Reason and emotion, according to this tradition, are oppositional forces locked in combat with each other. But in recent times this picture has been shown to be inaccurate on both scientific and philosophical grounds.

Neurobiologists have drawn attention to the ways in which mutual interactions between neural and chemical elements in our brains and our bodies produce emotional responses – in doing so, they have stressed the cognitive value of these interactive processes. As they see matters, so far from emotions and reason being locked in a constant struggle, emotions are, at least sometimes, indispensable for decision making. Granted that, on occasion, biological drives and emotions produce irrational responses by biasing our deliberations and distorting our judgment,[21] they are generally necessary for effective decision making.[22] Moreover, there is a rich diversity of psychological evidence to support the idea of the mutual interaction of thought and feeling in effective decision making.[23] Finally, we know that much of what we think of as rational reflection proves inadequate in everyday situations when it is called upon to cope with complex personal and social problems.[24] The assistance of our emotions has been identified as vital for overcoming these failures of 'calculating rationality'.

Various philosophers have stressed that emotions can be *appropriate* or *intelligible*[25] within particular contexts, and that, when they are appropriate, they make a vital contribution to decision making. There is, in fact, a complementarity between them and the reasons we have for pursuing

---

[21] See, for example, Gilbert and Wilson (2000).

[22] See, for example, Damasio (1994). Damasio's clinical subjects were unable to engage in effective practical reasoning – to plan for their futures, to act in ways that were in their best interests, and to maintain healthy and stable personal relationships – when the areas of the brain implicated in the processing of emotion were malfunctioning.

[23] See the evidence cited in Callahan (1988).

[24] Cf. Kahneman, *et al.* (1982) and Sutherland (1992).

[25] Cf. de Sousa (1987); Greenspan (1988) and (2000); Stocker (1996: 38–55); and Goldie (2000: 37ff). White (1994: 127–144, 167–175) helpfully discusses the place of affect in competent health care decision making. The connection between mental competence and appropriate emotions is discussed by Charland (1998a) and commented upon by Chadwick (1998); Elliott (1998); and Youngner (1998). Charland replies in (1998b).

particular courses of action. Emotions contribute to our assessment of the salience of the considerations that have to be taken into account when we engage in practical reasoning. Thus, without the sort of emotional attachment that provides the motivation for taking particular courses of action, much that we do would be rendered unintelligible. So, the contribution of our feelings, moods, and emotions to our decision making cannot be reduced to mere instrumental rationality; but that does not show that they are irrational or lack cognitive importance. Notice, first, that I have not said that our rational decision making cannot be overwhelmed by the emotions we are experiencing – clearly this can happen as, for instance, when we are in a fury – only that there is no need either to think of this as inevitable or as characteristic of all emotions. Neither, second, have I denied that emotions can, on occasion, be misplaced – simply consider an emotion like hope. Nor, third, have I suggested that emotions never obstruct decision making. They clearly can, and do, as, for instance, when a patient inappropriately allows himself to become resigned to a certain fate (perhaps, his imminent death) and so refuses to think about other realistic possibilities. My contention is only that the traditional picture of reason being locked in a struggle for superiority with emotion is inaccurate. The point is important in the present context because it helps bring out why we should expect a competent person to feel some emotional attachment to his decisions: having such an attachment shows that he cares, which, in turn, has a bearing on his decision making. Moreover, affording due recognition to the role of affect can serve to remind us that it is not necessary to agree with a person's values, goals or projects to view his decisions as competent in virtue of accurately reflecting his values, or promoting his goals and projects, for, as was seen earlier, all that is required is that those values be part of a consistent and stable set that he affirms as his own.

To illustrate the way that emotions can be relevant to an assessment of a patient's competence it will be instructive to consider fear. I choose it because it is one of the emotions that clinicians sometimes claim undermines the rationality of patient decision making, especially end-of-life decision making, not because it is especially helpful to my claim that there is no need to see emotions as at war with reason. It is quite appropriate to be afraid in the face of uncertainty or danger, and being appropriately afraid can assist in making a rationally defensible decision. In a case of physical danger, for instance, the decision may be a prudential one such as to beat a hasty retreat or to don protective gear. With moral danger, fear may help prompt a response like taking steps to distance oneself

from the circumstance giving rise to the danger in order to avoid temptation, or, perhaps, 'blowing the whistle', or even making it clear that, given
the circumstance one is facing, some of one's previous moral convictions
may no longer be sustainable.[26] Just as fear can play a positive role in
practical reasoning in these kinds of circumstance, it can also help galvanise
patients in clinical settings into thinking more rationally about their
situations. It is quite inappropriate, therefore, to suggest that patients
who are emotionally affected by their illness must *inevitably* fail a test of
rationality, let alone that they cannot be competent.

IV

The account of competence I have developed avoids implausibly having
to think of ourselves as narrowly rationalistic beings and, instead, takes
heed of other aspects of our natures, aspects that remain as relevant when
we are ill as when we are well. I have emphasised that competence is a
threshold notion, but I have also indicated that some individuals will,
nonetheless, be more competent than others in relation to a particular
task. This is compatible with each of the individuals reaching the
(minimal) threshold. A highly competent individual may have capacities
and attributes that take him well beyond the threshold requirement for a
particular task, whereas a less competent individual may only just achieve
the threshold. Moreover, an individual may be competent at certain times
to perform a particular task, or make a particular type of decision, but
not be competent at other times. Such an individual will be *intermittently
competent*. This idea of intermittent competence gives us a bridge to the
claim I made very early on that my account of competence would shed
light on decision making by psychiatric patients and those of uncertain
competence. I shall now make good on my promise.

While psychiatric patients will sometimes be quite generally lacking
in competence as a result, for example, of severe psychosis, it is more
common to find psychiatric patients suffering only intermittently from a
clouding of their consciousness, or other forms of confusion.[27] In those
periods when their psychiatric conditions do not undermine their capacities
to understand and assess their situations there will be no reason to judge
such individuals incompetent. Historically, of course, psychiatric patients
have far more frequently been deemed incompetent compared with patients
suffering debilitating physical illnesses. In particular, when psychiatric

---

[26] Bennett (1974).   [27] Cf. Culver and Gert (1982: 62).

patients have sought to refuse various kinds of medical treatment (from the administration of electric shock therapy through to the use of psychotropic drugs) the reaction has commonly been to certify them incompetent. No doubt, at least part of the explanation has been the way reason has been elevated above emotion, but among important lessons I hope have been learned from the preceding investigation of the concept of competence, two stand out, namely, that competence is not simply a function of the substantive content of a decision maker's decisions and that emotions play a vital role in decision making. A competent decision is not the same as a correct decision (always supposing that there is a correct decision and that it can be determined), or even a rationally justified decision. Where subjective considerations are involved, and there is no determinate, objectively correct answer, a competent decision need not even be one that is capable of being made convincing to others. To reiterate a point I have made several times: refusals by adult Jehovah's Witnesses of blood transfusions are unlikely ever to be found convincing by those who do not share their beliefs but that is no ground for objecting to the competency of their refusals.

Since competence is not to be decided by reference to the content of a decision, the practice of deeming psychiatric patients incompetent should they refuse treatments proposed by their care-givers is not justifiable. In a noteworthy recent British case[28] the judge found accordingly. Mr C, a sixty-eight year old paranoid schizophrenic, was resident in a secure hospital. He had a gangrenous foot that, according to his doctors, required amputation. C applied for an injunction to prevent his doctors doing what they judged to be in his best interests, namely, amputating his foot, in the event that they deemed him to be incompetent. At the time of making the application, he was suffering active delusions about being tortured by various doctors who, he believed, were involved in a conspiracy against him. The judge ruled that, despite C's psychosis, and its likely effects on his general competence, it had not been shown that he was incapable of understanding the choice he wished to make. C was, therefore, presumed to be competent to refuse the operation and, moreover, granted an injunction *in perpetuity*. He recovered despite not having the amputation; although his leg was somewhat withered, he still had some use of it.

The judge appears to have believed that C was competent at certain times and that the views he expressed during those times were unwaveringly against amputation. Thus, he was found competent to refuse the proposed

---

[28] *Re C* (Adult: Refusal of Treatment) [1993] 1 *Family Law Reports* 940; [1993] *Family Law* 404.

operation. This was despite the gangrenous condition of his leg being trace-able to his failure to seek early medical treatment, a failure that stemmed from his belief about his doctors having conspired to torture him. (The decision makes sense provided only that the judge accepted that C's desire to keep his leg was one he had specifically formed in light of his values and with an awareness that he might die if the operation were not authorised.)[29]

V

As previously mentioned, it has sometimes been claimed that dying persons who might seek to take advantage of the legalisation of voluntary medically assisted death should be prevented from doing so if their competence is doubtful because of cognitive impairment or depression. Now, even if the claim were sound it could have no bearing on whether those who are not cognitively impaired or depressed should be able competently to request medical assistance with dying. But I shall say no more about these latter because, for present purposes, I want to concentrate on those whose com-petence may be doubted.

   The first point to make is that sufferers from certain forms of dementia (like Alzheimer's disease), some geriatric patients suffering a degree of organic brain damage, and some severely depressed patients, may, like the psychiatric patients referred to above, be intermittently capable of compe-tently giving their consent or, alternatively, of refusing to do so. By empha-sising that competence is to be understood as involving a *process*[30] in which an individual exercises various deliberative capacities so as to reach a decision that furthers his values, goals and projects, the analysis I have offered justifies the inclusion of at least some sufferers from such conditions among the competent. They will be competent for those tasks and at those times when they exhibit the relevant capacities in an appropriate way.

---

[29] In a similar case in the United States, *Lane v. Candura* [1978] 376 N.E. 2d. Mass. App. Ct., Mrs Candura was found to be competent to refuse amputation of her leg, which was affected by gangrene. She did not wish to become an invalid and did not believe that having the operation would save her life. She vacillated about having the operation, found it difficult to concentrate on matters that were being discussed with her, and had a distorted sense of time. However, as the Court emphasised, she was aware of her circumstances and of the risks to which her refusal of the operation would expose her, and was able perceptively to answer pertinent questions. The Court could find '. . . no indication in any of the testimony that [her refusal] is not a choice with full appreciation of the consequences. The most that is shown is that the decision involves strong emotional factors, that she does not choose to discuss the decision with certain persons, and that occasionally her resolve against giving consent weakens' (at 1232). See further Demarco (2002: 242ff).

[30] This is a point much emphasised by Buchanan and Brock (1989: 48ff).

Needless to say, the competence of any such individual to make particular decisions can rightly be considered uncertain until the process followed in making those decisions has been examined and found to be both apt for the purpose *and* consonant with the individual's values. Oregon's *Death With Dignity Act*, for example, requires physicians to order an evaluation of the mental health of patients whom they suspect are suffering from a 'psychiatric or psychological disorder or depression causing impaired judgment' before responding to a request from them for medical assistance with suicide.

Though there is much to be said for having such evaluations conducted within an ongoing doctor–patient relationship, research suggests there are also some significant disadvantages because many doctors are not especially well qualified to assess whether decision making competency is impaired.[31] But, even if they were better qualified, there would still be philosophical reasons for resisting the idea that medical professionals are well placed, let alone uniquely well placed, to make assessments of patient competence and incompetence. It *is* true that physicians know better than their patients about the medical status of those patients. That is why they have such an important role to play in the provision of information, and in ensuring that decisions are taken in circumstances conducive to that information being understood and evaluated. But it will be rare for a patient's medical situation to be the only thing he needs to take into account in making decisions about his medical treatment, particularly his end-of-life treatment. To the extent that his values, goals and projects are central to the decisions he makes, it will be him, not his attending physician, who will be best placed to make a decision that accords those considerations their due place. To maintain the contrary position is to embrace a form of medical paternalism.

There is a further point to be made in response to those who challenge the competence of the dying to choose physician-assisted suicide or voluntary euthanasia. It is that relevant empirical research provides no good reason to believe the challenge is well-founded, because it reveals only 'a relatively weak relationship between severity of depression and decision-making impairment'.[32] Indeed, as Rosenfeld observes, even in cases of severe depression the extent of decision-making impairment is not pronounced. That is, of course, distinct from whether depression has any significant influence on opinions about which end-of-life decisions the

---

[31] For a helpful account of the relevant empirical research that has been carried out in recent years see Rosenfeld (2004: 114–118).
[32] Rosenfeld (2004: 122ff). Cf. Appelbaum, *et al.* (1999).

dying may make. But, even supposing there is some influence, to infer that depressed dying patients are, therefore, incompetent would be invalid. As well as the research just mentioned, there is other relevant research relating to the influence of depression on requests for medically assisted death in both The Netherlands and Oregon. Though depression has, unsurprisingly, been identified among those making such requests, it has not rated as a significant reason for the requests.[33] So much for depression, but what about cognitive impairment and its effect on end-of-life decision making? As Rosenfeld remarks, the literature investigating the relationship between these matters is scant but what there is (mainly based on studies of patients with forms of dementia) 'supports the hypothesis that cognitive impairment significantly impedes decision-making ability'.[34] Let this be agreed. Nothing follows from it as to whether those who have sought and been given medical assistance with dying (where it has been legal to do so) have, in fact, been cognitively impaired and hence, at the very least, are of doubtful competence. More importantly, no evidence has been produced to demonstrate that those who have exercised their legal entitlement to assistance have done so while cognitively impaired.[35] No advocate of the legalisation of voluntary medically assisted dying should object to doctors making every effort to ensure that those who seek medical assistance with dying are competent to do so. It is surely unobjectionable, for instance, for physicians to call upon the services of other medical personnel with greater expertise in the assessment of depression or cognitive impairment, and their impact on competence, before agreeing to a request for medical assistance in dying. Ensuring that only those competent to do so are able to take advantage of the legalisation of medically assisted death has always been a priority among its supporters.

---

[33] Rosenfeld (2004: ch. 7) discusses relevant studies in some detail. For information on the Dutch situation see van der Maas, et al. (1996). For information on Oregon see Ganzini, et al. (2000).

[34] (2004: 122).

[35] Two important recent studies lend support to this conclusion, at least in relation to Oregon. See Bharucha, et al. (2003) and Pearlman, et al. (2005). In the former survey, depressive symptoms were not found to be an influential factor in patients' pursuit of physician-assisted suicide and no evidence was uncovered of depression-related decisional incapacity. In the latter study, none of the patients in the sample was acutely depressed either when planning or requesting physician-assisted suicide. Finally, the major studies of the practice of medically assisted death in The Netherlands have not attributed a significant role either to depression or to other psychiatric conditions.

CHAPTER 9

Advance directives

To this point my focus has largely been on the permissibility of competent dying patients choosing the manner and timing of their death, including, where necessary, with medical assistance. However, it is a fact of life for many patients that by the time death looms they are no longer competent and so are unable to make autonomous decisions. For these dying patients, it is, therefore, of great significance whether reliance can be placed on end-of-life choices made while they were competent. In particular, it is of great significance whether careful, written specifications of those choices (in the form of advance directives, or what are sometimes called 'living wills') should be accorded a privileged status as conveying competently formed convictions that are to bind their end-of-life treatment.[1]

To decide these matters it will be necessary to consider whether the 'prior consent' recorded in an advance directive can be considered authentic given the impossibility of confirming or ratifying it once competence is lost. (When a patient remains competent, and so is able to confirm the instructions in his advance directive, this issue will not arise.[2] No competent individual can be bound by what he earlier decided, so a competent individual can simply overturn an advance directive if he undergoes a change of mind. Not to allow him to change his mind would itself be a serious infringement of his autonomy.) To determine the evidential value of 'prior consent' it will be necessary to consider, first, whether a competent person can have sufficient information and imagination to make choices that bind how he may be treated when he is no longer competent. A particular, but largely neglected, instance of this problem has to do with whether clinicians are

[1] I shall not consider the contention that precedence should instead be given to the views of a patient's family, particularly when that entails overriding the autonomous wishes of the patient. For such a contention see Chan (2004).
[2] Francis (1993) claims that where (voluntary) euthanasia is concerned, advance directives should be permitted to come into play *only* in such instances. I will show that this is to adopt an excessively sceptical attitude toward advance directives.

entitled to ignore the advance directives of those suffering psychiatric illnesses. In countries influenced by Anglo-American law, considerable powers are given to clinicians under mental health legislation to discount or even override certain judgments of the mentally ill. Since this arrangement has implications for the use of advance directives I will canvass it to see what lessons, if any, are to be learned. Second, I will consider whether it even makes sense to think of a competent chooser and the incompetent individual he subsequently becomes, as one and the same person, and, thus, whether he can coherently be considered to have the authority to decide how the person he will become should be cared for. Third, I will consider what should happen when an advance directive fails to give clear instructions about how a no longer competent person should be treated. This will also provide an opportunity to reflect on the duties and responsibilities of health care providers in relation to the implementation of advance directives, especially as they bear on medical assistance with dying.

I

Individuals who are competent, able to perform the relevant means–end reasoning, able to understand the implications of their choices, and informed about what their medical treatment involves, are entitled to refuse that type of treatment even when it seems likely to be beneficial to their health. This is because a competent person is entitled to give greater weight to personal values, ideals or goals than to the achievement of a particular standard of health. As was seen in the previous chapter, this entitlement is simply an expression of the value of individual autonomy.[3] That same value is also expressed in the fact that we are entitled to make decisions about our futures.

These points find classic illustration in the fact that competent Jehovah's Witnesses are legally entitled in various jurisdictions to refuse life-saving blood transfusions.[4] Moreover, because a competent Jehovah's Witness is

---

[3] Cf., for example, Buchanan and Brock (1989: ch. 2); King (1991: chs. 2–3); and Davis (1996).

[4] Cf., for example, *Malette v. Shulman* [1990] 67 *Dominion Law Reports* (4th) 321. It is fascinating that the most significant English court decision about an advance directive to date concerned a (former) Jehovah's Witness. *HE v. A Hospital NHS Trust* [2003] EWHC 1017 (Fam) concerned a twenty-four year old patient with a congenital heart problem who required surgery involving a blood transfusion. Though brought up initially as a Muslim, HE and her mother became Jehovah's Witnesses after her parents separated. In 2001, while still a Jehovah's Witness, HE signed an advance directive in which she indicated her unwillingness to accept blood and primary blood components should the need arise. She also stated that her advance directive could only be revoked in writing. Subsequently she became engaged to a Muslim and stopped attending meetings of the Witnesses. In April 2003 she was rushed to hospital by ambulance in need of emergency heart surgery. In the course of the journey

entitled to refuse such a transfusion prior to undergoing surgery he can effectively prevent the administration of a transfusion needed to save his life.[5] What these considerations make clear is that a competent Jehovah's Witness may exercise his autonomy in such a way as to control what happens to him at a future date when, for whatever reason, he cannot exercise his occurrent autonomy. In this respect there is an exact parallel with the way that prior consent is recorded in an advance directive. When a competent Jehovah's Witness deliberately withholds his consent to a blood transfusion, the procedure cannot legally be carried out. Whatever we might think of the choice not to have a transfusion, in the absence of evidence to the contrary his choice must be respected. The situation is no different from a competent person refusing to give informed consent to a proposed medical procedure or to a proxy applying a 'substituted judgment standard'[6] in refusing such a procedure.[7]

Given these considerations, if there are reasons to object to the use of advance directives those reasons cannot concern the giving in advance of authentic consent about how we may be treated (in the future) when we are no longer in a position to speak for ourselves. But, as was indicated earlier, other reasons have been offered which purport to show that

she told her brother and aunt that she did not want to die. By the time she arrived at the hospital she was unconscious and required emergency surgery necessitating the use of blood products. Her mother informed the hospital of the advance directive refusing such products. This action prompted HE's father to make an application to the court to authorise the surgery, including any necessary blood transfusion. The judge held that just as advance directives can be made orally or in writing, so, too, can they be revoked orally or in writing, and that the 'inherent revocability' of advance directives voids any attempt to make them irrevocable. He further ruled that, because HE's life was at stake, great weight had to be placed on her renunciation of her beliefs as a Jehovah's Witness (which had formed the foundation for the advance directive) *and* the wish she had expressed not to be allowed to die. He held that the burden of proof had to be borne by those opposing medical treatment clearly in HE's best interests, and concluded that it had not been. However, nothing in his judgment gainsays the fact that advance directives clearly have legal effect in English law.

[5] In the United States, various courts have ruled that in circumstances where the state can establish a 'compelling state interest' in overriding the patient's self-determination, a patient's choice to refuse medical treatment may be set aside. Four such compelling state interests have been affirmed in different cases: 1. to preserve life; 2. to prevent suicide; 3. to protect innocent third parties (such as the unborn child(ren) of a female patient); 4. to safeguard the integrity of the medical profession (as when a professional wishes to disengage from providing treatment she judges unethical).King (1991: 44–55) gives several reasons why a patient's right of self-determination, should, nevertheless, normally prevail.

[6] According to the substituted judgment standard, a proxy ought to attempt to make decisions by choosing as the no longer competent individual would have chosen had he remained competent. See further Buchanan and Brock (1989: 112–122) and King (1991: 152–156).

[7] Though refusals are permitted in these ways, the situation is quite different if patients or their proxies wish to insist on particular treatments being administered. As was noted when I discussed the issue of medical futility, doctors are under no obligation to provide treatments that they do not consider to be medically indicated. Cf. Skene (2006).

advance directives lack the evidential value needed for them to be reliable expressions of our views about how we are to be treated when we are no longer competent to make decisions on our own behalf. I will now consider these reasons in turn.

II

A first objection to the use of an advance directive in end-of-life medical care is that its having been devised by a competent agent is not enough on its own to make it evidentially useful. Those who advance this objection contend that the agent needs, as well, to be both informed and imaginative. How much would an agent need to know to be suitably informed? How much, for instance, would an agent need to know about the range of possible medical circumstances to be covered in the directive, and about the variety of medical treatments relevant to that range, in order to be suitably informed? Care must be taken to avoid giving an answer that is too demanding lest advance directives be simply ruled out altogether. What is true is that the further in advance of the onset of any particular life-threatening medical condition that a directive is devised, the harder it is to ensure that the instructions are precise enough to be helpful. A directive devised decades prior to the need to make an end-of-life decision, and never subsequently revisited, let alone modified, would probably be of little evidential value concerning a person's preferences near the time of death. An initial response to the objection then might be that it serves only as a reminder of the need for those issuing advance directives to update them continually while competent. But much more needs to be said because it is clear that many advance directives also suffer from their reliance on vague or ambiguous terms (like 'terminal condition', 'quality of life', 'extreme mental deterioration' and 'being without hope of significant recovery'[8]), whose use is best explained as a cloak for the issuer's lack of precise information.

Is it possible to obviate this sort of deficiency? At first glance it may seem that it is not. For one thing, medical progress itself ensures that advance directives will often be premised on an understanding of the treatment possibilities that becomes outmoded. Second, since the medical circumstances in which an individual devises an advance directive may be quite different from those that apply at the time when the directive has a part to play, there is further scope for slippage. If advance directives are based on

---

[8] As outlined by Stone (1994: 225–234). Cf. King (1991: ch. 4) and Francis (1993: 300ff).

assumptions that reflect what people anticipate their medical circumstances will be in the future, and those circumstances do not eventuate, the advice given in the directive will not be accurate. This is especially apt to occur when disease-specific directives are issued.[9] These two points indicate why there may be slippage between what is indicated in an advance directive and what would be appropriate at the time when such a directive has to be put into effect.

Fortunately, however, all is not lost. The most effective way to minimise slippage is (obviously enough) to reduce the time between the formulation of the directive and its use. Fewer matters will then be left hostage to fortune. Notwithstanding this point, it is unrealistic to think that all possibilities for slippage can be removed, but, more importantly, it would be unwise to try. The reason is that, to eliminate the slippage, it would be necessary to insist on an unrealistically demanding standard of decision making capacity because the threshold for competent decision making in such instances would have to be set far too high. To do this would deny many individuals of undoubted competence the opportunity to make decisions for themselves. In other contexts than end-of-life decision making individuals do not have to be able to anticipate every possible development that may have a bearing on the decisions they make before they can be considered competent. And, even when developments occur that call into question decisions taken previously, it would be absurd to conclude that those who took those decisions were, therefore, not competent. As long as agents satisfy the requirements for competent decision making *at the time when they make their decisions* their lack of a god's eye view of the future is not a reason to challenge the competency of their decisions. It was pointed out in the previous chapter that a competent decision is to be distinguished from a rationally justifiable decision. Of course, to the extent that making a competent decision under conditions of uncertainty necessitates investigating all reasonably likely possibilities, those investigations should be undertaken.[10] But that is consistent with everything I have said.

So, there will be slippage. Nonetheless, in addition to the point already made about keeping advance directives as current as possible, there are two other points of relevance to the containment of any slippage. First, advance directives should be easily alterable and easily revocable. Anyone who issues a directive should (while ever he remains competent) be able straightforwardly to change his mind about any aspect of the directive, as

[9] Peter A. Singer (1994).   [10] Cf. Savulescu (1994: 197f).

well as to annul it. Second, advance directives may take the form of a *proxy* decision making arrangement, not just the *instructive* form that I have hitherto been considering. Under a proxy decision making arrangement the person appointed as proxy is able to make decisions for, and on behalf of, the person who established the arrangement when he is no longer competent. Unless otherwise specified, the proxy is expected to satisfy the standard required of a substituted judgment, namely, to make the decision the patient would have made in the prevailing circumstances. To manage this, the proxy needs to be very familiar with the views and values of the patient. However, as has already been seen, the patient may not have considered all of the relevant possibilities, or had access to all relevant information, or be in circumstances like those he had imagined. Some take these to be reasons for favouring the practice of individuals issuing both an advance directive *and* appointing a proxy, with the proxy being empowered to promote the patient's choices. Such a strategy makes it harder for those who would rather not act on the preferences expressed in a directive to dismiss them (by, for example, claiming that they were formed under duress), since the issuer's authorisation of a proxy decision maker is a way of insisting on being heard. But, whatever the advantages of this dual strategy, when a proxy cannot be sure of what the patient would have decided in the particular circumstances prevailing at the time a decision has to be made (because such a circumstance was not discussed), the proxy must make a good faith effort to decide for, and on behalf of, the patient. At the very least this will mean deciding in accordance with the best interests standard should the uncertainty preclude satisfying the substituted judgment standard. Either way, the proxy needs to make decisions that will survive the critical scrutiny of the patient's medical team, his family, and, should it come to it, the courts.

As foreshadowed, I want to take up the issue of whether advance directives made by those diagnosed with psychiatric illnesses can have any standing, given that legislation dealing with the psychiatrically ill typically permits clinicians to administer treatment to those at risk of harming themselves, or others, without first needing to obtain consent. Should previous expressions of competent views by such mentally ill persons be honoured? In particular, should clinicians honour previous competent refusals of medical treatment *for conditions other than the mental illness*?[11]

---

[11] Cf. Savulescu and Dickenson (1998a) and their commentators Brock (1998); Burgess (1998); Dresser (1998); and Eastman (1998). Savulescu and Dickenson reply in (1998b).

I contend that there is no essential difference in the evidential value of an advance directive issued by a competent individual to cover a physical illness he later suffers (like a severe brain injury) that robs him of his competency, and one issued by a competent individual who later suffers a psychiatric illness (including something foreseeable like Alzheimer's), which robs him of his competency. Since the issuer of each of the directives is competent at the time of its being issued, and the evidential value is to be measured in relation to the competent person not the person each becomes, the evidential value has to be the same. Nonetheless, it might be thought that there are greater limits on our capacity imaginatively to envisage what it would be like to suffer a mental illness than to suffer a physical illness. Even if that is true, the focus of an advance directive concerning end-of-life care (as against one covering health care more generally) will be on treatment for the mentally ill sufferer's physical illness. In cases involving dementia, the form of mental illness most commonly singled out in this context, access to the legalised medical assistance with dying for which I have been arguing should only be available to terminally ill demented patients who previously issued an advance directive covering their end-of-life care. Let me return to the main point I want to make: to the extent that mental health legislation has in the past encouraged clinicians to reject competently devised advance directives issued by those who later succumb to mental illness, such clinicians have surely been in error. Physical illness and psychiatric illness may well contribute in differential ways to *loss of competence*, and it may be much harder for the well to imagine the impact on their future selves of the latter than the former, but that does not show the evidential worth of an advance directive about his end-of-life care made by a competent person who never succumbs to a psychiatric illness exceeds that of one who does.

The value of advance directives issued by individuals who are chronically psychiatrically unwell, but who have periods in which they are competent to make decisions about aspects of their health care, may seem less straightforward. However, for these individuals, who suffer conditions ranging from anorexia nervosa[12] to bipolar disorder,[13] it is equally unfair to regard their decisions as tainted by their mental illness. Consider again the British case of Mr C, which I mentioned in the preceding

---

[12] Anorexia nervosa is an eating disorder that involves a refusal to maintain body weight at or above a minimally normal weight for age and height because of an intense fear of gaining weight or becoming fat.

[13] Bipolar disorder (popularly known as 'manic depression') is an illness marked by extreme changes in mood, thought, energy, and behaviour.

chapter.[14] C, it will be recalled, was a sixty-eight year old paranoid schizophrenic who was resident in a secure hospital. His gangrenous foot, according to his doctors, required amputation. C applied for an injunction against
his doctors to prevent them amputating his foot in the event that they
deemed him to be incompetent. In successfully applying for the injunction,
C, in effect, made an advance directive. Even though he was suffering active
delusions about being tortured by various doctors at the time when he
formed his view, the judge ruled that it had not been shown that he was
incompetent, at that time, to refuse the operation, and hence that the
presumption in favour of his having decided competently must stand.[15]
He found that mentally ill individuals are entitled to seek a judicial determination of their capability to make decisions about their medical treatment, and, except where they are judged to be incapable, they retain the
right to consent to, or to refuse, medical treatment. He further found
that, once judged capable, the decisions they make, or the intentions they
form, constitute an advance directive for future medical treatment.[16]

C's mental illness did not bar him from making known in advance his
preference about a particular form of medical treatment, or from having
it endorsed by the court. As Savulescu and Dickenson put it: 'The judgment . . . states clearly that the preferences of people with mental illness
may be valid if the treatment being refused is not for the mental condition.'[17] Even if certain forms of mental illness diminish the autonomy
of sufferers (and conditions like paranoia must surely do so), it does not
follow that the choices of mentally ill persons can always be traced to
their illnesses, or that mentally ill persons will always be incompetent to
deliberate about treatment options for their other medical conditions.

---

[14] Re C (Adult: Refusal of Treatment) [1993] 1 Family Law Reports 940; 1993 Family Law 404.
[15] Mason, et al. (2002: 332f) criticise the judgment for being vague. In particular, they think that in
saying C had to understand the 'nature, purpose and effects' of the treatment in order to qualify
as competent it was left unclear just what he needed to do to establish that he had understood
these matters. Even if they are right about this, in a subsequent judgment concerning a woman
who refused an anaesthetic for a caesarean section because of her fear of needles, Re MB [1997] 8
Med LR 217, the English Court of Appeal set out basic principles to be considered in cases involving
refusal of consent which are very like those I have adumbrated. The Court acknowledged that the
judgment in Re C was tantamount to a judicial recognition of the validity of advance refusals of
treatment, a position reinforced in a subsequent British case, Re AK (Medical treatment: consent)
[2001] 1 FLR 129, [2001] 58 BMLR 151.
[16] The United Kingdom recently introduced the Mental Capacity Act which enables those who have the
mental capacity to appoint a Lasting Power of Attorney to take decisions on their behalf should they
lose that capacity, and authorises the appointment of an Independent Mental Capacity Advocate for
those who lack mental capacity and are without a family member or friend to advocate on their
behalf.
[17] Savulescu and Dickenson (1998a: 236).

The implications this has for end-of-life decision making by those suffering mental illnesses should be obvious.[18]

Clearly, it is one thing to suggest that some decisions of the mentally ill (namely, those made while competent) should be afforded the same protection as the competent decisions of others, and yet another for this to become widely adhered to in clinical practice.[19] It would be a mistake, however, to think that C's case has dramatic implications, for the stand he took is quite intelligible given that others with vascular conditions sometimes express similar preferences, albeit they may not be so insistent about dying with their legs intact. The more resistance there is to acknowledging, especially in practice, that the mentally ill can competently make certain decisions, the greater the importance that will attach to the view expressed by, for example, Dan Brock,[20] that a carefully specified public policy is needed to ensure that mentally ill patients are both given protection against abuse and given support to make the decisions they are capable of making. Because there is still significant resistance to the view I have been putting, the next section will be devoted to consideration of a problem about advance directives that is often thought to have special force in relation to the mentally ill, even though it is also raised in connection with those whose mental well-being is not in doubt.

III

I will suppose, in light of the preceding discussion, that, at least at first glance, an advance directive (whether in instructive or proxy form) is a valuable source of evidence for those making end-of-life decisions on behalf of the issuer. There are those who argue, nonetheless, that, on a second look, such directives prove to have no evidential worth. They argue that, when a competent individual who has drawn up an advance directive becomes incompetent, he is no longer *the same person* he was when he issued the directive. Even if the now incompetent individual remains a person (and, as will become clear, some dispute that this is true of certain incompetents), the issuer's views cannot be binding in relation to his end-of-life treatment. So, according to these critics, no directive made in advance can have morally

---

[18] The Dutch Supreme Court held in the *Chabot* case that it is possible for a psychiatric patient voluntarily to request assistance with dying. For details see Griffiths, *et al.* (1998: 329–340).

[19] Schermer (2002) provides a salutary reminder of how the ethical and legal requirements for informed consent are frequently ignored in the practice of medicine within hospitals.

[20] (1998: 253) and (1991).

binding authority in relation to the end-of-life care of a no longer competent individual.

As well as turning on a specific understanding of the potentially ambiguous term 'person', the objection is underpinned by a philosophical theory about personal identity, namely, the theory that some present person, X, is the same as some past person, Y, if and only if there is psychological continuity between X and Y and this continuity is the result of the right sort of causal process. As stated, this theory (known as the 'psychological continuity' theory) is concerned with both necessary and sufficient conditions for identity but, in what follows, I will be concerned only with the supposed necessary condition. Some (but by no means all) who accept the psychological continuity theory endorse, as well, what Derek Parfit[21] has termed 'the simple view' of what it is to be a person, namely, that a person is a self-conscious being, aware of his identity and his continued existence over time.

Though accounts of personal identity based on psychological continuity vary, an assumption they hold in common is 'that our persistence depends on some psychological relation: a relation having to do with mental contents or capacities'.[22] In other words, what is necessary for personal identity is continuity of mental life, the continuity of the relatively sophisticated mental life characteristic of persons.[23] (As I use the term, 'persons' are not to be *identified with* 'human beings' – the former refers to a psychological category, whereas the latter refers to a biological category.)

It will help to show how the criticism of advance directives I am considering can be met if I first note some of the challenges that have recently been made to the defensibility of psychological accounts of personal identity. I shall begin with Parfit's views because they have greatly influenced recent debates about personal identity.

In his early, more reductionist, writings on the identity of persons, Parfit contended that persons were just logical constructions of (and, so, were reducible to) more fundamental elements, in particular, to mental states and relations between those states. He argued that since psychological continuity was a matter of degree this needed to be recognised in our

---

[21] (1984: 202).

[22] Olson (1997: 16). 'Mental contents' will include memories, desires, beliefs, dispositions and so forth; 'mental capacities' will include the capacity for conscious experience, the capacity for self-awareness, the capacity to speak a language, the capacity to reason, and so on.

[23] On this Lockean view of what it is to be a person – so described because a view of this type was first proposed by Locke (1706: Book II, xxvii, ζ9) – the mental capacities of persons include self-awareness and thus they are able to think of themselves as continuants. It is this that distinguishes persons from beings of other kinds.

moral and social practices.[24] Hence, instead of thinking of judgments of personal identity as all-or-nothing judgments, he urged that they be thought of in terms of degree. An earlier self and a later self might, in consequence, be connected only tenuously (that is, to only a very low degree). That being so, the following argument becomes attractive: if advance directives depend on the preservation of personal identity, we should be very cautious about allowing those issued far in advance of the need to implement them to hold sway in end-of-life decision making.

There are at least two points to offer in response. The first is a reiteration of a point made previously concerning the importance of the currency of advance directives. Even if Parfit's early views about personal identity could be sustained, they would have little significance in circumstances where a directive was issued only shortly in advance of its implementation, for then any diminution in the degree of psychological continuity would be kept to a minimum and the directive would maintain its worth as evidence of the issuer's convictions. Second, and more importantly, if Parfit's early position on personal identity were sustainable it would have far-reaching consequences for our moral, legal and other social practices and institutions. However, the arguments he offered are not so compelling as to warrant the overthrow of those practices and institutions. Indeed, one of the more significant rejoinders that was made to his reductionist position was that, contrary to his contention that it is psychological connectedness, rather than personal identity, that is fundamental, neither our projects nor our social practices can be coherently conceptualised in the absence of a unified sense of self. For agency to be practically effective, an agent has to have a unified sense of self.[25] So, there is no need to concede to Parfit that psychological continuity is a matter of degree. But, if it were conceded, the degree of psychological continuity necessary to uphold judgments about the preservation of personal identity would simply become a matter for decision.[26] If, for example, something less than the highest degree of psychological continuity were agreed to be sufficient for the preservation of personal identity, Parfit's arguments could be taken on board without there being any need to make radical revisions to our moral, legal, and other social practices and institutions.

[24] (1984: ch. 15). Later (1986), he acknowledged that personal identity fails to provide a 'deep enough' fact on which to base practical concerns about punishment and compensation, or even attitudes to our own death.

[25] See, for example, Wolf (1986) – Parfit (1986) is a reply to Wolf; Adams (1989: 454ff); and Korsgaard (1989). For other important critical discussions see Johnston (1987); Buchanan and Brock (1989); and Unger (1990).

[26] Cf. Buchanan and Brock (1989: ch. 3) and Francis (1993: 303f).

Parfit subsequently came to think[27] that it is survival rather than identity that matters and shifted his focus away from psychological accounts of personal identity as such. Having discarded the idea that it is identity that is the basis of a rational egoistic concern about the future, he came to believe, for example, that it is not irrational for a person at the onset of dementia to be less egoistically concerned about his future than would be the case if he did not have a demented future in prospect. If he wished to devise an advance directive this would have obvious implications.

Jeff McMahan shares Parfit's conviction that identity does not matter. He urges that identity is not the basis of egoistic concern (for instance, about one's future should one become demented), and thinks that if a person at the onset of dementia is thinking *egoistically*, then, from his present point of view, he 'ought rationally to be less concerned about the particular goods and evils in [his] own future life'.[28] By contrast, if his concern is moral, rather than egoistic, he 'may rationally care as much about [his] future, demented self as [he] cares about [himself] now'.[29] Since McMahan believes the unity between the life of a person at the onset of dementia and at a more advanced stage of dementia is only very slight, he suggests that greater significance should be attached to the *segments* of the life that make up the whole, than to the life considered as a whole. Suppose a person suffers from severe dementia. If the segment of his life that coincides with the severe dementia holds no significance for him it would be right, on McMahan's account, to implement his advance directive requesting that in such circumstances his life not be prolonged. However, if the segment of life during the severe dementia still has significance for him, an advance directive specifying that no life-sustaining treatment be given should he suffer from severe dementia may rightly be ignored.[30]

A separate challenge to psychological accounts of personal identity has stemmed from the concern that if psychological continuity is *essential* to my identity as a person then, prior to my becoming conscious, I (the person I am now) did not exist. It follows that *I* was never a foetus, or, at least, that *I* was not a foetus while ever it lacked consciousness (and, so, was certainly not a foetus prior to the second part of the second trimester of foetal development). Just as obviously, if the simple view about what it is to be a person is

---

[27] The chief ground for his change of mind was the possibility of cases involving 'branching', viz., cases in which there are two (or more) individuals who enjoy psychological continuity with an earlier person. Since identity is a one-to-one phenomenon it cannot be preserved in such cases despite the psychological continuity. In contrast, survival may be a one-to-many phenomenon, so it is compatible with branching. Given that branching is a mere possibility, there will, in practice, be no distinction between identity and survival, but the possibility is enough, Parfit thinks, to show that it is not identity that matters.

[28] (2002: 496).　　[29] (2002: 496).　　[30] (2002: 501f).

correct, *I* (the person I am now) did not exist prior to becoming *self-conscious* (which, everyone agrees, post-dates my becoming conscious). On the latter view, therefore, *I* was never even a newly born infant.

The implication that I am not numerically identical, on the first view, with the foetus from which I developed, or, on the second, with the infant from whom I developed, strikes many as absurd. Eric Olson believes that the absurdity of these implications should lead to the rejection of psychological accounts of personal identity in favour of an account based on the fact that we are biological organisms.[31] He takes the term 'person' to be a *phase sortal*, and so to refer to a kind to which an individual belongs only for part of his history, namely, for a phase of it. On Olson's biological continuity account,[32] identity is a matter of the persistence of a biological organism, like a human animal. Thus, psychological continuity is neither necessary nor sufficient for personal identity; it is, in fact, irrelevant. If someone who has issued an advance directive subsequently falls into a persistent vegetative state,[33] there is, on Olson's account, no loss of identity. Hence, an advance directive would be binding as regards treatment of the organism in the persistent vegetative state. That the organism would no longer be a person would be irrelevant. Accordingly, if a biological continuity account of identity is correct, the objection I have been considering in this section will be without force.

Those who subscribe to a psychological account of personal identity *and* consider that the term 'person' denotes a *substance sortal* (the kind of thing something is essentially) are committed to person essentialism. For them, a person exists essentially and thus can only exist as such when the requirements for being a person are satisfied. Among those who appear committed to person essentialism are influential writers like Michael Tooley, Peter Singer and Helga Kuhse.[34] Quite apart from whether they are committed

---

[31] Olson's objection is, nevertheless, indecisive against the version of person essentialism formulated by Nozick, viz., one in which 'it is part of the essence of selves that they are selves *or have the capacity to be selves*' (1981: 78, my italics).

[32] (1997: chs. 1, 4 and 5).

[33] As mentioned in Chapter 1, I am relying on the taxonomy of vegetative and related states proposed by Jennett (2002).

[34] McMahan (2002: 350) argues that even though Singer, at least, *appears to be* committed in some of his writings to person essentialism, he cannot be a person essentialist because he believes we are organisms that can continue to exist after we have ceased to be persons. McMahan takes Singer's claim that the life of a person begins only with the advent of self-consciousness to be no more than an exaggerated way of emphasising that it is only after we become self-conscious that we have an interest in our future existence. The term 'person' is thus to be regarded as a phase sortal. Even if this is right – and I have to say I am unpersuaded – Singer's subjective understanding of what it is to have an interest in our future existence need not be accepted. I will show this in Chapter 11 below.

to person essentialism, and from the plausibility of their view that a person was never a foetus or an infant, their espousal of the simple view of what it is to be a person has implications for the use of advance directives when, according to the simple view, someone is no longer a person. Since Kuhse has given an explicit statement of her position on this matter I will target it. It will, however, be easier to see what is wrong with her position if I prepare the ground for my critique by considering some influential views about the reliability of advance directives for those afflicted with dementia.

Olson's rejection of psychological accounts of identity enables him to avoid the problem of whether there is identity between a competent issuer of an advance directive and a subsequent incompetent to whom it is supposed to apply. Those, like Parfit and McMahan, who contend that identity is not what matters do not have to face that problem, but they do have to confront the issue of whether the former person has a prudential interest in what happens to his survivor. But those who believe in the necessity of psychological continuity for identity, and those who believe both in the necessity of psychological continuity for identity *and* the simple view of what it is to be a person, must squarely face the problem I outlined earlier.

According to accounts of personal identity based on psychological continuity, whenever an individual suffers an irreversible loss of mental capacity, or no longer has any higher cognitive function, that is, no longer has a mental life, the individual suffers a loss of identity. Consider, for illustrative purposes, someone who lapses into a persistent vegetative state. A psychological continuity account of personal identity entails that an individual who lapses into a persistent vegetative state has irretrievably lost the capacity to think and the capacity to remember, and, so, is no longer a person (let alone the same person). The person the individual once was no longer exists. In other cases where there is loss of access to mental contents, as can occur with dementia, or Korsakoff's syndrome,[35] the question of whether the same person exists cannot be answered as straightforwardly.

When I stated the objection to the worth of advance directives based on loss of personal identity I put it in terms of one person (a competent person) not being able to bind a subsequent (supposedly different and incompetent) person. My claim is that the objection has its greatest force when the simple

---

[35] Korsakoff's syndrome is a form of mental illness commonly found in brain-damaged patients suffering from alcoholism, though it can be associated with brain damage resulting from cerebral tumours, head injuries and minor strokes. Sufferers are unable to remember recent events – in extreme cases sufferers cannot remember immediately preceding events – and are, in consequence, prone to invent implausible accounts of their recent activities.

view of what it is to be a person is conjoined with the psychological continuity theory of personal identity. For those who endorse a psychological basis for identity *and* the simple view of what it is to be a person, the loss by an individual of self-awareness must signal the end of personhood. Many, including me, who do not accept the simple view, but believe that psychological continuity is one of the evidential bases for identity, consider that, in cases like those mentioned at the end of the previous paragraph, the same person may still exist, notwithstanding the psychological discontinuities.

Suppose that an advance directive makes it clear that the issuer does not want treatment to be continued if it would be clearly medically futile. Presumably the issuer of such a directive has it in mind to rule out senseless prolongation of the biological life form that he may become in the event that he ceases to be a person, and, *as well*, to rule out the senseless prolongation of his life should he remain a person. This sits well with the contention by Allen Buchanan and Dan Brock[36] that a person who issues such a directive has an interest in (a stake in) avoiding needless prolongation of his life. They hold, accordingly, that to implement an advance directive is to acknowledge a competent person's rights over his body, including over its disposal. They acknowledge that there are conceivable circumstances in which such a right might justifiably be overridden (for example, to keep the issuer's body alive longer than he directed but long enough to allow his organs to be harvested for transplantation in accordance with a policy of routine harvesting that the issuer never opposed). Otherwise, however, the implementation of an advance directive ensures that the issuer is able to achieve his intended goals (for example, not to be kept alive in an undignified condition; or, to ensure that his loved ones are not put through emotional distress; or, to ensure that his loved ones do not have to pay for expensive, but futile, life-sustaining treatment), and is, therefore, the best way to respect his autonomous wishes. Indeed, even if the issuer has ceased to be a person this will still be the best way to respect his autonomous wishes.

Notwithstanding that Buchanan and Brock's position is attractive in just such instances, some may think it lacks the same attraction in cases involving severe forms of dementia like Alzheimer's disease, where a minimal mental capacity is retained but there is, for example, little or no memory of earlier life. Consider an advance directive issued by a person who directs that no life-prolonging medical treatment be provided should he

---

[36] (1989: 165ff).

succumb to a severe form of dementia *and* his intellectual life degenerate to a point where he lacks competence. Suppose that he does become demented and does suffer a loss of competency. Suppose, however, that, unlike many sufferers from dementia, he continues to enjoy his life and is calm and contented. Buchanan and Brock discuss cases of this type only indirectly but several other writers, including various critics of the use of advance directives, think them pivotal.[37]

Ronald Dworkin urges that, in such an instance, we should honour the values and projects that were critical for the person, not the person's present interest in having enjoyable experiences. Hence, he thinks the advance directive should be implemented because it best protects the integrity of the decisions the person arrived at via 'precedent autonomy' before the onset of dementia, where precedent autonomy is defined in terms of preferences formed at some earlier time (and expressed in an instrument like an advance directive).[38] Dworkin clearly thinks that because the earlier preference was arrived at when the agent was competent and capable of reflecting critically on the fit between it and his values and projects, whereas the latter was not, the earlier preference should prevail.

In contrast, Rebecca Dresser thinks there is insufficient continuity between the interests of the former, competent person and the demented one for the advance directive to have any force and so believes the directive should be disregarded whenever a minimally intrusive life-sustaining intervention would preserve the life of someone who is as contented and active as, say, Andrew Firlik's Margo. Agnieszka Jaworska, like Dresser, also thinks that the current interests of demented individuals should be given greater respect. However, her case for this view differs from that put forward by Dresser. She contends that when a demented individual holds to certain values, those values must be given greater weight than any mentioned in an advance directive, should they come into conflict. She claims that clinical

---

[37] The case resembles that of 'Margo' first reported by Firlik (1991). Firlik visited Margo on a daily basis while he was a medical student. She was fifty-five years old but already suffering the effects of Alzheimer's. Despite her incapacity to remember, she continued to be cheerful, even carefree, about her life. Hers and similar cases have been commented on by, among others, Rhoden (1990); Dworkin (1993: 221ff); Finnis (1994: 172, note 7), where he criticises Dworkin's handling of such cases; Post (1995); Dresser (1995); Kuhse (1999); Jaworska (1999); DeGrazia (1999) and (2005); Hughes (2001); McMahan (2002: 496–503); and Harvey (2006).

[38] For discussion of the idea of precedent autonomy see Davis (2002). Davis argues that precedent autonomy should be defined more strictly as comprising acts of self-determination under conditions such that the agent's earlier preference is a 'former preference' during at least part of the time for which it was intended to be satisfied. A preference is 'former' if we suppose the agent would not now reaffirm it under hypothetical circumstances just like the agent's actual circumstances except that the agent is assumed to have full mental capacity. See, too, Newton (1999).

evidence supports the idea that despite the impact on the ability of someone suffering Alzheimer's to engage in means–end reasoning, there is none on his ability to value. The ability of a sufferer to implement his values will be hampered, but it does not follow that he will lack the basic form of autonomy for which the ability to value is sufficient. An advance directive made out by a person who subsequently becomes demented, but remains a valuer, is thus akin to a 'Ulysses contract' (wherein a person, while competent, agrees to have others make decisions for him at some later stage in anticipation of not being competent at that later time, regardless of whether he is, in fact, incompetent when that time comes).[39] Jaworska disapproves of this type of arrangement – because it is unwarrantedly paternalistic – and so she rejects a role for advance directives in the lives of those who continue to be valuers.

There is no difficulty in reconciling Dworkin's position with the one defended by Buchanan and Brock, but Dresser's and Jaworska's positions are clearly at odds with Dworkin's (and, by extension, with that of Buchanan and Brock). Jaworska's understanding of autonomy is too thin to be compelling. Nonetheless, she makes an important point against Dworkin about those victims of dementia whose current wishes are both consistent and unwavering and, more pertinently, in conflict with the choices reflected in their advance directives. Those of us who believe that an advance directive provides *presumptive evidence* of a person's wishes can agree that in such circumstances the current wishes of a victim of dementia should not be automatically overridden by those he previously expressed. Since this point bears, as well, on what Dresser has had to say, I will expand on it further in a moment.

In addition to urging that precedent autonomy should be set aside in instances where the psychological continuity of a patient is open to challenge, Dresser thinks there is a compelling state interest in the preservation of life which overrides not only a person's precedent autonomy as expressed, for example, in an advance directive, but also certain choices a proxy may wish to make on the person's behalf. Two points need to be made in reply. First, Dresser makes much of the shortcomings she believes are

[39] Cf. Homer, *The Odyssey*, bk. 12, lines 44–60. On his return from the abode of the shades, Ulysses recounted to Circe wondrous visions of Hell. She rewarded him by helping speed his homeward voyage, instructing him particularly how to pass safely by the coast of the Sirens. These nymphs had the power, through their singing, of charming all who heard them, and, in particular, of impelling mariners to self-destruct by casting themselves into the sea. Circe directed Ulysses to stop the ears of his seamen with wax, so that they would not hear the strain. She also advised him to have himself bound to the mast and to enjoin his crew not to release him until they had passed the Sirens' island, whatever he might say or do once in its vicinity.

present in the process of making advance directives, but Dworkin's response to a case like Margo's is premised on Margo having produced an advance directive that gives a high priority to protection of her critical interests should she later suffer a loss of competence. To that extent a good deal of what Dresser says in criticism of Dworkin is beside the point, for there is nothing in Dworkin's characterisation of circumstances like Margo's *as such* that is at odds with Dresser's claim that precedent autonomy has less moral authority than contemporaneous autonomy (a point that can readily be granted by supporters of advance directives). What remains is simply a reiteration of the argument that there is 'insufficient continuity' between the interests of the competent person Margo once was, and those of the demented person she has become, for her advance directive to have force. Quite apart from the success or otherwise of that argument, Dworkin believes (and I agree with him) that the salient consideration is whether a person is to be *made to go on living* in circumstances that he previously competently indicated would be unacceptable to him. Nonetheless, some elaboration of this point is necessary to avoid misunderstanding. First, Dresser is right that someone who issues an advance directive that ignores the possibility of ending up in a condition like Margo's has produced an ill-considered document. (Though Dworkin might still wish to insist that Margo's advance directive should be implemented in full, it is only fair to point out that the cases on which he bases his support for precedent autonomy are generally more tractable than Margo's.) Second, and more importantly, when a victim of dementia is leading a contented existence and is still able to access things he considers of value,[40] to end his life would be inappropriate if the purpose he had in mind in devising his advance directive was to ensure that he did not suffer needlessly, or did not end up in an undignified state. In the absence of a detailed spelling out in the directive of the sort of future that would be unacceptable to him, including a clear specification that the type Margo experienced would be unacceptable, no grounds would exist to override his consistent and unwavering current wishes to go on enjoying an experience like Margo's.

The second element in Dresser's position, the supposed compelling state interest in sustaining life, has to be linked to her understanding of what

---

[40] As Jaworska (1999: 112, 124) points out, with dementia sufferers it is more likely that some of their previous values will drop out of consideration rather than that they will develop new values. Hence, the values that remain will typically be traceable to previous values. Doukas and McCullough (1991) advocated drawing up a 'values history' at the same time as an advance directive to help identify and explain the issuer's values. Such a history would, no doubt, prove useful as a supplementary source of information.

would constitute a 'minimally intrusive life sustaining intervention'. There might be some such interventions that would be compatible with the sentiments expressed in a carefully composed advance directive. For example, if the issuer had specifically excluded palliative care, but such care was medically indicated, it would be appropriate to override his specific direction if doing so would be compatible with the achievement of his main goal of not being subjected to a prolonged process of dying. But, equally, there would be other interventions that would not be compatible with his intent in issuing the directive. Dresser's remarks about when experiential interests should have priority over wishes expressed via precedent autonomy are vague and it is, therefore, difficult to know what she would say about the overriding of expressions of precedent autonomy in carefully composed advance directives in circumstances like those just mentioned. Hence, there is no good reason to agree with her view that, until we know competent patients are not victims of 'error and abuse', the state is entitled paternalistically to protect its interest in the preservation of life. If an advance directive drawn up by a competent person is subject to 'error and abuse', paternalistic intervention will be in order, but in the absence of evidence that advance directives are uniformly affected by error and abuse, there is no warrant to presume that they are. They should, therefore, continue to be scrutinised on a case-by-case basis.

Helga Kuhse's position differs from those just considered and is offered as a challenge to the adequacy of a position like that of Buchanan and Brock (and the one I am advocating). She holds that a severely demented patient has no awareness of being a continuing self and for that reason can no longer be regarded as a person (because a person must conceive of himself as existing over time). In other words, she endorses the simple view of what it is to be a person. Though I will not make anything of it here, even if the simple view states a sufficient condition for being a person, it is far from obvious that it states a necessary condition, as can be made clear by considering the difficulties amnesia cases (to say nothing of cases like Margo's) pose for Locke's original psychological continuity account (in which memory provides us with the best evidence for such continuity).

Kuhse believes that Buchanan and Brock fail to provide a satisfactory reason for implementing an advance directive on behalf of a once competent but now severely demented individual. Buchanan and Brock agree that a once competent individual may cease to be a person despite continuing to live,[41] but they hold that even if this happens, some of the interests of

---

[41] As, indeed, I do, for instances like those involving persistent vegetative states.

the once competent individual may survive the loss of personhood and warrant protection. Kuhse provides no serious criticism of this crucial claim; instead, she merely asks rhetorically whether interests can survive the profound changes the person has undergone.[42] I believe that she does this because she conflates interests and preferences.[43] Buchanan and Brock do not think preferences and interests are to be identified, as can be gleaned from the fact that they think some of a person's interests can survive even death.[44] Given this, there can be no doubt that some of the interests of a once competent individual can survive the loss of personhood consequent upon severe dementia. Hence, a severely demented patient can have an interest in an outcome even though he takes no interest in it.

I want now to raise a separate question about Kuhse's claim that a calm and contented victim of severe dementia is no longer a person.[45] As a consequence of her account of the nature of persons, Kuhse believes that an advance directive cannot be binding in relation to the medical treatment to be provided at life's end to a severely demented individual, no matter what that individual's outlook is while severely demented; hence, no direct wrong is done if a severely demented individual is allowed to die (as long as the dying is painless) because such an individual has no interest in being kept alive. According to Kuhse, although severely demented patients may appropriately be given palliative care, life-prolonging treatment should be withheld from them because they no longer have an interest in their own continued existence. In this respect they are, for her, like neonates and so, like them, can (in appropriate circumstances) be allowed to die. Those, like me, who do not subscribe to the 'simple view' of personhood (with its insistence that only those with a continuing sense of self can be persons), consider it highly implausible to infer that someone like Margo is merely a living organism rather than a person, and so believe that, other things being equal, she should be treated in the way she intended when she devised her advance directive.

Suppose, however, that I am wrong to think that Margo remains a person. It is worth remembering, in that case, that the objection to the

---

[42] Kuhse (1999: 357).

[43] Kuhse thinks that having an interest (in continuing to live) is simply having a desire or preference (to continue living). However, the latter, unlike the former, is a wholly subjective matter. (I will make a similar point in Chapter 11, in connection with a passage in a work she co-wrote with Peter Singer.) On Kuhse's account, a severely demented patient can no longer be regarded as a person (because a person must conceive of himself as existing over time), but may still have desires to enjoy pleasurable experiences, or to avoid painful ones.

[44] (1989: 162–164).

[45] McMahan (2002: 497) makes a similar claim about some victims of advanced dementia.

use of advance directives from which I began will still fail because it was based on the claim that one person should not be allowed to impose his wishes on a different person at some later date. If Margo is not a person, then, as Buchanan and Brock suggest, acting on the instructions she issued in an advance directive devised when she was a person cannot amount to inflicting her wishes on a different person.[46]

IV

In my introductory remarks I mentioned that it would be necessary to consider whether advance directives may at least sometimes prove unreliable because they fail to give clear instructions about how to treat a no longer competent person. Of course, in such circumstances, recourse could be had to a standard based on the person's best interests (as happens in emergency situations when it is not possible to obtain informed, voluntary consent), or to a substituted judgment standard. Suppose, for instance, that the issuer of an advance directive becomes seriously demented and loses competency, and, as death approaches, palliative care is medically indicated. Provided that giving care of this sort would not significantly undermine central elements in his directive (for instance, by bringing about a situation where life was prolonged beyond what he clearly would have wanted), it would be appropriate to override his specific instructions about palliative care to avoid a substantial harm. Nonetheless, any appeal to either of these standards can, at best, represent a default position whenever an advance directive exists, a default position to which recourse should be had only if the directive is so seriously flawed as to be of little or no operational use.

Suppose, however, that a no longer competent person's directive includes insufficient guidance on how he prefers to be cared for as a dying patient. What should happen then? If the matter goes before a court the evidentiary standards to be applied will in general be those employed in civil suits, namely, the matter will have to be decided by 'the preponderance of the evidence' or, more simply, by what is most probable.[47] But in some cases (e.g. *Cruzan v. Director, Missouri Department of Health*), a tougher standard – that of requiring 'clear and convincing evidence' – has been applied. If the decision to be made concerns whether to commence a form of treatment, then, when an institution like a hospital considers that that would be appropriate, the effect of making the evidentiary standard tougher will be

[46] (1989: 168).   [47] Cf. King (1991: 162).

to strengthen the institution's hand. Even though a competent patient may refuse treatment for a treatable condition, it would be unjustifiable for an institution to withhold treatment from a no longer competent patient with a treatable condition in the absence of an advance directive giving clear instructions to withhold just such treatment.

A related issue arises with those patients whose competence at the time of apparently intending to revoke a previous directive is doubtful. Consider a patient suffering a cognitive impairment who requests ventilator support during a respiratory crisis, despite having issued an advance directive explicitly prohibiting the use of a ventilator. Since a competent patient can override a prior directive, whether the patient is competent is of paramount significance. To be judged competent a patient need only meet the threshold requirement (a minimal requirement), but because his advance directive was produced in cooler circumstances it might be thought to represent a more thoughtful expression of his settled view. Be that as it may, a later competent judgment still takes precedence over an earlier one (for otherwise there could be no basis for the idea of revoking an earlier point of view).

Given these competing considerations, it is critical that medical caregivers be as clear as they can be as to whether a revocation order has been competently issued. If medical care-givers proceed simply on the basis that *apparent* revocations are good enough, they run the risk of undermining the evidentiary value of advance directives. Consider again the sort of case mentioned in the previous paragraph. Suppose that ventilator support is provided and the patient becomes dependent on the respirator. Strictly, it will then be improper to switch off the respirator until it is judged to be medically futile to continue. This is presumably a far cry from what the issuer of the advance directive had in mind in rejecting respirator support. As King points out,[48] allowing revocation in circumstances where a person's competence has become uncertain denigrates other evidence (for example, from the patient's family) that is consistent with the values espoused in the advance directive. Moreover, it has the potential, as well, to make all decisions taken after that revocation problematic. For example, in a case like the one just mentioned, it could reasonably be asked whether it would lead to the adoption of a life-at-all-costs approach to subsequent medical care. That would be consistent with honouring the revocation but not with the more reflective judgment contained in the advance directive. Thus, to go along with a revocation order when there

[48] King (1991: 167f).

is uncertainty about the revoker's competence is a risky thing to do, and, hence, not to be recommended.

However, there is an alternative perspective that has much to recommend it. To the extent that it is possible to have greater confidence in an advance directive that clearly expresses the well thought-out, settled preferences of a competent individual, than in any subsequent request he makes to set aside those preferences (because his competence is by then uncertain), the views expressed in the directive should prevail. Moreover, the more it is insisted that those who issue directives must meet high standards for imaginative and autonomous decision making, the higher the confidence that their autonomy is being respected when their directives are implemented.

It is not difficult to see why some health care-givers doubt that they should honour the autonomous choices of an individual made at an earlier time, once he is no longer competent to confirm those choices, especially if he seems capable of living for quite some time without suffering significantly in the process. The fact that there is no difficulty in making sense of such a standpoint is no reason to sympathise with them if they propose to give precedence to a revocation whose status is uncertain rather than to a directive that satisfied high standards for autonomous decision making. This is particularly so when family and friends can testify to the importance the individual placed on the choices reflected in the advance directive. The point has its greatest significance in relation to advance directives that authorise medical assistance with dying.

CHAPTER 10

Voluntary medically assisted death and slippery slope arguments

Proposals to legalise voluntary euthanasia (as distinct from physician-assisted suicide) have commonly been met with counter-arguments to the effect that legalisation would put society on a slippery slope that will inevitably result in non-voluntary euthanasia being widely practised. They were again prominent in the debates surrounding the Bill recently introduced by Lord Joffe into the UK House of Lords concerning *Assisted Dying for the Terminally Ill*. Given that they are so persistently relied on by opponents of voluntary medically assisted death it is important to make a thorough assessment of their worth. Here are three variants on the theme.

1. If voluntary euthanasia were to be legalised it would prove impossible to avoid the legalisation, or, at least, toleration, of non-voluntary euthanasia. But, even if the former can be justified, the latter clearly cannot. Hence, it is better that the first step (legalising voluntary euthanasia) not be taken so as to prevent a slide into non-voluntary euthanasia.[1]

2. If voluntary euthanasia were to be legalised it would signal society's approval of medically assisted death as a means of escape from life's difficulties and so would open the floodgates to requests from people not suffering from a terminal illness who want to be assisted to die while they are relatively healthy, because they dread having to face a problematic future existence (perhaps, for example, because of having been diagnosed with Alzheimer's disease), or because they are depressed, or disabled, or just feel excluded from their community. To avoid any such slide, society should resist the legalisation of voluntary medically assisted death and, instead, provide those who request it with the support necessary to enable them to make decisions free from the effects of socially coercive forces (like lacking access to adequate resources, or being victims of social discrimination).[2]

---

[1] Cf. Keown (1994a), (1994b) and (1995b).   [2] Verhey (1998: 357–360).

3. If voluntary euthanasia were to be legalised it would result in abuse or neglect of the vulnerable, and mistakes in the treatment of patients. So, whatever the merits of legalising voluntary euthanasia, it would inflict a terrible cost via the resultant abuse, neglect and mistaken killings. Since the costs to be borne by the abused, neglected and mistakenly killed would outweigh the benefits to be had from legalising voluntary euthanasia, it would be foolish to legalise it.[3]

As stated here, the last of these three arguments is not strictly a slippery slope argument but it can be turned into one by construing it – as it often, in fact, has been – as an argument to the effect that legalising voluntary euthanasia would lead both to vulnerable patients being subjected to non-voluntary euthanasia, and to patients being subjected to non-voluntary euthanasia because of mistakes in diagnosis.[4]

In order properly to assess these counter-arguments to proposals to legalise voluntary euthanasia, it is necessary both to understand the nature of slippery slope arguments and to assess the evidence offered in support of the claims outlined above. This is not to say that advocates of the legalisation of voluntary euthanasia have failed to carry out either of these tasks; in fact, they have energetically undertaken both tasks.[5] However, because they have typically considered slippery slope arguments only as they bear on the legalisation of voluntary euthanasia, they have not made use of recent assessments of the logic of various forms of slippery slope argument. Those whose opposition to the legalisation of voluntary euthanasia is based on one or other of the slippery slope arguments outlined above may not cease to be opposed after being informed of this recent work, but, at the very least, they will need to review the worth of those arguments. In the process of assessing these arguments, I will consider the evidence that their advocates have appealed to, particularly evidence relating to the impact that, initially, the legal toleration, and, subsequently, the legalisation, of voluntary medically assisted death has had in The Netherlands.

I

Recent work by applied logicians has emphasised the importance of distinguishing various quite different forms of slippery slope argument. Trudy Govier (1982) distinguished four sorts of slippery slope argument: a

---

[3] New York State Task Force on Life and the Law (1994).
[4] Foot (1977); New York State Task Force on Life and the Law (1994); and House of Lords (1994).
[5] Rachels (1986); Battin (1992); and Burgess (1993).

conceptual form which is associated with issues of vagueness, and, so, raises the question of whether it is possible non-arbitrarily to distinguish between instances within a series where there are no sharp cut-off points between the instances; a *precedential* form relating to the requirement for consistent treatment of similar cases; a *causal* form concerned with the avoidance of actions that will, or likely will, cause undesirable consequences; and a *mixed* form combining elements of the other three forms of argument. In the most comprehensive study of slippery slope arguments to date, Douglas Walton (1992) has offered a similar taxonomy using the following labels: the *sorites*[6] slippery slope argument; the *precedent* slippery slope argument; the *causal* slippery slope argument; and what he terms the *full* slippery slope argument (which is similar to Govier's mixed form).

This recent work has shone fresh light not only on the variety of these arguments but also on their validity. Consider, for instance, *sorites* arguments: they are problematic, but, whatever the problem, it is not that they are invalid. The reason is that a sorites argument can be presented as a series of steps, each of which relies on the valid rule of inference known as *modus ponens*.[7] What makes them problematic is their reliance on doubtful premises.

It has become clear that the evaluation of the different forms of slippery slope argument requires careful consideration of different types of evidence. The evidence relevant, for instance, to the proper drawing of conceptual lines will be different from what is relevant to the determination of logical consistency, and, in turn, to the justification of claims about the relationship between causes and consequences. All three sorts of evidence will be relevant to the assessment of those arguments that combine elements from the conceptual, precedential, and causal forms. I will now briefly consider each of the forms in turn.

A conceptual or *sorites* slippery slope argument is rhetorically most effective when it is difficult to distinguish between the contiguous members of a series because they vary only by apparently insignificant degrees, despite it being easy to distinguish widely separated members. The reason is that the more apparently insignificant the differences between contiguous members of the series, the harder it will be on

---

[6] The ancient Greeks used this term in connection with the problem of drawing conceptual lines. Thus, for instance, they applied it to puzzles like: 'when does a man suffering hair loss become bald?', and 'when does a collection of items become a heap?'.

[7] From the Latin *ponere* meaning 'to affirm'. In *modus ponens* the antecedent of a hypothetical premise is affirmed to yield the valid argument form 'if p, then q; p; therefore q'.

conceptual grounds to justify drawing a line at a particular cut-off point.[8] If a key term is vague, so that it would be arbitrary to attempt to draw a line marking the divide between appropriate and inappropriate uses, it will be difficult to counter a slippery slope argument based on the vagueness of the key term.[9]

To distinguish between voluntary euthanasia and non-voluntary euthanasia as concepts is not difficult – no more difficult, in fact, than distinguishing the concept of baldness from that of non-baldness. Each pair consists of conceptually distinct notions. However, some who advance the conceptual form of the slippery slope argument contend that the issue is whether there are instances of euthanasia whose classification is an open question (just as there are instances in which it is open to debate whether someone is bald). Those who advance the conceptual form of the slippery slope argument against the legalisation of voluntary euthanasia claim that it is only when a cut-off point is *arbitrarily* established that it is possible to classify instances as either voluntary euthanasia or non-voluntary euthanasia. This is allegedly because decisions involving assistance with dying (including whether an illness is terminal, and whether a request for assistance has been competently made) are essentially matters of degree. I do not accept this claim. First, there is no matter of degree as to whether someone is terminally ill – there is a fact of the matter even in cases where doubt exists about the imminence of death. (For legislative purposes, of course, it may be necessary to stipulate that a terminal illness will result in death within a particular time frame, such as 'within six months' or 'within twelve months', but that simply reflects the necessity for legal purposes of establishing a determinate time frame.) Second, as I argued above in Chapter 8, whether someone is competent is not a matter of degree but of whether he satisfies a threshold requirement. Nonetheless, in order to explore the following interesting suggestion made to me by Lynda Burns, I will temporarily waive my rejection of the claim that it is only by arbitrary means that voluntary and non-voluntary euthanasia may be distinguished.

Burns suggests that those who understand vagueness as akin to a no-man's land between two clearly marked territories are apt to think

---

[8] An argument like this has sometimes (e.g. Glover (1977)) been employed in discussions about whether late term abortions are morally distinct from infanticide.

[9] Williams (1985) and van der Burg (1991) have made helpful contributions to our understanding of how to counter such arguments. Among recent discussions critical of slippery slope arguments specifically in relation to voluntary medically assisted death are those by Frey in Dworkin, *et al.* (1998: ch. 3) and Griffiths (1998).

that any resort to an arbitrary cut-off point will involve *unacceptable stipu-lation* because it amounts to a demand to make the indefinite definite. But she believes this misunderstands the social function of language and so fails to acknowledge that, for various social purposes, we sometimes need to stipulate sticking points, which then determine how we should classify contentious instances. This happens very commonly in the formal setting of the law.[10] The legalisation of voluntary euthanasia would be a case in point. So, on her account, whether someone who requests assistance with dying does so voluntarily, or is coerced, or manipulated, into making such a request, may not be conclusively decidable by empirical means. Even though I am not convinced that cases that are undecidable will arise (since I am not persuaded that there is an exact parallel with disputes about baldness and non-baldness), I am prepared to grant, for the sake of argument, that there might be such cases. Were such cases to eventuate, Burns would surely be right that legislators ought to be empowered to stipulate sharp boundaries for voluntariness in order to regulate voluntary euthanasia (and, by implication, non-voluntary euthanasia). They might, for instance, stipulate a far more stringent set of requirements to be met to establish a person's competence to seek assistance with dying, than they would for the same person's competence to make his last will and testament.

Critics who believe it can be shown that to favour the legalisation of voluntary euthanasia is to be *logically committed* to permitting non-voluntary euthanasia, are unlikely to be persuaded. They contend that if death is supposed to be a 'benefit' to competent patients who request assis-tance with dying in the belief that their lives are no longer worth living, it must logically be supposed to be a benefit to non-competent patients who are suffering in similar ways. So, anyone who supports voluntary eutha-nasia logically ought to support non-voluntary euthanasia. This is the basis for the claim that there is a valid conceptual slippery slope argument against the legalisation of voluntary euthanasia. I will consider two distinct argu-ments that have been put forward in support of this claim and show that neither of them is sound.

John Finnis contends that there are moral norms that apply to far more than the practice of medicine which prohibit assisting a dying patient to die even if the patient believes he would be better off dead. According to

---

[10] In a discussion of some of the moral issues raised by developments in biotechnology, Buckle (1990) makes a similar suggestion about the way it is sometimes necessary to draw precise (or, as they are often called, 'bright') lines for legal purposes, even though our central concern may be with qualities that emerge gradually and continuously.

Finnis, if medically terminating a patient's life when his life had become a burden were not morally prohibited, it would become morally permissible to 'terminate people's lives outside the context of medical care, and/or on the ground that doing so would benefit *other people* at least by alleviating their proportionately greater burdens'.[11] This implies obviously enough that there is nothing morally special about the medical context on which I have been concentrating. But the heart of the matter for Finnis is that it implies the existence of a slippery slope, one that, according to him, adverts 'not so much to predictions and attempted evaluative assessments of future consequences and states of affairs, but rather to the implications of consistency in judgment'.[12] It is difficult, however, to make sense of his contention that, *on the basis of consistency in judgment*, permitting the termination of a competent dying person's life on request would license the termination of the lives of other people who would be better off dead, unless he thinks that advocacy of *voluntary* medically assisted death is based on a crude calculation of consequences. Even if, from a consequentialist perspective, the world would be a better (less bad) place in the event that assistance with dying were afforded to those who did not ask for it, this is beside the point as far as advocates of voluntary medically assisted death are concerned. Finnis' argument echoes an idea first floated in Germany last century in a publication about the destruction of 'worthless life'.[13] However, it has no more credibility in the present context than it did then because there is no reason at all to think that support for voluntary medically assisted death is based on ridding the world of burdensome lives in order to make it a less bad place. I pointed out in Chapter 1 that voluntary euthanasia is distinct from 'mercy killing', but, if Finnis were right, there would be no distinction. What Finnis terms 'the central case of euthanasia' is easily distinguished conceptually from mercy killing because, as I previously pointed out, the main moral foundation for voluntary euthanasia is respect for the autonomy of competent, dying patients. Mercy killing requires no such moral foundation. To accord respect to the choices of those who competently conclude that their lives are no longer valuable to them is not a licence for the termination of the lives of others society considers would be better off dead (that is, for whom being killed would be a mercy), *despite their never having competently arrived at any such conclusion.*

According to John Keown's version of the argument, voluntary euthanasia is not justified in virtue of a dying patient's request but in

---

[11] (1995: 24f).   [12] (1995: 24f).   [13] Binding and Hoche (1920).

consequence of 'the doctor's judgment that the request is justified because the patient no longer has a life "worth" living'.[14] In other words, according to Keown, medical professionals do not simply agree to requests from their patients, but agree to them only when they judge that fulfilling the request would be in a patient's best interests. This reasoning may seem convincing at first sight but I think it exemplifies a common error: it is the error of assuming that a patient's best interests can be judged entirely by reference to the patient's *medical* interests (since it is only in relation to these latter that the medical professional could possibly lay claim to having a better vantage point from which to determine a patient's interests than the patient). Since patients have other interests, including interests in shaping and directing their own lives (that is, in acting autonomously), it is an error in reasoning to conclude that medical professionals should treat the competent and the non-competent as though they are alike when assessing what will be in their best interests. Hence, Keown's slippery slope argument is fallacious.

Is there a lesson to be learned from the failure of the two preceding arguments to show that the legalisation of voluntary euthanasia would lead (by way of a conceptual slippery slope) to non-voluntary euthanasia? I believe the lesson to be learned is that for purposes of drafting relevant legislation it is vital to set out precise requirements that a competent person who requests medically assisted death must satisfy. That is the best way to reinforce the clear conceptual line between voluntary medically assisted death and non-voluntary euthanasia. Furthermore, it is the very path that has been followed in the Northern Territory, Oregon, The Netherlands and Belgium.

II

I turn now to slippery slope arguments based on precedent. When a precedent is established it binds those who have to deal with all similar, subsequent instances. Accordingly, precedential slippery slope arguments have the following form: if a certain thing is permitted (or, done) it will establish a precedent that will justify permitting (or, doing) the same thing in similar, subsequent circumstances; permitting (or, doing) the same thing in these subsequent instances will, in turn, become a precedent for other similar circumstances; and, so on, via a chain of precedents, to permitting (or, doing) something that is unacceptable; therefore, the first instance should not be permitted. To prevent having to permit the unacceptable outcome at the

[14] (1995b: 262).

end of the series, the first step must be disallowed lest it establish a precedent. Whatever plausibility these arguments have depends on whether the cases used in the case-by-case reasoning are strictly analogous, for only then will there be consistency of reasoning.[15]

This form of argument appears irrelevant to the claim that the legalisation of voluntary euthanasia would initiate a slippery slope leading inevitably to the countenancing of non-voluntary euthanasia. There is no significant analogical connection between voluntary euthanasia and non-voluntary euthanasia because there are key differences between the two forms of euthanasia. In consequence, logical consistency does not require that cases of voluntary euthanasia be treated similarly to cases of non-voluntary euthanasia. Indeed, the very fact that someone who competently requests voluntary euthanasia asks to be helped to die, while someone who is administered non-voluntary euthanasia does not, is enough to show that approving the former yields no precedent for approving the latter.[16] Hence, those in favour of legalising voluntary euthanasia need have no fear of precedential slippery slope reasoning.

III

It is causal forms of slippery slope argument that are most often employed by opponents of the legalisation of voluntary euthanasia. Sometimes the causal process is supposed to be a psychological one, sometimes the nature of the causal process is not spelled out but it is claimed that those who take a specified first step will inexorably be driven (by an unstated causal process) to an unacceptable outcome. Since psychological factors are the most prominent of the driving forces appealed to in causal slippery slope arguments I shall concentrate on them. There are several ways in which a psychologically based account of the causal process from first step to unacceptable outcome may be formulated.[17] Thus, for instance, it may be said that it will become easier, psychologically, to take subsequent steps once the first step (of tolerating or legalising voluntary medically assisted death) is taken. Alternatively, it may be said that once any exception, other than for self-defence, is allowed to the prohibition on killing, it will be easier to justify yet further exceptions. So, if an exception is

[15] Cf. Walton (1992: 153ff).
[16] Rachels (1986: 172f). I interpret his 'logical' version of the slippery slope as the precedential form of slippery slope argument.
[17] Those, like Pellegrino (2001a), who advance arguments of these forms do not always distinguish between them.

allowed for competent, dying persons who request medical assistance with dying, it will become easier to assist someone to die who has not requested such assistance (than would have been the case had the first exception never been allowed). A third alternative is exemplified in the following comment by Philippa Foot in which she speaks of changes being occasioned in our expectations:

> The possibility of active voluntary euthanasia might change the social scene in ways that would be very bad. As things are, people do, by and large, expect to be looked after if they are old or ill. This is one of the good things that we have, but we might lose it, and be much worse off without it. It might come to be expected that someone likely to need a lot of looking after should call for the doctor and demand his own death.[18]

Clearly, Foot thinks that as a result of changes in expectations that would follow the legalisation of active voluntary euthanasia, some who wish to live would feel they were expected to request medical assistance to die. In other words, there would be an unacceptable slide into a situation where people would feel psychologically coerced into asking to be helped to die.

As with all causal forms of slippery slope argument, it is crucial to assess the empirical likelihood of the predicted future outcomes. Those versions of the argument that proclaim that a particular (unacceptable) outcome will *inevitably* occur can have little credibility simply because the most that it is possible to justify empirically is the likelihood or probability of an outcome's occurring.[19] What, though, are we to make of the predictions embodied in the three variants of the psychological version of the slippery slope argument?

According to the first variant, it is predicted that it will become psychologically easier to agree to non-voluntary euthanasia once voluntary euthanasia is legalised. The proper response to this prediction about what would be likely to happen if voluntary euthanasia were to be legalised is to acknowledge that no one can be certain that instances of non-voluntary euthanasia would not be carried out as a result of society becoming accustomed psychologically to the idea of medical killing. However, there are two important riders to this response. First, based on what we know from jurisdictions where voluntary euthanasia is legally permissible, there is reason to

---

[18] (1977: 112). Cf., too, Battin (1994b); Hardwig (1997); and various essays in Humber and Almeder (2000).

[19] It is this that accounts for the vigour with which causal forms of slippery slope argument have been criticised by, for example, Schauer (1985) and by Frey in Dworkin, *et al.* (1998: 45ff).

believe that those doctors who administer it legally will be motivated by their respect for the autonomy of their dying patients.[20] It is no more than a mere possibility that doctors with this motivation will find it easier psychologically to kill someone they know has not made a request to be helped to die. No doubt some diehards will think that the slippery slope would extend as far as *involuntary* euthanasia, but it is altogether implausible to think that, once it became legal to offer medical assistance with dying, medical professionals who are motivated to help those who expressly request it would proceed to kill others known to have expressed their opposition to being assisted to die.[21] Second, there is good reason to believe that non-voluntary euthanasia is already a frequent occurrence. It takes place whenever, for instance, those who are not competent to ask for life-sustaining treatment to be withheld, or withdrawn, nevertheless have it withheld, or withdrawn, by medical personnel. As I have already emphasised, those who oppose the legalisation of voluntary medically assisted death do not consider that the withholding, or withdrawal, of life-sustaining treatment is euthanasia, let alone that it amounts to non-voluntary euthanasia.[22] But that is what it sometimes is. Since non-voluntary euthanasia in this guise is quite prevalent even in those jurisdictions where voluntary euthanasia is neither legally tolerated nor legally permissible,[23] it is utterly implausible to claim that there is a psychological basis for an inevitable slippery slope running from the legalisation of voluntary euthanasia to non-voluntary euthanasia.

In addition to the two points just made, the experience over recent decades in The Netherlands has provided us with relevant empirical evidence about the first of the psychological bases alleged to ground a slippery slope argument. I will introduce this evidence in the next and final section of the chapter but I will first complete my survey of forms of slippery slope argument.

---

[20] An overwhelming majority of Dutch physicians, for example, believe that competent patients have the right to make their own end-of-life decisions. See Onwuteaka-Philipsen, *et al.* (2003).

[21] Jack Kevorkian, for example, only ever assisted those who requested his help. As for doctors who have murdered patients, there is no need to look beyond Harold Shipman, the infamous Manchester doctor who was convicted of murdering fifteen of his patients, and suspected of murdering more than two hundred others, between 1971 and 1998. The official inquiry into his activities could find no rational motive for his conduct, but speculated that he had been motivated variously by a desire to experiment with certain drugs, by greed, and by sheer conceit. While it is true that some of his victims were near death, nothing in the record indicates that he was concerned to end their suffering. Indeed, he consistently denied that he had killed anyone.

[22] Several Catholic critics of legalising voluntary euthanasia, like Gormally (1993) and (1995); Finnis (1995); Fisher (1995: 332f); and Keown (2002: 14–15), agree that euthanasia can occur by deliberate omission but go on to deny that withholding of burdensome or futile treatment amounts to a deliberate omission to treat.

[23] Kuhse, *et al.* (1997).

According to the second of the psychological variants, once an exception is made to the moral prohibition on killing the innocent, human life will suffer a devaluation that will make it psychologically easier for doctors to kill those who lack the competence to ask for medical assistance with dying. The points made in response to the previous argument apply here, too, but additional ones are required for completeness.

Given that it would be medical personnel who administer voluntary medically assisted death,[24] it is necessary to ask on what basis it is being predicted that there will be a devaluation of human life and a consequent breakdown in inhibitions about killing. The available evidence (from studies of clandestine administration of voluntary euthanasia in places where it remains illegal[25] as well as from studies carried out in The Netherlands[26]), strongly indicates that medical personnel participate in voluntary euthanasia and physician assisted suicide with trepidation and a sense of regret as professionals about having run out of options to offer their patients. Such personnel are not at all likely to become blasé about killing or, worse still, to become inured to it.

The third variant of a psychological slippery slope, the one suggested by Philippa Foot, concerned what medical personnel might come to be prepared to do as expectations of what is morally permissible change, particularly in Western societies. However, as James Rachels pointed out in reply to Foot, any change in relevant expectations would take place within a context in which the law would permit doctors 'to administer voluntary euthanasia only to terminal patients in special circumstances'.[27] Thus, there is little or no reason to think that those not wishing to be assisted to die would come to think they were expected to seek such assistance, and even less to think that they would be given it. Again, the evidence from The Netherlands is instructive, in that doctors there refuse many more requests for medically assisted death than they facilitate.[28]

IV

Since none of the three forms of slippery slope argument that I have considered – the *sorites*, precedential and causal forms – has provided any

[24] It has sometimes been suggested that the task could be assigned to trained technicians rather than physicians. There are many reasons for rejecting this suggestion, but the most important of them is that medically assisted death should be seen as a legitimate form of end-of-life medical care, a point already made several times.
[25] Magnusson (2002).   [26] Griffiths, *et al.* (1998).   [27] (1986: 175) and Battin (2005b).
[28] van der Maas, *et al.* (1996) and Onwuteaka-Philipsen, *et al.* (2003).

basis for the claimed descent down a slippery slope from the legalisation of voluntary euthanasia to the administration of non-voluntary euthanasia, the fourth form – the full, or, mixed form – will not do so either. That is because it simply incorporates elements from the other forms.

Accordingly, I will put to one side issues having to do with the *form* of slippery slope argument used to criticise proposals to legalise voluntary euthanasia, and focus on the evidence relating to the impact that the legal toleration of voluntary medically assisted death has had in The Netherlands in the last couple of decades. (As was noted in the opening chapter, legislation in favour of voluntary medically assisted death was not enacted in The Netherlands until 2001, but the practice had been legally tolerated within established guidelines for several decades. The evidence I will consider relates chiefly to the period of legal toleration. I concentrate on The Netherlands rather than, for example, on Oregon because there is more evidence relating to the former than to the latter.) Critics of the legal toleration of voluntary medically assisted death in The Netherlands have claimed that the evidence shows that its toleration has led to the frequent practice of non-voluntary euthanasia, and to a culture of death. They contend, in consequence, that it would be unsafe to legalise it in other jurisdictions (and, of course, that the Dutch should repeal their legislation). Any of the following three claims may be made: first, that non-voluntary euthanasia is morally impermissible and so we should not do anything that will lead to it; second, that the legalisation of voluntary euthanasia and physician-assisted suicide will lead to some individuals who are not terminally ill being helped to die; and, third, that the legalisation of voluntary euthanasia and physician-assisted suicide will inevitably result in abuses (and thus that euthanasia will sometimes be administered to those not competent to seek it, who will, therefore, become victims of the legal changes).

Three major investigations have been carried out in The Netherlands to ascertain the impact of the legal toleration of voluntary medically assisted death: the first was in 1990–1991, and produced the so-called 'Remmelink Report'[29]; the second was carried out by a team led by Paul J. van der Maas, and covered the period 1990–1995. There was a third follow-up study in 2001.[30] These investigations are of great importance not only because they provide us with the best evidence we as yet have of the impact of

---

[29] The findings of the Remmelink Committee are most easily accessed via the following articles: van der Maas *et al.* (1991) and van der Wal, *et al.* (1992a) and (1992b). Keown (2002: Part III) critiques the first two surveys; Fenigsen (2004) critiques the third survey.

[30] See van der Maas, *et al.* (1996); van der Wal, *et al.* (1996); and Onwuteaka-Philipsen, *et al.* (2003).

legally tolerating voluntary medically assisted death (since the Northern Territory of Australia's legislation operated for less than a year and the experience in the State of Oregon in the United States with the legal toleration of physician assisted suicide is still relatively new[31]), but also because there has been a concerted effort in The Netherlands to put safeguards in place to minimise, if not prevent, abuse.[32]

What the long-term studies have shown is that in nearly sixty per cent of the instances where doctors have assisted terminally ill persons to die, an explicit request for medically assisted death was made near to the time of death. Of the remaining instances, namely, those where there was no explicit request for assistance with dying near the time of death, about half had previously discussed their wish for euthanasia with their doctor or doctors. More importantly, for those from this latter group who were no longer competent, the decision to end life was taken in the overwhelming majority of instances only after consultation between medical staff and family members to ascertain what the patients would have wanted had they remained competent. In almost all of these latter instances – around ninety-five per cent of them – the decision was agreed between medical personnel and the patient's loved ones. In the remaining instances (those where there was no such consultation), the decision shortened life by no more than a day or two except in a very small number of instances involving intense suffering. The investigators remarked that 'most of the cases in which life was ended without the patient's explicit request were more similar to cases involving the use of large doses of opioids than to cases of euthanasia'.[33] This is an important remark in the present context because, as was seen in Chapter 6, opponents of the legalisation of medically assisted death, without exception, have no moral qualms about giving large doses of opioids to patients so long as they are not given with the intention of killing them, even when it is foreseen that giving the drugs will cause death. Thus, the upshot of the extensive investigations in The Netherlands into the alleged slippery slope from toleration, and subsequently legalisation, of voluntary medically assisted death to the practice of non-voluntary euthanasia is that such non-voluntary euthanasia as occurs in The Netherlands is indistinguishable from what in other

---

[31] Some early findings are, however, available. See Ganzini, et al. (2000); Wineberg (2000); and Ganzini (2004).

[32] For more on the safeguards designed to protect the quality of the choices made by patients, particularly against institutional and professional manipulation of those choices, see Battin (1992: 139ff). For a dissenting view see Hendin (1998).

[33] Cf. van der Maas, et al. (1996: 1702). The Dutch use the term 'euthanasia' to signify 'voluntary euthanasia'.

jurisdictions is accepted as normal medical practice regarding the termination of the lives of no longer competent, dying patients.[34] Furthermore, the incidence of termination of life without an explicit request actually declined in The Netherlands during the period 1990–1995 and thereafter remained virtually unchanged in the period to 2001. There has, therefore, been no slide from voluntary medically assisted death to nonvoluntary euthanasia in the period surveyed, nor (to anticipate a possible line of reply) is there any reliable evidence to suggest that there was a sudden increase in non-voluntary euthanasia prior to the period surveyed but subsequent to the commencement of the legal toleration of voluntary medically assisted death. Finally, I wish to draw attention to several significant features of the practical operation of Dutch public policy on medically assisted death. These features are incapable of showing that Dutch public policy on medically assisted death is ethically justified, but their political significance is clear. First, the people of The Netherlands have regularly given overwhelming support to the continuation of the practice of voluntary medically assisted death. If the policy were as dangerous as its opponents claim it surely would have come under greater challenge in a modern democratic setting than it has. Second, as previously noted, the majority of requests for help with dying are not acceded to, which has built confidence that doctors do not behave recklessly in these matters. Third, that confidence has been further increased by there having been only a few prosecutions of doctors for failing to follow the guidelines for the administration of medically assisted death, and fewer still that have given rise to controversy. I will detail the most controversial of these latter cases below.

The second of the arguments set out at the beginning of the chapter concerned the alleged existence of a slippery slope from the legalisation of voluntary euthanasia to the offering of medically assisted death to people who are not terminally ill, and who, therefore, must fail to satisfy the criteria for legalised voluntary medical assisted death. A case from The Netherlands involving a psychiatrist, Dr Boudewijn Chabot,[35] is often

---

[34] Cf. Dworkin, *et al.* (1997) as regards the situation in the US, and Kuhse, *et al.* (1997) for the situation in Australia. The latter study was modelled on the one carried out by van der Maas and his associates, so the similarity of result is revealing. If anything, the practice was more common in Australia than in The Netherlands despite the fact that voluntary medically assisted death is not legally tolerated in Australia (setting to one side the brief period when it was legal in the Northern Territory).

[35] Though *Chabot* has attracted most of the attention, there have been at least two other cases concerning the legitimacy of offering assistance with dying to patients whose suffering was not physical that have gone to trial in The Netherlands – see Griffiths, *et al.* (1998: 80, note 123). *Chabot* is discussed in connection with several other cases of patients with psychiatric illnesses who sought medical

cited to illustrate the point, though similar things have been said in relation to cases involving medically assisted death administered to disabled individuals,[36] including infants with spina bifida.[37]

In 1991 Chabot supplied a woman, Mrs B, who asked to be helped to die, with lethal drugs that she administered to herself in the presence of Chabot, a general practitioner, and one of her friends. She died shortly thereafter. Chabot reported her death to the coroner as an assisted suicide. Mrs B had suffered a series of traumatic experiences, including the loss of her first son to suicide and of her second to cancer, which left her in a severely depressed state. When the psychiatric treatment she sought had no effect on her depression she made one serious attempt to take her own life. After this failed attempt she suffered a loss of desire to live and declined all further therapy. Chabot considered that her suffering was enduring and intense, and her request for assisted suicide well-considered. He consulted seven other expert psychiatrists, who all largely agreed with his assessment of Mrs B and his proposed course of action, though none of them examined her.

When the matter reached the Supreme Court in 1994 (after earlier trials in the District Court in Assen and the Court of Appeals in Leeuwarden), Chabot argued that he had acted out of *necessity*. He contended that he had faced a conflict between his duty to relieve Mrs B's unbearable suffering by the only effective means available to him, and his duty to preserve her life. He chose to fulfil the former because he considered it the more stringent duty. The Supreme Court rejected the contention of the prosecution that a defence of necessity in connection with assisted suicide can only be relied upon if a patient is both suffering and in the terminal phase of a physical illness. However, even though it ruled that necessity could be claimed in instances where there was non-physical illness, it found that there was insufficient evidence to justify necessity in Mrs B's case because there was no corroborating evidence from a medical expert who had personally examined Mrs B. In particular, it found that there was no corroborating evidence in relation to: the seriousness of her suffering; whether any options other than assisted suicide were canvassed; and, whether her

---

assistance with dying in Burgess and Hawton (1998). For discussion of cases involving disability see, for example, Kirschner (1997) and Silvers (1998).

[36] See, for example, *The Age Newspaper* (Melbourne) (2005: 11).

[37] Spina bifida is a neural tube defect. It occurs when the spinal column fails to close completely in the first month of pregnancy. The effects of spina bifida vary quite markedly, but severely affected infants have hydrocephalus and suffer paralysis, bladder and bowel dysfunction, and learning disabilities.

request for medically assisted death was voluntary and well-considered. Nonetheless, despite finding that Chabot was guilty of the offence of assisting a suicide (under Article 294 of the Dutch Penal Code), in virtue of failing to fulfil the requirements for corroboration, the Supreme Court imposed no penalty. The statutory penalty for the offence is imprisonment for up to three years. This suggests that the Court did not consider Chabot had done anything seriously wrong and was only at fault in failing to get confirmation of the matters he relied on for his defence of necessity.

That there has been a case in The Netherlands like the one involving Chabot certainly does not show that legal toleration, or legalisation, of voluntary medically assisted death will lead inevitably to significant numbers of people who are not terminally ill being assisted to die. The Dutch courts have made it clear that a person whose suffering is psychological can competently choose to die. They have also made it clear that when a person's psychological suffering is intolerable, it is permissible for him to request medical assistance with dying if he is incapable of ending his own life unaided. The empirical evidence is equally clear that the floodgates have not opened in consequence of these findings.

The third and final of the arguments set out at the start of the chapter expressed concern that the legalisation of voluntary euthanasia would result in abuses. Among the abuses that some opponents of legalisation have suggested as likely to occur are that the demented, the comatose, and those dependent on the public purse who would be expensive to keep alive would become victims of non-voluntary euthanasia.

The evidence from The Netherlands is, again, revealing. The numbers requesting medically assisted death increased between 1990 and 1995 and were stable between then and 2001. Researchers think the initial increase is best explained as a function of an ageing population, and that continuing efforts to ensure procedural transparency have contributed to the stabilisation that has occurred since 1995. It is also relevant that there has been no change over the course of the studies in the sorts of conditions for which patients have sought medically assisted death. The conditions most represented throughout the whole of the period in question were cancers, diseases of the respiratory system, and diseases of the circulatory system. There is no evidence, in other words, that the demented, the comatose, or the indigent have been treated worse as a result of the legal toleration of voluntary euthanasia. The efforts made to establish protocols for dealing with these matters as a direct result of the legal toleration and subsequent legalisation of medically assisted death would appear to have borne fruit.

Consider another sort of abuse that opponents have claimed would follow the legalisation of voluntary medically assisted death, which I referred to in the second argument outlined at the start of the chapter, namely, that the sick and dying would be pressured by others, or talk themselves, into asking for assistance to die, despite not really wanting it. Once again, no evidence has been found to suggest that this has occurred in The Netherlands. And, as was pointed out above, the fact that more requests for help are denied than are agreed to, yields a powerful reason to reject the suggestion that abuse of this sort must inevitably follow the legalisation of voluntary medically assisted death. Moreover, since the key conviction of supporters of the legalisation of voluntary medically assisted death is that decisions made by competent patients should be respected, it is these very supporters who are among those most concerned to ensure that it is only decisions untainted by the above-mentioned sorts of pressures that trigger the requested assistance. Finally, as noted above, the Dutch have introduced a range of safeguards to protect patients, and have striven to develop an acceptable body of legal rules covering medical behaviour that shortens life. These rules cover cases like those of newborn babies (on which I will have more to say in the next chapter), comatose patients, patients suffering from senile dementia, and patients who are in the last throes of life but are incapable of expressing their wishes.[38]

Some remarks of John Griffiths state an appropriate conclusion to my investigation of slippery slope arguments:

The slippery-slope argument, applied to the Dutch experience . . . seems in a paradoxical way to get the direction of legal development backwards. It assumes a tendency toward relaxing legal control over medical behaviour, whereas what is really going on is a quite massive *increase* of control.[39] [italics in original]

V

In sum, none of the forms of slippery slope argument that I have considered gives reason to think that support for voluntary medically assisted death must inevitably lead to support for non-voluntary euthanasia. There is no conceptual basis, no basis in precedent, and no causal psychological basis

[38] Cf. Griffiths, *et al.* (1998: ch. 6).   [39] (1998: 103).

for endorsing such an inference. Contrary to what is often claimed, the evidence from the legal toleration of voluntary medically assisted death in The Netherlands – the most significant evidence available as to whether *in practice* there is a slippery slope from voluntary medically assisted death to non-voluntary euthanasia, or to any other supposedly catastrophic outcome – shows no slide into abuse.

CHAPTER 11

Non-voluntary euthanasia

In previous chapters I have focused chiefly on decisions by competent individuals about the timing and manner of their own death (either, indirectly, by way of an advance directive, or, directly, when death is imminent). In this chapter I will be considering decisions about death and dying made on behalf of those who are not competent (either because they are no longer competent and have never issued an advance directive that sets out their considered wishes, or because they have never been, nor, as best we can judge, ever will be, competent). There is a risk inherent in proceeding straight from a discussion of voluntary medically assisted death to the topic of non-voluntary euthanasia, namely the risk of giving credence to the criticism that the legalisation of voluntary euthanasia and physician-assisted suicide would inevitably lead to non-voluntary euthanasia being practised. I have argued that that is not inevitable, so nothing hinges on the order in which the chapters appear. Moreover, I have contended that opponents of the legalisation of voluntary medically assisted death already embrace medical practices that, properly understood, amount to non-voluntary euthanasia (for instance, the withholding and withdrawal of life-prolonging treatment from patients whom it is judged futile to continue to treat, but who have given no indication as to whether they wish to be kept alive for as long as medically possible). If those practices are considered defensible (and I am not going to raise a challenge to them), the criticism that the legalisation of voluntary medically assisted death would inevitably lead down a slippery slope to (the allegedly morally outrageous practice of) non-voluntary euthanasia must lack credibility.[1]

---

[1] Some argue that the only way to ensure equal rights for all is for voluntary medically assisted death to remain illegal for everybody, lest any right to assistance with dying has to be made available to the incompetent as well as the competent. They claim that legalising a right to these forms of medically assisted death would lead to discrimination against those disabled individuals whose medical situations resemble those of competent individuals seeking to be helped to die, but who themselves are not competent to request such assistance (and cite efforts to ensure that there is no such discrimination like the

I shall begin my consideration of the justifiability of the practice of non-voluntary euthanasia by looking at the situation of those who were once competent, but no longer are: for example, sufferers of the more severe forms of adult onset dementia. Where such individuals have omitted, while competent, to provide legally recognised guidance as to how they want to be treated in the event of loss of competence, and have not given anyone a medical power of attorney, they are likely to be given all medically indicated care unless, and until, it is considered medically futile to continue doing so.[2] When patients have had opportunity both to issue an advance directive to indicate their wishes concerning medical treatment in the event of loss of competence, and to appoint a proxy, but have done neither, their carers may have to make a substituted judgment. If making such a judgment is not feasible, carers are legally obligated to act in the best interests of those for whom they have a duty of care. I am not suggesting that acting in accordance with what are judged to be a patient's best interests will always be straightforward since that can sometimes be subject to debate. One reason, as previously noted, is that the best interests standard is sometimes interpreted very narrowly as referring only to a patient's best *health care* interests, when it is more correctly interpreted as referring to what would be in his best interests *all things considered*. But even supposing that the best interests standard is understood in the latter, more comprehensive, sense, its application in decisions about appropriate treatment for a once, but no longer, competent person whose death is imminent, may still be complicated by difficulties in determining what would be best all things considered for *him*. Notwithstanding this, the final section of the chapter will be devoted to showing that the problems facing its application need not be intractable. That task will be made easier if I first consider those far more troubling instances where decisions have to be made about what constitutes appropriate medical care for

---

Americans with Disabilities Act of 1990). However, the argument is easily disposed of since, even supposing there is a right to a voluntary medically assisted death, the right can only be exercised by those competent to request assistance; hence, it is not discriminatory to permit the right to be exercised by those who are competent, *and only by them* (or, their proxies). For related discussion see Bickenbach (1998) and Silvers (1998).

[2] In an illuminating discussion of how to develop an end-of-life policy for those suffering from Alzheimer's disease, Battin (1994c) argues that permitting active (non-voluntary) euthanasia would be the best policy to adopt. However, because she doubts this will find acceptance, she outlines a thought experiment to explore the option of empowering victims to take their own lives prior to descending into incompetence. Her point is that, if society considers active non-voluntary euthanasia to be out of the frame, it needs an imaginative alternative to the present widespread practice of only providing maintenance care. Cf. Prado (1990).

someone who has never been, nor, as can best be judged, ever will be, competent. The next two sections will focus on just such instances.

From an emotional perspective, decisions that have to be made on behalf of infants born with severe impairments and poor prognoses will always be hard, even when those decisions are guided by the best interests standard. Because they have had no life to speak of, there will typically be insufficient specific information available on which to base judgments concerning what would be best for them. Given that the right sort of information is unlikely to become available before any final decision has to be made, little is to be gained by delaying a decision.

Perhaps harder still, emotionally, are decisions concerning young children who, in addition to lacking competence, are suffering from conditions which afford no hope of recovery, but who, nonetheless, have been around long enough to become individuals in their own right and to establish relationships with their families, their care-givers, and with others. These very considerations make it difficult to ascertain what is in such children's best interests. I will argue, nonetheless, that it will sometimes be in the best interests of infants and young children, whose circumstances are like those I have been describing, to be allowed to die provided this can be managed without needlessly prolonging their suffering. The situation is like that with other patients for whom further medical treatment is deemed to be futile. With each it is morally justifiable to cease aggressive attempts to prolong life. In arguing in the way that I have foreshadowed, I am not resiling from my claim (in Chapter 6) that killing, in such circumstances, would be morally no worse than letting die. But I will contend that there is no need to give ammunition to those opposed to the legalisation of voluntary medically assisted death by insisting that the means for administering non-voluntary euthanasia to incompetent patients be no different than for administering voluntary medically assisted death to competent patients.[3] In what follows I will first set out the considerations of relevance to any decision to allow, or assist, an infant to die, and then I will discuss who should make the decision.

---

[3] Publication in recent years of information about the way some neonates and young infants have been actively helped to die in The Netherlands and in Belgium has led to strident criticism of its defenders. For the details see, in particular, van der Heide, et al. (1997) and Provoost, et al. (2005). These studies revealed that even though a large proportion in each country of non-sudden neonatal and infant deaths are attributable to the practice of withdrawing and withholding further medical care, a small proportion involves active non-voluntary euthanasia via lethal drugs administered by doctors. The main reasons given by doctors for using these means to end the lives of neonates and infants were the absence of real prospects of survival and expected poor quality of life. A protocol for handling these issues has been developed in The Netherlands – for the details see Verhagen and Sauer (2005).

I

Advances in genetic detection, foetal diagnosis and monitoring, improved surgical techniques, and the development of sophisticated ventilatory and other support systems, like gastrostomy tubes for feeding, have combined in recent decades to ensure the survival of many neonates who would previously not have survived birth, or, if they had, would either have died soon after birth or in early infancy. But, some of those who owe their lives to these developments survive only to suffer conditions that drastically impair their chances of leading a worthwhile life. They may have to cope with frequent and ongoing hospitalisations, shunts, colostomy bags, exposure to serious infections and so on. At the extreme, sufferers of genetic conditions like Tay-Sachs disease,[4] Lesch-Nyhan syndrome,[5] and Sanfilippo's disease,[6] as well as severe congenital conditions like very premature birth, birth trauma, and infectious disease, may face a life which, for all its brief duration, is dominated by intense suffering that is never compensated for with worthwhile experiences. By this I mean experiences that would make the infant's life of value *to the infant* (not to others, like other members of the infant's family or circle). Since it is sufferers from such conditions whose interests seem least likely to be served by continuing to live, and who, therefore, are at risk of being allowed to die, I need to say how the judgment might be reached that their lives lack value (for them).

As I indicated in Chapter 7, philosophers have tackled the question of what it is that makes our lives valuable by asking what it is about death that is bad. As mentioned there, the most widely supported answer has been that death is bad for us when the goods we realistically would have had access to (or, in all probability, would have been able to have access to) can be considered of positive

---

[4] Tay-Sachs is a genetic condition most common among Ashkenazi Jews (i.e. Jews of East European origin) and certain French-Canadian and Cajun French families. The absence of an enzyme necessary for breaking down gangliosides (fatty substances needed for the normal development of the brain and nerve cells) allows gangliosides to accumulate throughout the brain. This results in neural degeneration and disability. Death typically occurs within the first few years of life.

[5] Lesch-Nyhan is caused by a mutation in the HPRT gene that results in an absence of enzyme activity needed to keep uric acid levels in balance. Because the HPRT gene is located on the X chromosome the disease affects only infant males. It results in compulsive self-mutilation, head banging, and severe intellectual disability. Victims typically die within the first few years of life but some have survived for a couple of decades.

[6] Sanfilippo's is one of the lysomal diseases, a group of diseases responsible for different types of neurodegenerative disorders. In lysomal storage disorders, the activity of one or more of the lysomal degrading enzymes is deficient, leading to interference with cell function. The lysomal diseases are categorised into four sub-categories, according to the class of substance stored, and Sanfilippo's falls within the sub-category of mucopolysaccharidoses (which in turn is sub-divided, at present, into six varieties). The clinical indicators are mildly coarse facial features, corneal clouding, mild joint stiffness, progressive intellectual and motor retardation, and disruption of cognitive and emotional development.

value to us, or, as it will sometimes be more idiomatic to say, for us. Contrariwise, death is good for us when no (or, perhaps, few) goods of positive value would have been accessible to us had we continued to live; that is, death is bad, when it is bad, because of the possible future goods of which it deprives us.

In the context of end-of-life decision making for newborns this answer raises at least two critical questions, namely: 'does it not follow from that answer that an early death will sometimes represent less of a loss than a later death?' and 'is that not counter-intuitive?'. It will help me respond more effectively to these questions if I first comment on a contentious, connected issue concerning the value of (human) life. Michael Tooley endorses what I have previously referred to as the 'simple view' of personhood, namely, that only a being conscious of existing over time as a continuing self, can have a right to life. He adds that this consciousness does not develop until at least three months after birth. Hence, prior to that marker point, an infant cannot have a 'serious' right to life.[7] Tooley puts his point in terms of 'rights', but it can be restated without loss as the claim that it is wrong to deprive another of life only when doing so prevents a self-aware being from accessing the future goods it would realistically otherwise have been able to access. A clear implication of Tooley's contention is that until a being is self-aware it does not have a life of value *to* (or, *for*) *it*. So, death does not deprive a being lacking self-consciousness of anything of value; strictly, therefore, such a being cannot be wronged.[8]

In their widely debated defence of infanticide, Helga Kuhse and Peter Singer[9] take Tooley's position to be basically sound. However, they depart from it in two ways. First, unlike Tooley, who thinks self-awareness is not achieved in humans before three months of age and probably not until much later, Kuhse and Singer say only that the self-aware life of a person does not begin until some time after birth – they hint at a month or so after birth. Second, and more importantly, Kuhse and Singer list a number of reasons why Tooley's position ought to be modified so as to ensure that the lives of newborn humans should generally, even if not

---

[7] (1983: ch. 11). Contrary to Tooley's claim that 'A has a right to X' is roughly synonymous with 'If A desires X, then others are under a prima facie obligation to refrain from actions that would deprive him or her of X', Carter shows that it is more accurate to think of it as roughly synonymous with 'Unless A expresses his or her desire that not-X, then others are under a prima facie obligation to refrain from actions that would deprive him or her of X' (1997: 6). Given this alternative analysis, there is no reason to think that desiring to continue to be a subject of experiences is a necessary condition for having a serious right to life.

[8] Brock (1993a: 385, note 14).   [9] (1985: ch. 6).

always, be protected, despite their lack of self-awareness (and thus they contend that their position is not as radical as it might appear).[10] Among the reasons they give, one has to do with an infant being valued by others (such as biological or adoptive parents); another is based on other rights the infant may have quite apart from his right to life (for instance, the right not to be needlessly caused pain[11]), which presumably are based on relevant interests of the infant. But the chief reason that they advance as to why their position is not particularly radical has a different character altogether. It is that because the newborn infant has a life of no greater value to (or, for) the infant than a foetus' life has to a foetus (since in neither case is the life of value to the being in question), *and* abortion is permitted, infanticide should likewise be permitted because birth does not mark a morally significant boundary (between being and not being morally considerable).

Because I believe the crucial question is whether the life available to an infant will be of value *to the infant*,[12] I will concentrate on the final reason they offer in support of their position. First, though, I should register a major difference between their normative outlook and my own. Kuhse and Singer are consequentialists, who characterise the morally right in terms of consequences, whereas I think that in addition to taking account of the consequences of our actions it is also necessary to take account of certain constraints on what moral agents may do (like affording protection to individual rights), and certain prerogatives they may assume (like autonomously pursuing projects and goals that are not harmful to others). A normative pluralist like me has to acknowledge that on occasion morality demands the avoidance of extremely serious bad consequences and thus that constraints and prerogatives may be outweighed. It is, therefore, an important normative difference between us that I do not accept that, when the life available to an infant is of value to that infant, this consideration

---

[10] (1985: 134–139).

[11] Warren (1997: 219) claims that Tooley's (and, hence, Kuhse and Singer's) point about the infant's lack of self-awareness establishes only that an infant cannot value its life to the extent that a self-aware being can, but that insofar as infants 'experience their existence as (on the whole) pleasurable' they have an interest in continued life, and so a right to life. See also Warren (2000). Her focus is on how pleasurable the infant's experiences appear to be. While the pleasure an infant appears to take in life will undoubtedly have a significant influence on the motivation of the infant's carers, the move from pleasure to interests that Warren makes is, as I will shortly explain, no more convincing than the one Kuhse and Singer make from desires to interests.

[12] I will discuss the interests of other parties (such as parents, siblings and other relatives) in section II, but I will continue to insist that the prime concern has to be whether an infant or child's life has positive value.

may simply be overridden by consequentialist considerations in the manner proposed by Kuhse and Singer.[13]

With that preliminary point made, let me turn to the final reason they give for thinking that a newborn's life is of no value to the newborn. I agree with Kuhse and Singer that birth is not as such a morally significant marker. But this concession does not establish their position because it is in virtue of having an interest in the continuation of its life that an infant (or, a late term foetus, for that matter) has a life of value to, or, for, itself, and this holds even though it lacks a sense of itself as a continuing self.

In thinking about these matters, it is vital to bear in mind that 'having an interest in the continuation of life' is not to be construed as 'being interested in going on living'. Kuhse and Singer conflate these very different ideas when they claim that:

. . . only a being capable of understanding that it has a prospect of future existence can have a desire to go on living, and only a continuing self can have an interest in continued life.[14]

There is a world of difference between '*desiring x*', which necessitates being interested in *x*, and '*having an interest in x*', which requires only that the occurrence of *x*, or the coming into existence of *x*, be to one's advantage.[15] That world of difference can be illustrated as follows: a trustee charged with protecting an individual's interests ought to protect them regardless of whether the individual takes any interest in (that is, has desires about) their protection. The final part of the passage quoted above follows logically only if 'interest' is taken in the former (subjective) way, but it then expresses a trivial truth. If 'interest' is understood, instead, in the latter (non-subjective) way, the second part of the passage fails to follow logically from the first – it is simply an assertion, and a question-begging one to boot. Contrary to what Kuhse and Singer claim, whenever a newborn's life will be of positive value to, or for, the newborn, it will, other things being equal, be in the newborn's interests to go on living even though it makes no sense to say that it has a desire to go on living.

Let me elaborate on the notion of its being in the interests of a newborn, or, more generally, of an infant, to go on living. Jeff McMahan has distinguished interests *simpliciter* from what he labels 'time-relative interests'.

[13] Kuhse and Singer are not the only ones who advance such a view. Kitcher (2002) explicitly and vigorously does so, too.
[14] (1985: 132).   [15] Cf. Feinberg (1984: 38–45).

Though his introduction of this distinction gives rise to important philosophical issues, these can be set to one side for present purposes. I will assume, for the purposes of my argument, that an infant has a 'time-relative interest' in continuing to live because a time-relative interest is what a person has 'egoistic reason to care about now (or, in the case of a non-self-conscious being incapable of being egoistically concerned about the future, the time-relative interests it presently has are what a third party would have reason now to care about for the being's own sake)'.[16] A time-relative interest is thus relativised to a being's state at a particular time. Hence, 'the strength of an individual's time-relative interest in continuing to live is . . . the extent to which it matters, for his sake now or from his present point of view, that he should continue to live'.[17] In effect, the degree of egoistic concern a person has about his future varies with the extent of the psychological continuity between that individual and the future individual he will become. This is how McMahan elaborates the point: '[it] varies primarily with either or both . . . the net amount of good that the individual's future would contain if he were to continue to live and . . . the extent to which [psychological connectedness and psychological continuity] would hold between the individual now and himself later when the goods of his future life would occur'.[18] Doubtless, the time-relative interests of, for example, an infant are weak in virtue of the weakness of the psychological connections between the infant and the egoistic concerns of the being he will become in the future. But, since it is these psychological connections that are the foundation for an individual's concern for his future, the fact that they are *weak* affords us no licence to *disregard* them. All that is necessary for an infant's life to be of value to him is that there be the relevant psychological connections between him and the being he will become in the future.[19]

---

[16] (2002: 80).   [17] (2002: 105).   [18] (2002: 233).

[19] While McMahan considers that an account of the value of a person's life (for the person living it) in terms of time-relative interests is more plausible than the alternatives, he thinks it counter-intuitively implies that the wrongness of killing is a function of the time-relative interests of particular individuals. This is counter-intuitive because it implies that killing some persons (whose lives are of more value to them) is worse than killing others (whose lives are of less value to them), rather than that it is just as wrong to kill one innocent human being as to kill another. Since belief in the equal wrongness of killing is grounded in belief in the equal worth of persons, the wrongness of killing does not vary as between individuals like badness of deaths does. The badness of death is a function of the value of a person's future life to the person, whereas the wrongness of killing is a function of a failure to give due respect to the victim as a person. McMahan's strategy is to try to make this implication of his position more palatable by proposing the need for *both* a morality of interests *and* a morality of respect, the former applying to non-persons (non-human animals, human foetuses, and so forth), the latter applying to persons. Because his book is concerned with individuals who are below the threshold of respect (those who are at 'the margins of life'), his account of the morality of interests

To sum up the argument to date: where death frustrates our interest in continued life, because it deprives us of accessible future possible goods that would generate positive value to, or for, us, death is a bad thing. Indirectly, this tells us what it is that makes our lives of value to, or for, us (as distinct from any social value they may have). An individual's life can have value for him regardless of whether he is aware of being a continuing self, that is, a self-conscious being. Nor is there any inconsistency in affirming this while holding, at the same time, that death is, other things being equal, worse for those who *are* aware of being continuing selves. The more we have invested in shaping and directing our life, the more psychologically connected our life is, and the more we lose when that life is cut short. It is for this reason that an individual is thought to lose more if death terminates his life when it is in full flight rather than in its infancy. That is not to say that the latter sort of death will not be experienced as an enormous tragedy by others, including most obviously the parents of such an infant. There can be no doubt that the grief of parents of infants who die of 'cot death syndrome', for instance, is grief occasioned by the tragic loss of the infant's life regardless of whether the death is a loss to the infant. But, if so, is that not at odds with any attempt to value a person's life by reference to how much is lost if the person dies? Does it not imply that death in infancy must be worse than death at, say, thirty-five years of age (contrary to what I claimed earlier)? No, it does not, because the view I have been defending has neither of these implications.

Recall that I endorsed McMahan's claim that an infant's life is only weakly psychologically connected to the life of the future being he will become. To evaluate the badness of death for an individual it is necessary to make the evaluation in relation to the effect death has on the individual *at the time of the death* rather than the effect it has on the individual's life *as a whole*. The distinction is well illustrated by McMahan.[20] Suppose a child is born with a condition which, if left untreated, will lead to a very early death, but which, if treated, will not result in death until early adulthood. Everyone will agree that the child's condition should be treated. This may appear to be at odds with the claim that death is generally worse for someone when his life is in full flight. But appearances, as we know, can sometimes be deceptive. The claim that death is generally worse for someone when his life is in full flight is relativised to

is developed to a far greater extent than that of the morality of respect. For quite different accounts of these matters see DeGrazia (2003); Broome (2004); and Kittay (2005).

[20] (1988: 58ff) and (2002: 185ff).

the time when death occurs. When treating a treatable infant, our concern is for his whole life. It is critically important to distinguish between judgments about the value someone's life has to him, at a particular time, and judgments concerning the value to him of his life as a whole. The latter sort of judgment is made when assessing whether a person's life is, or has been valuable for him, but that does not preclude making judgments based on how bad death is for him at the time when his death occurs.

With this brief account in place of what it is that makes someone's life of value to, or for, him, I wish to return to the claim I made that an infant's life may sometimes be of no positive value to, or for, that infant, and hence that it may be warranted to allow such an infant to die (in virtue of the futility of providing life-prolonging treatment). Obviously, consultation with an infant to try to determine whether his life will be of positive value is out of the question, whereas it is possible with a competent adult. The judgment that has to be made is whether the future accessible to the infant will contain sufficient possible good things (experiences, opportunities, development of capacities, and so forth) to make his life on the whole worth living, despite any bad it will contain. The bad will include: the extent of pain and suffering he will face; intellectual and physical disabilities he will suffer; trauma he will experience in undergoing medical treatments he cannot understand; and, the difficulties he will have in forming meaningful relationships with others.[21] Any judgment that is made (in light of these sorts of consideration) to the effect that a particular infant's life will not be positively valuable for him will need to be clear cut. Where there is uncertainty this must count in favour of the infant being given every reasonable form of assistance since the goal must be to act in the infant's best interests.[22] Thus, suppose that there is an experimental procedure that carries a minuscule hope of making it possible for an infant to enjoy a life of positive value that would otherwise be unavailable to him, but which may also shorten his life. In such a circumstance the odds of the procedure being successful obviously must be carefully assessed before the infant is made to undergo it. However, since there is no reason to think that it is always worse mistakenly to let someone die than it is mistakenly to keep someone alive,[23] there is no need for anyone to think that

---

[21] See Young (1979: 129f); Bayles (1984: 93ff); Kuhse and Singer (1985: ch. 7); and Warren (1997: 217–219).

[22] As recently, for example, as March, 2006, in the United Kingdom, this was unequivocally stated to be the guiding principle by Justice Holman in *An NHS Trust v. MB and Anor.*

[23] See Feinberg (1991) and Richards (1992: 234).

they will have failed in their duty to the infant if the procedure is not administered. Even so, if it would not clearly be in the interests of a particular infant to be allowed to die, appropriate medical support should be provided, including support that cannot be guaranteed to be efficacious.[24]

As Bayles has pointed out,[25] some will object that it is impossible for anyone else to assess the value of someone else's life to that person, while others will object that, even if it were possible, it should not be done. Neither claim is plausible. The best evidence that such assessments *can* be made is that they *are* made. Consider, for instance, how assessments are made about the medical futility of continuing to treat someone on the ground that there is no prospect of his ever regaining a life he would value. There is, *in principle*, no difference between forming such an assessment in the case of an infant and doing so when it is an adult's existence that is near to its end. Furthermore, there often is justification for making such assessments (if only, for instance, because doing so will enable individuals, including infants, to avoid needless suffering, or, having to undergo futile treatments). Those who object to such assessments being made sometimes mistakenly claim that making them is tantamount to making the judgment made by the Nazis that some lives are 'not worthy to be lived'.[26] This is a mistake because it seriously misconstrues the nature of the judgments I have been proposing. It conflates judgments concerning the value of an individual's life to, or for, him, with judgments about the value of his life to, or for, the society in which he lives. Unlike the Nazis, I have said nothing about judgments of the latter sort because they have no relevance to the issue being investigated.

---

[24] Though their critics have often overlooked the qualifications they introduce, Kuhse and Singer sometimes (1985: 143, 152, 154) fail to make this point with sufficient firmness and clarity. Moreover, when they advance an argument based on 'the value of the next child' (1985: 155–161), and urge the *replacement* of an infant with poor prospects by one with better prospects, they muddy the waters even more. Because they consider infanticide to be, in crucial respects, morally on a par with abortion, the permissibility (for them) of replacing a foetus with poor prospects with one that has better prospects, applies also to infants. Quite apart from the fact that the premise of their argument has plausibility only if foetuses, *no matter how developed*, are assumed not to have lives of value, their argument unhelpfully draws attention away from the central issue of what would be in the infant's best interests.

[25] (1984: 94f).

[26] An idea first floated in Binding and Hoche (1920). For more on the origins and development of the idea see Lifton (1986) and Burleigh (1994).

How may the goal of acting in the best interests of an infant with poor prospects of a worthwhile life be achieved? In particular, once it has been decided that an infant would be better off dead, is the only morally defensible way to try to achieve it to allow the infant to die? And, who should decide? In this section I will endeavour to answer these questions.

Let me begin with instances where there are no, or few, complications arising from the effect an infant's continued existence would have on others – parents, siblings, extended family, and friends of the family – that is, instances concerned pretty well exclusively with the value to an infant of his expected life wherein it is judged that the infant will not enjoy a life of positive value. If the infant's condition is sufficiently bad that not treating him will quickly lead to his death, or if the degenerative process is so rapid that death will come swiftly and any aggressive intervention will only delay the inevitable, the infant's best interests can be promoted simply by refraining from doing anything beyond providing comfort care.

Unfortunately, things will rarely be as simple as this. For one thing, typically there will be interests of other parties to consider (even if, as I have been emphasising, the infant's best interests are the prime consideration). For another, it will be rare that medical staff will be able only to offer comfort care, so it will be necessary to consider whether, in such circumstances, they ought to do more. Let me take these points in turn.

How should medical staff handle instances where the best interests of an infant cannot be considered in total isolation from the interests of others, especially parents and siblings, but also, for example, of other infants (who may stand to benefit if trials of experimental treatments are initiated)? There will be instances where an infant's life is not expected to be of value to him, but the interests of others may be promoted if he is kept alive, but also instances where despite the fact that he may be expected to have a life of some value, keeping him alive will threaten the interests of others.

In the former circumstance, parents, or, if, for some reason, they cannot be consulted, an independent body like a court, should have to give informed consent for any deliberate prolongation of the infant's life. There obviously can be instances where keeping an infant alive would be of great benefit to others (not just via experimentation with medical treatments, but via observation of the progress of a condition, or to harvest organs for transplantation to others, and so on). Michael Bayles[27] objected to any prolongation of an infant's life for the benefit of others when obtaining the benefit would impose a burden (such as further suffering) on the infant. As plausible as this claim initially sounds, I think that it needs refinement. Exceptional circumstances aside, there must be proportionality between benefits and burdens. After all, a relatively minor additional burden could, in theory, lead to a major benefit for others (as with an organ donation that could save the life of another infant, or young child, if the donor were kept alive for a few hours). Nonetheless, if, as I have been urging, the prime consideration is the dying infant's interests, no delay in ending his life should be entertained that would be disproportionately burdensome for him.

However, it is the second type of circumstance identified above that poses the more serious problem. Even on the view that life is not of value *as such*, but, instead, of value to individuals because of the goods it makes realistically available to them, it remains important not to allow an individual to be used as a *mere* means to others' ends.[28] So, the question that has to be answered is whether Kant's important principle is violated if moral significance is accorded to the consequential effects on other people's lives of allowing an infant whose life has some value to him to continue living. I do not believe that it is violated since it is clear that, in those exceptional cases where the consequences for others of saving or prolonging one person's life will be horrendous, and the only way of avoiding those consequences is not to save or prolong the person's life, it is permissible not to save or prolong that life.[29] Taking account of the consequences that a particular way of dealing with a person will have for others is not treating that person merely as a means. Indeed, to fail to take account of the consequences for those others would be to deny *them* proper moral consideration. It would be to treat their lives as if they were of no account. In theory, at least in economically developed societies, there should be no cases where the life of an infant, which is of positive value to him, is not prolonged because prolonging it would seriously damage the interests of others. The reason I say this is that it should be possible to make use of social forms of support to minimise damage to the interests of others; if priority is to be given to the interests of the infant these forms of support should be

---

[27] (1984: 99).   [28] Kant (1785: second section).
[29] Cf. Foot (1967) for the case of an innocent fat man who becomes tightly wedged in the only exit of a cave about to be filled with water while leading a group of explorers. See, too, Kagan (1989: 141f).

enlisted before a decision is made to allow an infant to die.[30] Thus, for example, where the constancy of care an infant needs is so demanding as to threaten the individual and collective interests of the other members of the family, home help, respite care and other strategies can be utilised to avert, or ease, the threat, supposing that adoption, foster care, and institutionalisation are not viable options.

Unfortunately, what is possible in theory is not always achievable in practice, so, to the extent that it is not, the hand of those who urge infanticide (whether by allowing death to occur, or by hastening it) is strengthened. Kuhse and Singer, for example, cite evidence to back their claim that keeping severely disabled infants alive sometimes unfairly damages the interests of the families into which they are born.[31] I will mention some specifics that support their general point. Even in a wealthy country like Australia (and there is no reason to think the Australian situation differs dramatically from that in other Western countries), parents of severely disabled infants and young children may be unable to get access to sufficient support to ensure that other members of the family do not end up being greatly disadvantaged. First, accessing home help and respite care (which may only become available after time on a waiting list) typically involves significant extra expense for families even when they are afforded such assistance by the state, to say nothing of the disruption to family life that may be occasioned. Moreover, those in rural or outback locations not only face greater difficulty in accessing respite care but confront heavier expenses in obtaining it, as compared with those in metropolitan areas, when it is available. Second, if a severely disabled infant survives into childhood, there will commonly be extra costs incurred by families because of the need to: modify domestic architecture to incorporate access ramps, and renovate bathroom and toilet facilities; obtain a vehicle that is suitable for transporting the child to see doctors, and attend hospitals

---

[30]   In their discussion of this issue, Kuhse and Singer (1985: 146–155) give the impression that the interests of others will outweigh those of the infant far more often than should be necessary, at least in economically developed countries. Again, I think this is because of their underlying conviction that an infant (in the early months after birth) has the same inherent moral significance as a foetus, viz., none. That is why their discussion of 'the interests of the child versus the interests of the family' leads in to their appeal to the replaceability argument. Those, like me, who are unpersuaded by their position on the value of the lives, and hence the moral status, of young infants see this as a reason to consider other strategies than infanticide whenever an infant has a life of some positive value open to him. The burdens that would be placed on others can be a reason for not bringing a child into existence, and can be a reason for not prolonging the life of an infant. But, the onus of showing that the burdens on others are likely to be of greater moral moment than the loss to the infant of his life must be borne by those who advocate infanticide.

[31]   (1985: 146ff).

and schools; purchase special beds and mechanical lifting equipment; and so forth. Third, in cultures in which it is common for both parents to do paid work, whenever the constancy of the demand for care requires at least one parent to provide most of the care, the result will be that the family suffers financially. Given the difficulties in being able to access paid care outside normal working hours, even part-time paid work may be hard to manage. (A single parent is, of course, doubly disadvantaged.) Fourth, as well as occasioning additional financial burdens, the care of a severely disabled infant or young child typically imposes other burdens, including: having to deal with the almost inevitable medical issues that will arise; emotional strain; and, effects on the health and relationships of the carers themselves. Fifth, the overall quality of family life is likely to be affected – if only because of the time and energy that has to be devoted to the severely disabled child and the constant disruptions to family life.

Given these considerations, if a decision is taken to prolong the life of a severely disabled infant (even when that is done initially only to provide further time to assess the infant's life prospects), parents and siblings may fail to receive the support needed to minimise the impact of the decision on them. Nevertheless, each of the considerations I have mentioned is capable of being coped with if there exists a sufficiently strong social will to ensure support is adequate. But, until that social will becomes stronger than it is at present in most wealthy countries, including Australia, the argument of those who think that the damage done to the infant's family outweighs the loss to the infant in being denied the opportunity to live will be harder to resist than it should be.

I turn now from consideration of the importance of taking seriously the interests of others than the infant, to the second issue that I flagged, namely, what is to be done when it is judged that an infant's life lacks (and will always lack) value to the infant, but death will not come quickly even if further medical treatment is withheld. Publicity about the case of an infant left to die in the early nineteen seventies at the Johns Hopkins Hospital in Baltimore,[32] who took a couple of weeks to die (from starvation and dehydration), gave rise to discussions about the appropriateness of simply letting infants die once it had been decided that further treatment was futile. I will not repeat the argument I gave in Chapter 6 for the view that there is no intrinsic moral difference between allowing a person to die and killing him. As emerged there, even if there is no intrinsic

---

[32] President's Commission for the Study of Ethical Problems in Medicine and Biomedical and Bio-behavioral Research (1983: 198f).

moral difference between them it will sometimes be morally worse (on extrinsic grounds) to let a person die than to kill him. The Johns Hopkins Hospital case makes the point. Once the decision was taken that providing further medical treatment was futile, it was morally worse to allow the infant to die in the way that transpired, namely, by allowing death from dehydration and starvation. (The outcry about the way that that particular infant was allowed to die led to changes in the institutional care of infants from whom further life-prolonging treatment was to be withheld with the result that dehydration, for example, is nowadays avoided.) In making decisions more generally as to whether an infant whose life lacks positive value[33] should be allowed to die, the focus ought to be, first, on whether he will be subjected to any needless suffering and, second, on whether there will be any unnecessary prolongation of the trauma of his dying. Since improvements in palliative care have made it extremely unlikely that a dying infant will only be able to be spared unnecessary pain by being actively assisted to die, the contentious issue of the moral propriety of actively assisting an infant to die can largely be circumvented. This is not to go back on my claim that letting die may sometimes be morally worse than killing. That remains my position, but I wish to draw attention in the next paragraph to a number of considerations of strategic significance for the present discussion.

To begin with, an infant, by hypothesis, cannot competently consent to being helped to die and so the situation is quite different from that with competent adults who request medically assisted death. Certainly, if it were legal to do so, competent parents could request medical assistance with dying on their infant's or child's behalf just as they make other decisions on behalf of their children. But, given how morally fraught it would be to permit other parties to decide to kill non-competent adults, who would be better off dead, it should be seen as equally troubling to allow parents, or, others, to make similar decisions on behalf of infants or young children. Second, to adopt such a strategy would simply play into the hands of those who oppose the legalisation of medically assisted death for competent individuals on the ground that it will inevitably result in killings of those who lack competence.[34] Finally, as already indicated, it is not necessary to adopt such a strategy. Typically, a dying infant's pain and suffering will be able to be overcome with drugs, albeit at the expense of its

---

[33] For ease of exposition I will, from now on, ignore those instances where an infant has a life of so little value to him that his interests are clearly of less significance than those of others (like other members of his family).

[34] I have, in consequence, changed my position from that defended in my (1979).

awareness of others. The adoption of a strategy of, say, inducing pharmacological oblivion will, in such circumstances, be an appropriate way to bring the life of an infant to an end. As explained in the preceding chapter (in relation to adults who lack competence to consent to being allowed to die), this is properly characterised as non-voluntary euthanasia because the decision not to prolong the life of an infant, but to allow him to die, is taken with the aim of ensuring that he does not suffer needlessly. Such a strategy has the advantage that it is consistent with medical practices acceptable even to those opposed to voluntary medically assisted death.

Interestingly, among those who take seriously the role accorded to the moral significance of intentions in Catholic theology, some consider that the law concerning homicide is incorrectly interpreted when doctors are permitted intentionally to bring about a patient's death by omitting to provide further life-prolonging treatment.[35] They point to *Airedale N.H.S. Trust v. Bland*, in which the Law Lords permitted Anthony Bland's tube-feeding to be halted, as evidence of a lack of coherence in the interpretation of the law relating to homicide (specifically in England, but, by implication, elsewhere as well). Despite my many disagreements with them, I believe their opposition to the ending of human life both by active means *and* by omission makes them more consistent than those who consider that bringing about a patient's death by refraining from providing medical treatment[36] simply amounts to allowing the patient's medical condition to run its natural course.

It is an important implication of the position I have been arguing for that, when the life of an infant has previously been of some positive value to him, but it then deteriorates to a point of no return (as happens with victims of genetic conditions like Tay-Sachs disease, Lesch-Nyhan syndrome, and Sanfilippo's disease, and of certain congenital conditions like spinal muscular atrophy) there should be a preparedness to take the decision to allow such an infant to die. It is a further implication that this will be true as well when the loss of value to the infant does not come until childhood, but nevertheless before the child is capable of giving informed consent. I think it important to highlight these implications because doing so reinforces the importance of being sure that the infant's, or child's, life truly does lack positive value. This is especially important given a greater

---

[35] Keown (1993); Finnis (1993); and Gormally (1995).

[36] I here assume, as various recent court judgments in several countries have made clear, that artificial feeding and hydration are forms of *medical* treatment. For discussion of the consequences see McLean (2006).

reluctance to allow a child to die (whose life has no value for him) than a neonate (whose life similarly lacks value). Unfortunately, such an attitude can have appalling consequences as was shown in a recent Canadian case, the Latimer case.

Robert Latimer was convicted in 1993 of the second-degree murder of his twelve year old daughter, Tracy. Tracy was born with severe cerebral palsy as a result of being deprived of oxygen at birth. She was a spastic quadriplegic who only ever had the mental capacity of an infant a few months old. She suffered convulsions and seizures; had difficulty sleeping; was unable to swallow food; vomited frequently; and, had chronic respiratory problems. In her fourth year she underwent her first surgical operation to release muscle tension and pain in her leg caused by muscle degeneration. Over the next few years her scoliosis (curvature of the spine) rapidly progressed to the point where her body became severely contorted. Around age ten she underwent further surgery to relieve muscle tension. By 1992 her scoliosis had become so marked that it began to affect her vital organs. She underwent a third operation involving the insertion of steel rods to keep her body more rigid but this seems to have worsened her discomfort. In her final year of life she was unable to get significant relief from her pain and, in consequence, even rest, let alone sleep, was rare. A fourth surgical operation was proposed. The surgeon testified later at Robert Latimer's trial that this operation would have put Tracy through excruciating pain and would not have achieved more than a temporary slowing of the degeneration in her hips, pelvis and back. Her parents decided that she had suffered long enough and that further surgery would not only not make any significant difference to Tracy's situation but would worsen it, so Robert Latimer painlessly killed his daughter by way of carbon monoxide poisoning. When tried, he offered a defence of necessity.[37] The matter went on appeal from the Saskatchewan Court of Appeal to the Supreme Court of Canada.[38] Latimer appealed against both his conviction and sentence. The Supreme Court followed *Perka*[39] in declaring that the rationale for

---

[37] When the defence of necessity succeeds it mitigates rather than exculpates. It is worth noticing that since *R v. Dudley and Stephens* [1884] 14 QBD 273, British law has refused to countenance a defence of necessity in cases of intentional killing. Dudley and Stephens were tried for the murder of Richard Parker who was killed so that he could be eaten after the shipwreck of the vessel on which they were bound for Australia. In the recent case of *Re A (children)* [2000] 4 All ER 961, Lord Justice Brooke sought to argue against this traditional position when he offered the opinion that one of two conjoined twins could justifiably be killed to save the life of her sister (though he seems to have thought that there was no inconsistency between his position and the doctrine of double effect). For criticism see Annas (2001).

[38] *R v. Latimer* [2001] 1 S.C.R. 3.

[39] *Perka v. The Queen* [1984] 2 SCR 232. See also *R v. Perka* [1984] 2 SCR 233, 14 CCC (3d) 385.

the defence of necessity 'rests on a realistic assessment of human weakness, recognizing that a liberal and humane criminal law cannot hold people to the strict obedience of laws in emergency situations where normal human instincts, whether of self-preservation or of altruism, overwhelmingly impel disobedience. The objectivity of the criminal law is preserved; such acts are still wrongful, but in the circumstances they are excusable' (at 248). An act done out of necessity may thus be excusable even if it is, strictly, unlawful.

The Court ruled that Latimer's action could not be considered to have been done out of necessity because it did not satisfy any of the three requirements identified in *Perka* as essential for the defence of necessity to be applicable, namely, that there exist an urgent situation of clear and imminent threat to life; that there not be any reasonable, lawful alternative to disobeying the law; and, that any harm inflicted in disobeying the law be proportional to the harm thereby avoided. It contended, first, that Tracy Latimer's painful condition did not constitute an imminent threat to her life; second, that there was a reasonable, lawful alternative to killing her, namely using a feeding tube to improve her general health coupled with providing her with more effective medication for the relief of her pain; and, third, that the harm inflicted was not proportionate to the harm avoided.

I have previously argued that death is not always a greater harm than continued life (because those whose lives do not have, nor will in the future have, any positive value for them, are better off dead). I am in no position to claim that the Supreme Court of Canada was wrong to believe that Tracy Latimer was more harmed by being killed than she would have been had she been kept alive and supported in the ways it suggested (even though I find it astounding that the court thought her general health and pain relief could have been so much better managed that she would have had a worthwhile life). I do claim, however, that there can be instances of killing where the third requirement for the defence of necessity is satisfiable, regardless of whether the court was right to refuse to countenance this in the Latimer case. Second, even supposing that neither of the other two requirements for a defence of necessity was satisfied in Tracy Latimer's case, there can be no gainsaying the possibility that these requirements may be satisfiable in other cases involving a child being let die, or killed, because his life lacks positive value for him. In other words, regardless of whether the Court was right that Robert Latimer's conduct constituted second-degree murder under Canadian law, the possibility remains that a defence of necessity may be successful in other cases in which a child's life is ended because he would be better off dead.

Let me now turn to the final matter I flagged for discussion in relation to ending the lives of those who have never been competent, namely, who should make the decision not to continue aggressive medical treatment in favour of, for example, allowing an infant to die. Hitherto, it has frequently been assumed that the parents of an infant with very poor prospects of a worthwhile life could neither know enough, nor be sufficiently emotionally capable, to make a decision to allow their infant to die. This attitude dove-tailed well with the paternalistic attitudes and practices hitherto of many medical professionals. There is some empirical evidence that medical professionals still believe decisions of this kind are too harrowing for parents to make, despite parents wishing to make them, and, in consequence, that decisions made by parents are subject to quasi-paternalistic manipulation to ensure that they concur with those of the attending medical professionals.[40] Nonetheless, paternalistic and quasi-paternalistic attitudes lack any satisfactory justification in the present context since there is no reason to believe that parents are generally incapable of grasping the issues relevant to an assessment of their child's future prospects. I do not suggest that it is a simple matter to help parents reach such an understanding, especially in the midst of their distress over their child's prospects. It takes time; information has to be provided in an intelligible form so that they can understand it; counselling about options has to be made available; and, so forth. But none of these requirements can, nor should, be ruled out in principle. So, even parents who are emotionally distressed because of their infant's poor prospects should have the opportunity to receive assistance to help them in their decision-making. As was noted in Chapter 8, other major decisions in life often have to be taken under less than optimal circumstances but that is not thought to justify usurping the right of competent individuals to make their own decisions. If parents are incapable of making a reasonable decision even after extensive efforts to help them do so, and it can be established that it is their incapacity that is preventing a resolution, the issue should then be referred to a suitable tribunal or court for final determination.

Perhaps a more important reason for considering that parents are not best placed to make decisions to allow their infants to die is that they

---

[40] McHaffie, *et al.* (2001) reported this in relation to two studies carried out recently in Scotland. The findings in these studies should come as no surprise given that it has been known for some time that the way information is 'framed' is a major factor in determining the decisions people make based on that information. Framing occurs when an agent makes one possible outcome of behaviour the 'neutral' outcome. Other possible outcomes are considered to be either 'gains' or 'losses' relative to the 'neutral' outcome and, hence, are viewed as either positive or negative. For more on framing and related phenomena see, e.g., Kahneman, *et al.* (1982) and Horowitz (1998: 371).

may overrate the impact on their own interests, or those of other family members, of aggressively treating an infant with poor prospects.[41] This is not something on which it is sensible to generalise. Nor is it sensible to generalise about the inverse possibility, namely, that parents might wish to keep their infants alive even when this would not be in the best interests of those infants. Again, when there is reason to believe that a decision will be taken which is clearly not in the best interests of an infant, and all efforts to persuade the parents to reach a different decision have proved unsuccessful, the matter should be considered by an independent body such as a suitable tribunal or court. I think it will only rarely be the case that properly informed and counselled parents will choose to prolong the lives of their infant despite that not being in the infant's best interests. Moreover, it will be just as rare for parents to choose not to prolong the lives of their infant if the infant's prospects are positive, especially if they can be assured that they will have adequate backup support, including home help and respite care. But, in the unlikely event that such choices are made, they should be subject to scrutiny by a suitable tribunal or court to ensure that the best interests of the infants have been carefully considered. (This is not because tribunals and courts always make wise decisions, but because they provide an opportunity for serious and thorough consideration of weighty matters.)

It is not my intention to leave the impression that it is only parental decision-making that needs scrutiny in these matters. Suppose parents are acknowledged as having the right to decide their infants' fates, albeit after consultation with other concerned parties, including relevant medical personnel. Perhaps because of the nature of their training, medical professionals seem likely to be biased in favour of treating aggressively. Some, indeed, may wish to continue to treat when that would not, in fact, be in the best interests of a particular infant. Though parents must ultimately rely on information provided by medical care-givers they must endeavour to make decisions on behalf of their infant without allowing themselves simply to become mouthpieces for those care-givers (which may not be an easy task given the evidence from the Scottish studies cited above). They may need to seek other opinions to determine whether all appropriate options have been canvassed, or to consider whether to transfer their infant to another institution with better facilities. Above all, their endeavour must be to make decisions that are in their infant's best interests, and hence to do whatever that responsibility entails.

[41] Bayles (1984: 100f).

III

In this final section I shall consider whether non-voluntary euthanasia has any application in the end-of-life care of no longer competent patients. I will presume that no advance directive exists, because, if there is one, it will take precedence. I will also presume that a likely candidate will be someone for whom: further medical treatment is agreed to be futile; there is no likelihood of this outlook changing; and, there is no realistic prospect of him recovering to lead a worthwhile life in the time that remains. Individuals who fit the description I have just given are routinely allowed to die in hospitals and other facilities at the present time in Western countries (and, almost as certainly, elsewhere). Many medical practitioners have no difficulty with this state of affairs, but remain unwilling actively to assist such individuals to die. For some, this is because medically assisted death is at present against the law. But, for many other medical practitioners, it is because they consider that there is a fundamental moral and legal distinction between allowing someone to die in the sort of circumstance I have described, and helping him to die.

I have already argued that this distinction cannot bear the moral weight that many medical professionals place on it; furthermore, it is recognised in the common law that an omission is as capable of causing a death as an act. It is, nevertheless, highly unlikely that a contemporary court would find against a medical practitioner who refrained from giving further treatment to a dying patient whose prospects for recovery were poor, in the event that the patient then died. According to Margaret Otlowski's account of the common law (1997: 22–33), for an omission to be considered the cause of a death it must be both the *sine qua non* of the death (that is, it must be the case that, *but for the omission, the death would not have occurred*), and be sufficiently directly connected with the death that the agent of the omission – for present purposes, a medical practitioner – is the imputable cause of the death. To establish criminal liability for murder by omission, the failure to perform the relevant action must be accompanied by the requisite *mens rea* (or, guilty mind). Given the need to establish the presence of all these features before a medical practitioner, who omitted to treat a dying person, could be charged with, let alone convicted of, a criminal offence, it comes as no surprise that the courts have been very reluctant to consider doctors in violation of their legal duty when they omit to treat the terminally ill. Nonetheless, both the law and philosophical analysis agree that a person can cause another's death by omission as well as by commission. For this reason, if it is justifiable to allow no longer competent, terminally ill patients to die when nothing further can be done for them, and as already indicated, I believe it is, it should equally be justifiable to assist such people to die. I have not advocated this latter approach but that, as previously explained, is solely for strategic reasons.

The widespread practice of allowing no longer competent, terminally ill patients for whom further medical treatment would be futile, simply to die, accounts for the overwhelming majority of cases of non-voluntary euthanasia. As was shown to be the case for infants, only when it is no longer feasible to employ other means to alleviate pointless suffering is there any imperative to *assist* such individuals to die. Given the pharmacological resources available nowadays, such a circumstance is unlikely to eventuate very often.

In sum, I have argued that there is a crucial difference between the circumstances of competent agents who request help with dying because they cannot end their own lives but judge that they would be better off dead (and I include among their number those agents who, while competent, issued clear advance directives to that effect), and those who would equally be better off dead but are not competent to request assistance with dying. The capacity of the former to make autonomous choices about how and when they die makes all the difference to the propriety of helping them to die because the assistance they are rendered merely ensures that effect is given to their choices. It is they who act, albeit with assistance; so, in choosing whether to be assisted to die or to be allowed to die they remain self-governing, and making provision for their preferred mode of assistance respects their standing as autonomous beings.

Those who are incapable of making a competent decision about how their lives may be ended, regardless of whether this is because they have never been competent or because they simply never gave an indication of their preference before losing competence, have to be viewed differently. I have argued that many of these latter are effectively administered non-voluntary euthanasia when they are intentionally allowed to die. Most who oppose the views advocated in this book refuse to concede this last point but do not object to the practice. There is, however, no need to give them any cause to claim that the legalisation of voluntary medically assisted death will lead inevitably to terminally ill incompetent persons being killed (that is, to a more active form of non-voluntary euthanasia than I claim is already widely practised in hospitals). Since the competent are differently situated from the incompetent as regards their capacity to request assisted death, only the former may properly be afforded it. When it is evident that further treatment would be futile for a dying patient who lacks the competence to request assisted death, to allow him to die will be morally unobjectionable provided that does not exacerbate his suffering.

CHAPTER 12

Concluding remarks

Early in this essay (in Chapter 3) I defended the idea that it is sometimes medically futile to continue life-prolonging treatment. I claim that with this established the idea that human life has to be preserved at any cost has much less purchase. If human life does not have to be preserved at any cost, it is morally permissible to withhold or withdraw life-prolonging medical treatment. In jurisdictions that respect the moral importance of individual autonomy, the associated legal idea that competent patients are entitled to refuse medical treatment has become entrenched and is upheld even when refusal of medical treatment is tantamount to suicide.

Supporters of the legalisation of physician-assisted suicide and voluntary euthanasia believe that once there is agreement that dying persons may end their lives by, for example, requesting the withdrawal of medical treatment which is keeping them alive, there can be no logical obstacle to honouring their requests for help with dying when they are in a similar plight but are unable to die simply by having their medical means of support withdrawn. Others go further and argue that the same conclusion should hold for those who are not strictly dying but find themselves in an intolerably burdensome situation as a result, for example, of being a victim of one of the forms of motor neurone disease. I have lent my support to these conclusions in two main ways. First, in Chapter 2 I set out a moral case *in favour of* the legalisation of physician-assisted suicide and voluntary euthanasia based centrally on the entitlement of a competent individual to make choices about his life, including the manner and timing of his death. I then gave reasons why the most appropriate means of recognising the moral case in public policy would be to provide for a legal entitlement to medically assisted death for competent patients. Later (in Chapter 9) I argued that the same entitlement should be available to persons who provide guidance about their end-of-life care by issuing an advance directive or by appointing a proxy with a medical power of attorney. Second, I argued, in Chapters 4 to 10, that none of the various moral and policy objections that have been levelled *against* the legalisation of voluntary medically assisted death succeeds in justifying the claim that it should remain illegal (in those jurisdictions where it is presently illegal).

The position I have argued for has already come to prevail in several jurisdictions, but in most jurisdictions only two options are permissible: first, a person may be allowed to die if it is agreed to be medically futile to continue to treat him, and, second, a competent dying person may refuse life-prolonging medical treatment even when that is tantamount to ending his life. However, the former of these options draws attention to the following significant oddity. Not only is it permissible to allow someone to die if it is deemed medically futile to continue treating him, it is not even necessary to have obtained his consent (while he was competent) in order to do so. Moreover, in Chapter 5, I argued that the practice of allowing people to die when there is no technological obstacle to prolonging their lives is not reconcilable with the widely supported idea of the sanctity of human life. I sought to challenge opponents of voluntary medically assisted death further by arguing that the idea of the sanctity of human life is not defensible anyway and that concern for human life is better reflected through endeavouring to ensure that it is qualitatively valuable human life that warrants protection. I proceeded in the following chapter to argue that medico-legal thought countenances the practice of allowing dying patients to die, but spurns that of assisting them to do so, at least in part because of the influence of two connected principles, namely, that it is morally permissible to allow dying persons to die but morally impermissible intentionally to hasten their deaths. I showed that these dominant ideas are incapable of sustaining opposition to the legalisation of medically assisted death (where that requires more than merely allowing the dying to die).

In Chapters 7 to 10 I considered four matters that those opposed to the legalisation of medically assisted death have cited as reasons for their opposition, namely, that its legalisation would: conflict with the maintenance of professional integrity in medical practice; necessitate that society have unqualified confidence in the competence of those seeking medical assistance with dying; and, jeopardise the lives of vulnerable dying persons who have never competently requested that they be helped to die but would end up being assisted to die regardless of whether they requested such assistance. I argued that there is nothing in medical morality or the goals of medicine that precludes offering medical assistance with dying to those intolerably burdened patients who competently request it; that the imminence of death does not inevitably undermine competence; that directives made in advance of death have probative value in relation to a person's end-of-life care; and, that the evidence from the couple of jurisdictions where voluntary medically assisted death has been legalised give cause for confidence that its legalisation will not result in jeopardy to the life prospects of vulnerable incompetent persons. This last objection to the legalisation of medically assisted death, based on the existence of a supposed 'slippery slope' leading downwards from legalisation of voluntary medically assisted death to the practice of non-voluntary euthanasia, is often thought to be the most powerful reason for resisting change in the legal status of physician-assisted suicide and voluntary euthanasia. In addition to arguing that the evidence we have from those jurisdictions where there has been legal change shows there is no basis to the objection, I pointed out that a good deal of present medical practice, wherein dying patients are allowed to die when further treatment is considered futile is, *de facto*, a form of non-voluntary euthanasia.

Notwithstanding these two key points, I contended that advocates of medically assisted death need to ensure that they do not give ammunition to their opponents by endorsing practices that involve actively bringing about the deaths of those who cannot competently request help with dying. Accordingly, in Chapter 11, I argued that if there are circumstances in which non-voluntary euthanasia is justifiable it should be by way of strategies that opponents of voluntary medically assisted death cannot consistently oppose. They cannot consistently oppose them because they already endorse the very same strategies in other contexts and proclaim them to be safer than the legalisation of medically assisted death.

With the exception of Chapter 11, the central concern of this book has been those forms of medically assisted death requested by competent dying persons that require medical professionals to do more than terminally sedate their patients, encourage their patients to refuse nutrition and hydration, withdraw or withhold further life-prolonging treatment from their patients, or simply let their patients die. I have argued that it is morally justifiable for willing doctors to provide such help. With this in mind, and given that there are powerful positive reasons for legalisation and only a weak case against legalisation, I conclude that voluntary forms of medically assisted death should be made legal in jurisdictions beyond The Netherlands, Oregon, and Belgium.

References

Adams, Robert Merrihew (1989). 'Should Ethics Be More Impersonal?: A Critical Notice of [Derek Parfit] *Reasons and Persons*', *The Philosophical Review* 98: 439–484.

American Medical Association (1992). 'Physician-Assisted Suicide', *Journal of the American Medical Association* 267: 2229–2233.

American Medical Association Council on Ethical and Judicial Affairs (1998). *Code of Medical Ethics: Current Opinions with Annotations* (Chicago: American Medical Association).

Amundsen, Darrel W. (1996). *Medicine, Society, and Faith in the Ancient and Medieval Worlds* (Baltimore: The Johns Hopkins University Press).

Anderson, Elizabeth (1993). *Value in Ethics and Economics* (Cambridge, Mass.: Harvard University Press).

Angell, Marcia (1998). 'Helping Desperately Ill People to Die' in Linda L. Emanuel, ed., *Regulating How We Die: The Ethical, Medical and Legal Issues Surrounding Physician-Assisted Suicide* (Cambridge, Mass.: Harvard University Press): 2–20.

Anscombe, G. E. M. (1957). *Intention* (Oxford: Blackwell).

— (1958). 'Modern Moral Philosophy', *Philosophy* 33: 1–19.

— (1970). 'War and Murder' in Richard Wasserstrom, ed., *War and Morality* (Belmont, Calif.: Wadsworth): 42–53.

— (1982). 'Action, Intention and "Double Effect"', *Proceedings of the American Catholic Philosophical Association* 54: 12–25.

Appelbaum, Paul S., Charles W. Lidz and Alan Meisel (1987). *Informed Consent: Legal Theory and Clinical Practice* (New York: Oxford University Press).

— and T. Grisso (1988). 'Assessing Patients' Capacities to Consent to Treatment', *The New England Journal of Medicine* 319: 1635–1638.

—, T. Grisso, E. Frank, S. O'Donnell and D. J. Kupfer (1999). 'Competence of Depressed Patients for Consent to Research', *American Journal of Psychiatry* 156: 1380–1384.

Aquinas. *Summa Theologiae*.

Aristotle. *Nicomachean Ethics*.

Australian Medical Association (2002). Position Statement on 'Care of Severely and Terminally Ill Patients', URL=<http://www.ama.com.au/web.nsf/ topic/policy-medical-ethics/>.

Bachman, Jerald G., Kirsten H. Alcser, David J. Doukas, Richard L. Lichtenstein, Amy D. Corling and Howard Brody (1996). 'Attitudes of Michigan Physicians and the Public Toward Legalizing Physician-Assisted Suicide and Voluntary Euthanasia', *The New England Journal of Medicine* 334: 303–309.

Barker, Stephen F., ed. (1976). *Respect for Life in Medicine, Philosophy and Law* (Baltimore: The Johns Hopkins University Press).

Batavia, Andrew I. (2004). 'Disability and Physician-Assisted Dying' in Quill and Battin (2004): 55–74.

Battin, Margaret P. (1992). 'Voluntary Euthanasia and the Risks of Abuse: Can We Learn Anything from The Netherlands?', *Law, Medicine and Health Care* 20: 133–143.

— (1994a). *The Least Worst Death: Essays in Bioethics on the End of Life* (New York: Oxford University Press).

— (1994b). 'Is There a Duty to Die: Age Rationing and the Just Distribution of Health Care?' in Battin (1994a): 58–79.

— (1994c). 'Fiction as Forecast: Euthanasia in Alzheimer's Disease' in Battin (1994a): 145–162.

— (1994d). 'Voluntary Euthanasia and the Risks of Abuse' in Battin (1994a): 163–181.

— (1995). *Ethical Issues in Suicide* (Upper Saddle River, N.J.: Prentice-Hall).

— (2003). 'Euthanasia and Physician-Assisted Suicide' in Hugh LaFollette, ed., *The Oxford Handbook of Practical Ethics* (Oxford: Oxford University Press): 673–704.

— (2005a). 'New Life in the Assisted-Death Debate: Scheduled Drugs versus NuTech' in Battin, ed., *Ending Life: Ethics and the Way We Die* (New York: Oxford University Press, 2005): 301–315.

— (2005b). 'Safe, Legal, Rare?: Physician-Assisted Suicide and Cultural Change in the Future' in Battin, ed., *Ending Life: Ethics and the Way We Die* (New York: Oxford University Press): 321–331.

—, Rosamond Rhodes and Anita Silvers, eds. (1998). *Physician Assisted Suicide: Expanding the Debate* (New York: Routledge).

Baumrin, Bernard (1998). 'Physician, Stay Thy Hand!' in Battin, *et al.* (1998): 177–181.

Bayles, Michael (1979). 'A Problem of Clean Hands: Refusals to Provide Professional Services', *Social Theory and Practice* 5: 165–181.

— (1984). *Reproductive Ethics* (Englewood Cliffs, N. J.: Prentice Hall).

Beauchamp, Tom, ed. (1996). *Intending Death* (Englewood Cliffs, N.J.: Prentice-Hall).

— (1999). 'Competence' in Cutter and Shelp (1999): 49–77.

— (2001). 'Internal and External Standards for Medical Morality', *The Journal of Medicine and Philosophy* 26: 601–619.

Benn, Stanley (1973). 'Abortion, Infanticide and Respect for Persons' in Feinberg (1973): 92–104.

Bennett, Jonathan (1974). 'The Conscience of Huckleberry Finn', *Philosophy* 49: 123–134.

— (1994). 'Whatever the Consequences' in Steinbock and Norcross (1994): 167–191.

— (1995). *The Act Itself* (Oxford: Clarendon Press).

Bernat, James L., Bernard Gert and R. Peter Mogielnicki (1993). 'Patient Refusal of Hydration and Nutrition: An Alternative to Physician Assisted Suicide or Voluntary Euthanasia', *Archives of Internal Medicine* 153: 2723–2728.

Bharucha, Ashok J., Robert A. Pearlman, Anthony L. Back, Judith R. Gordon, Helene Starks and Clarissa Hsu (2003). 'The Pursuit of Physician-Assisted Suicide: Role of Psychiatric Factors', *Journal of Palliative Medicine* 6: 873–883.

Bickenbach, Jerome E. (1998). 'Disability and Life-Ending Decisions' in Battin, *et al.* (1998): 123–132.

Biggar, Nigel (2004). *Aiming to Kill: The Ethics of Suicide and Euthanasia* (London: Darton, Longman and Todd).

Binding, K. and A. Hoche (1920). *Die Freigabe der Vernichtung Lebensunwerten Lebens. Ihr Mass und ihre Form* (Leipzig: Felix Meiner), translated by W. E. Wright, P. G. Derr and R. Solomon as 'Permitting the Destruction of Worthless Life: Its Extent and Its Form', *Issues in Law and Medicine 8* (1992): 231–265.

Blustein, Jeffrey (1991). *Care and Commitment: Taking the Personal Point of View* (New York: Oxford University Press).

— (1993). 'Doing What the Patient Orders: Maintaining Integrity in the Doctor-Patient Relationship', *Bioethics* 7: 289–314.

Botros, Sophie (1999). 'An Error About the Doctrine of Double Effect', *Philosophy* 74: 71–83.

Boyd, K. (2002). 'The Law, Death and Medical Ethics: Mrs Pretty and Ms B', *Journal of Medical Ethics* 28: 211–212.

Boyle, Joseph (1989). 'Sanctity of Life and Suicide: Tensions and Developments Within Common Morality' in Baruch Brody, ed., *Suicide and Euthanasia: Historical and Contemporary Themes* (Dordrecht: Kluwer, 1989): 221–250.

— (1991). 'Who Is Entitled to Double Effect?', *The Journal of Medicine and Philosophy* 16: 475–494.

Bradley, Ben (2004). 'When Is Death Bad for the One Who Dies?', *Nous* 38: 1–28.

Bratman, Michael (1987). *Intention, Plans and Practical Reason* (Cambridge, Mass.: Harvard University Press).

British Medical Association (2006). 'End of Life Decisions', URL=<http://web.bma.org.uk/ap.nsf/Content/Hubendoflifeissues>.

Brock, Dan (1987). 'Informed Consent' in Tom Regan and Donald VanDeVeer, eds., *Health Care Ethics* (Philadelphia: Temple University Press, 1987): 98–126.

— (1989). 'Children's Competence for Health Care Decisionmaking' in Loretta M. Kopelman and John C. Moskop, eds., *Children and Health Care: Moral and Social Issues* (Dordrecht: Kluwer, 1989): 181–212.

— (1991). 'Decisionmaking Competence and Risk – Comments on Wicclair', *Bioethics* 5: 105–112.

— (1993a). 'Justice and the Severely Demented Elderly' in Brock, *Life and Death: Philosophical Essays in Biomedical Ethics* (New York: Cambridge University Press, 1993): 356–387.

— (1993b). 'Quality of Life Measures in Health Care and Medical Ethics' in Nussbaum and Sen (1993): 95–132.

— (1993c). 'Voluntary Active Euthanasia', *Hastings Center Report* 22, no. 2: 10–22.

— (1998). 'Commentary', *Philosophy, Psychiatry and Psychology* 5: 251–253.

— (1999). 'A Critique of Three Objections to Physician-Assisted Suicide', *Ethics* 109: 519–547.

Brody, Baruch and Amir Halevy (1995). 'Is Futility a Futile Concept?', *The Journal of Medicine and Philosophy* 20: 123–144.

Broome, John (2004). *Weighing Lives* (Oxford: Oxford University Press).

Buchanan, Allen (1996). 'Intending Death: The Structure of the Problem and Proposed Solutions' in Beauchamp (1996): 23–41.

— and Dan Brock (1989). *Deciding for Others: The Ethics of Surrogate Decision Making* (Cambridge: Cambridge University Press).

Buckle, Stephen (1990). 'Biological Processes and Moral Events' in Peter Singer, Helga Kuhse, Stephen Buckle, Karen Dawson and Pascal Kasimba, eds., *Embryo Experimentation* (Cambridge: Cambridge University Press, 1990): 195–201.

Buller, Tom (2001). 'Competence and Risk-Relativity', *Bioethics* 15: 93–109.

Burgess, J. A. (1993). 'The Great Slippery Slope Argument', *Journal of Medical Ethics* 19: 169–174.

Burgess, Sally and Keith Hawton (1998). 'Suicide, Euthanasia, and the Psychiatrist', *Philosophy, Psychiatry and Psychology* 5: 113–126.

— (1998). 'Commentary', *Philosophy, Psychiatry and Psychology* 5: 255–258.

Burleigh, Michael (1994). *Death and Deliverance: 'Euthanasia' in Germany c.1900–1945* (Cambridge: Cambridge University Press).

Calhoun, Cheshire (1995). 'Standing for Something', *The Journal of Philosophy* 92: 235–260.

Callahan, Sidney (1988). 'The Role of Emotion in Ethical Decisionmaking', *Hastings Center Report* 18, no. 3: 9–14.

Carter, Alan (1997). 'Infanticide and the Right to Life', *Ratio (new series)* 10: 1–9.

Cartwright, Will (1994). 'The Sterilisation of the Mentally Disabled: Competence, the Right to Reproduce and Discrimination' in Grubb (1994): 67–88.

Casey, John (1980). 'Killing and Letting Die: A Reply to Bennett' in Steinbock (1980): 132–138.

Chadwick, Ruth (1998). 'Commentary on Charland', *Philosophy, Psychiatry and Psychology* 5: 83–86.

Chan, Ho Mun (2004). 'Sharing Death and Dying: Advance Directives, Autonomy and the Family', *Bioethics* 18: 87–103.

Charland, Louis C. (1998a). 'Is Mr Spock Mentally Competent?: Competence to Consent and Emotion', *Philosophy, Psychiatry and Psychology* 5: 67–81.

— (1998b). 'Response to the Commentaries', *Philosophy, Psychiatry and Psychology* 5: 93–95.

Childress, James F. (1979). 'Appeals to Conscience', *Ethics* 89: 315–335.

Cohen-Almagor, Raphael (2001). *The Right to Die: An Argument in Ethics, Medicine and Law* (New Brunswick, N.J.: Rutgers University Press).

Commission on the Study of Medical Practice Concerning Euthanasia (1991). *Medical Decisions Concerning the End of Life* (The Hague: SdU) – known widely as 'the Remmelink Report'.

Connell, F. J. (1967). 'Double Effect, Principle of', entry in William J. McDonald (ed.), *The New Catholic Encyclopedia*, vol. 4 (New York: McGraw Hill): 1020–1022.

Cosic, Miriam (2003). *The Right to Die: An Examination of the Euthanasia Debate* (Sydney: New Holland Publishers).

Council on Ethical and Judicial Affairs, American Medical Association (1999). 'Medical Futility in End-of-Life Care', *Journal of the American Medical Association* 281: 937–941.

Crisp, Roger (1994). 'Quality of Life and Health Care' in Fulford, *et al.* (1994): 171–183.

Cullmann, Oscar (1958). *Immortality of the Soul or Resurrection of the Dead? The Witness of the New Testament* (London: Epworth Press).

Culver, Charles and Bernard Gert (1982). *Philosophy in Medicine: Conceptual and Ethical Issues in Medicine and Psychiatry* (New York: Oxford University Press).

— (1990). 'The Inadequacy of Incompetence', *The Milbank Memorial Fund Quarterly* 68: 619–643.

Curtis, J. Randall, David R. Park, Melissa R. Krone and Robert A. Pearlman (1995). 'Use of the Medical Futility Rationale in Do-Not-Attempt-Resuscitation Orders', *Journal of the American Medical Association* 273: 124–128.

Cutter, Mary Ann Gardell and Earl E. Shelp, eds. (1999). *Competency: A Study of Informal Determinations in Primary Care* (Dordrecht: Kluwer).

Daar, Judith F. (1993). 'A Clash at the Bedside: Patient Autonomy v. A Physician's Professional Conscience', *Hastings Law Journal* 44: 1241–1289.

Dal Pont, G. E. (2001). *Lawyers' Professional Responsibility in Australia and New Zealand* (Sydney: LBC Information Services, 2nd edn).

Damasio, Antonio (1994). *Descartes' Error* (New York: Putnam).

Darwall, Stephen (1986). 'Agent-centered Restrictions from the Inside Out', *Philosophical Studies* 50: 291–319.

Davis, John K. (2002). 'The Concept of Precedent Autonomy', *Bioethics* 16: 114–133.

— (2004). 'Conscientious Refusal and a Doctor's Right to Quit', *The Journal of Medicine and Philosophy* 29: 75–91.

Davis, Nancy Ann (1984). 'The Doctrine of Double Effect: Problems of Interpretation', *Pacific Philosophical Quarterly* 65: 107–123.

— (1996). 'The Right to Refuse Treatment' in Beauchamp (1996): 109–130.

de Sousa, Ronald (1987). *The Rationality of Emotion* (Cambridge, Mass.: MIT Press).

DeGrazia, David (1999). 'Advance Directives, Dementia, and the "Someone Else Problem"', *Bioethics* 13: 373–391.

— (2003). 'Identity, Killing, and the Boundaries of Our Existence', *Philosophy and Public Affairs* 31: 413–442.

— (2005). *Human Identity and Bioethics* (New York: Cambridge University Press).

Demarco, Joseph P. (2002). 'Competence and Paternalism', *Bioethics* 16: 231–245.

Devine, Philip E. (2000). 'Capital Punishment and the Sanctity of Life', *Midwest Studies in Philosophy* 24: 229–243.

Dinello, Daniel (1994). 'On Killing and Letting Die' in Steinbock and Norcross (1994): 192–196.

Donagan, Alan (1977). *The Theory of Morality* (Chicago: Chicago University Press).

Doukas, David J. and Laurence B. McCullough (1991). 'The Values History: The Evaluation of the Patient's Values and Advance Directives', *Journal of Family Practice* 32: 145–153.

Dresser, Rebecca (1995). 'Dworkin on Dementia: Elegant Theory, Questionable Policy', *Hastings Center Report* 25, no. 6: 32–38.

— (1998). 'Commentary', *Philosophy, Psychiatry and Psychology* 5: 247–250.

DuBose, R. A. and C. B. Berde (1997). 'Respiratory Effects of Opioids', *IASP Newsletter*, July/August: 3–5.

Dundas, P. (1992). *The Jains* (London: Routledge).

Dworkin, Gerald (1987). 'Intention, Foreseeability and Responsibility' in Ferdinand Schoeman, ed., *Responsibility, Character and the Emotions* (New York: Cambridge University Press): 338–354.

— (1988). *The Theory and Practice of Autonomy* (Cambridge: Cambridge University Press).

—, R. G. Frey and Sissela Bok (1998). *Euthanasia and Physician-Assisted Suicide: For and Against* (Cambridge: Cambridge University Press).

Dworkin, Ronald (1993). *Life's Dominion: An Argument About Abortion, Euthanasia, and Individual Freedom* (New York: Alfred A. Knopf).

—, Thomas Nagel, Robert Nozick, John Rawls, Thomas Scanlon and Judith Jarvis Thomson (1997). 'Assisted Suicide: The Philosophers' Brief', *The New York Review of Books*, March 27: 41–47.

Dyck, Arthur (2002). *Life's Worth: The Case Against Assisted Suicide* (Grand Rapids, Mich.: William B. Eerdmans Publishing Company).

Eastman, Nigel (1998). 'Commentary', *Philosophy, Psychiatry and Psychology* 5: 259–261.

Elliott, Carl (1998). 'Commentary on Charland', *Philosophy, Psychiatry and Psychology* 5: 87–88.

Emanuel, Ezekiel J. (1999). 'What Is the Great Benefit of Legalizing Euthanasia or Physician-Assisted Suicide?', *Ethics* 109: 629–642.

— and Margaret P. Battin (1998). 'What Are the Potential Cost Savings From Legalising Physician-Assisted Suicide?', *The New England Journal of Medicine* 339: 167–172.

Emergency Cardiac Care Committee and Subcommittees of the American Heart Association (1992). 'Guidelines for Cardiopulmonary Resuscitation and Emergency Cardiac Care', *Journal of the American Medical Association* 268: 2282–2288.

Epictetus. *Discourses*.

Erde, Edmund L. (1999). 'Breaking Up the Shell Game of Consequentialism: Incompetence – Concept and Ethics' in Cutter and Shelp (1999): 237–252.

Faden, Ruth and Tom Beauchamp, in collaboration with Nancy M. P. King (1986). *A History and Theory of Informed Consent* (New York: Oxford University Press).

Feinberg, Joel, ed. (1973). *The Problem of Abortion* (Belmont, Calif: Wadsworth).

— (1984). *Harm to Others* (New York: Oxford University Press).

— (1986). *Harm to Self* (New York: Oxford University Press).

— (1991). 'Overlooking the Merits of the Individual Case: An Unpromising Approach to the Right to Die', *Ratio Juris* 4: 131–151.

Feldman, Fred (1991). 'Some Puzzles About the Evil of Death', *The Philosophical Review* 100: 205–227.

— (1992). *Confrontations with the Reaper: A Philosophical Study of the Nature and Value of Death* (New York: Oxford University Press).

Fenigsen, Richard (2004). 'Dutch Euthanasia: The New Government Ordered Survey', *Issues in Law and Medicine* 20: 73–79.

Fine, Robert L. and Thomas Wm. Mayo (2003). 'Resolution of Futility by Due Process: Early Experience with the Texas Advance Directives Act', *Annals of Internal Medicine* 138: 743–746.

Finnis, John (1991). 'Intention and Side-effects' in R. G. Frey and Christopher W. Morris, eds., *Liability and Responsibility* (Cambridge: Cambridge University Press): 32–64.

— (1993). '*Bland*: Crossing the Rubicon?', *The Law Quarterly Review* 109: 329–337.

— (1994). '"Living Will" Legislation' in Gormally (1994): 167–176.

— (1995). 'A Philosophical Case Against Euthanasia' in Keown (1995a): 23–35.

Firlik, Andrew (1991). 'Margo's Logo', *Journal of the American Medical Association* 265: 201.

Fischer, John Martin, ed. (1993). *The Metaphysics of Death* (Stanford, Calif.: Stanford University Press).

Fisher, Anthony (1995). 'Theological Aspects of Euthanasia' in Keown (1995a): 315–332.

Foley, Kathleen and Herbert Hendin, eds. (2002). *The Case Against Assisted Suicide: For the Right to End-of-Life Care* (Baltimore: The Johns Hopkins University Press).

Foot, Philippa (1967). 'The Problem of Abortion and the Doctrine of Double Effect', *The Oxford Review* 5: 5–15.

— (1977). 'Euthanasia', *Philosophy and Public Affairs* 6: 85–112.

— (1994). 'Killing and Letting Die' in Steinbock and Norcross (1994): 280–289.

Francis, Leslie Pickering (1993). 'Advance Directives for Voluntary Euthanasia: A Volatile Combination?', *The Journal of Medicine and Philosophy* 18: 297–322.

Frankena, William K. (1976). 'The Ethics of Respect for Life' in Barker (1976): 24–62.

Freedman, Monroe H. (1988). 'Professional Responsibility of the Criminal Defense Lawyer: The Three Hardest Questions' in Joan C. Callahan, ed., *Ethical Issues in Professional Life* (New York: Oxford University Press): 51–58.

Frey, R. G. (1996). 'Medicine, Animal Experimentation, and the Moral Problem of Unfortunate Humans', *Social Philosophy and Policy* 13: 181–211.

Fulford K. W. M., Grant R. Gillett and Janet Martin Soskice, eds. (1994). *Medicine and Moral Reasoning* (Cambridge: Cambridge University Press).

Gampel, Eric (2006). 'Does Professional Autonomy Protect Medical Futility Judgments?', *Bioethics* 20: 92–104.

Ganzini, Linda (2004). 'The Oregon Experience' in Quill and Battin (2004): 165–183.

—, Heide D. Nelson, Terri A. Schmidt, Dale F. Kraemer, Molly A. Delorit and Melinda A. Lee (2000). 'Physicians' Experiences with the Oregon Death with Dignity Act', *The New England Journal of Medicine* 342: 557–561.

—, Steven K. Dobscha, Ronald T. Heintz and Nancy Press (2003a). 'Oregon Physicians' Perceptions of Patients Who Request Assisted Suicide and Their Families', *Journal of Palliative Medicine* 6: 381–390.

—, Elizabeth R. Goy, Lois L. Miller, Theresa A. Harvath, Ann Jackson and Molly A. Delorit (2003b). 'Nurses' Experiences With Hospice Patients Who Refuse Food and Fluids to Hasten Death', *The New England Journal of Medicine* 349: 359–365.

Gaylin, Willard, Leon Kass, Edmund Pellegrino and Mark Siegler (1988). 'Doctors Must Not Kill', *Journal of the American Medical Association* 259: 2139–2140.

Gert, Bernard, Charles M. Culver and K. Danner Clouser (1997). *Bioethics: A Return to Fundamentals* (New York: Oxford University Press).

Gert, Bernard, Charles M. Culver and K. Danner Clouser (1998). 'An Alternative to Physician-Assisted Suicide: Conceptual and Moral Analysis' in Battin, *et al.* (1998): 182–202.

Gilbert, Daniel T. and Timothy D. Wilson (2000). 'Miswanting' in Joseph P. Forgas, ed., *Feeling and Thinking: The Role of Affect in Social Cognition* (New York: Cambridge University Press): 178–197.

Glover, Jonathan (1975). 'It Makes No Difference Whether or Not I Do It', *The Aristotelian Society: Supplementary Volume* 49: 171–190.

— (1977). *Causing Death and Saving Lives* (Harmondsworth: Penguin Books).

Goldie, Peter (2000). *The Emotions: A Philosophical Exploration* (Oxford: Clarendon Press).

Gormally, Luke (1993). 'Definitions of Personhood: Implications for the Care of PVS Patients', *Catholic Medical Quarterly* 44: 7–12.

— ed. (1994). *Euthanasia, Clinical Practice and the Law* (London: The Linacre Centre for Health Care Ethics).

— (1995). 'Walton, Davies, Boyd and the Legalisation of Euthanasia' in Keown (1995a): 113–140.

Govier, Trudy (1982). 'What's Wrong with Slippery Slope Arguments?', *Canadian Journal of Philosophy* 12: 303–316.

Greenspan, Patricia (1988). *Emotions and Reasons* (New York: Routledge).

— (2000). 'Emotional Strategies and Rationality', *Ethics* 110: 469–487.

Griener, Glenn G. (1995). 'The Physician's Authority to Withhold Futile Treatment', *The Journal of Medicine and Philosophy* 20: 207–224.

Griffin, James (1986). *Well-Being* (Oxford: Clarendon Press).

— (1993). 'Reply' in Nussbaum and Sen (1993): 133–139.

Griffiths, John (1998). 'The Slippery Slope: Are the Dutch Sliding Down or Are They Clambering Up?' in Thomasma, *et al.* (1998): 93–104.

—, Alex Bood and Heleen Wyers (1998). *Euthanasia and the Law in The Netherlands* (Amsterdam: Amsterdam University Press).

Grisso, T. and P. S. Appelbaum (1998). *Assessing Competence to Consent to Treatment: A Guide for Physicians and Other Health Professionals* (New York: Oxford University Press).

Groenewoud, Johanna H., Agnes van der Heide, Bregje D. Onwuteaka-Philipsen, Dick L. Willems, Paul J. van der Maas and Gerrit van der Wal (2000). 'Clinical Problems with the Performance of Euthanasia and Physician-Assisted Suicide in The Netherlands', *The New England Journal of Medicine* 342: 551–556.

Grubb, Andrew, ed. (1994). *Decision-Making and Problems of Incompetence* (Chichester: John Wiley and Sons).

Hallenbeck J. (2000). 'Terminal Sedation: Ethical Implications in Different Situations', *Journal of Palliative Medicine* 3: 313–320.

Hampton, Jean (1988). 'Forgiveness, Resentment and Hatred' in Jeffrie Murphy and Jean Hampton, *Forgiveness and Mercy* (Cambridge: Cambridge University Press).

Hanson M. J. and D. Callahan, eds. (1999). *The Goals of Medicine: The Forgotten Issue in Health Care* (Washington, D.C.: Georgetown University Press).

Hardwig, John (1997). 'Is There a Duty to Die?', *Hastings Center Report* 27, no. 2: 34–42.

Harris, John (1980). *Violence and Responsibility* (London: Routledge and Kegan Paul).

— (1987). 'QALYfying the Value of Life', *Journal of Medical Ethics* 13: 117–123.

— (2000). 'The Doctrine of Triple Effect and Why a Rational Agent Need Not Intend The Means to His End', *The Aristotelian Society: Supplementary Volume* 74: 41–57.

Harvey, Martin (2006). 'Advance Directives and the Severely Demented', *The Journal of Medicine and Philosophy* 31: 47–64.

Hendin, Herbert (1998). *Seduced by Death: Doctors, Patients and the Dutch Cure* (New York: W.W. Norton).

Hill, Thomas E. Jr. (1991). 'Self-Regarding Suicide: A Modified Kantian View' in Hill, ed., *Autonomy and Self-Respect* (Cambridge: Cambridge University Press): 85–103.

— (1998). 'Four Conceptions of Conscience' in Ian Shapiro and Robert Merrihew Adams, eds., *Integrity and Conscience: Nomos XL* (New York: New York University Press): 13–52.

Homer. *The Odyssey*.

Hope, Tony, David Sprigings and Roger Crisp (1993). '"Not Clinically Indicated": Patients' Interests or Resource Allocation', *British Medical Journal* 306: 379–381.

Horowitz, Tamara (1998). 'Philosophical Intuitions and Psychological Theory', *Ethics* 108: 367–385.

House of Lords (1994). *Report of the Select Committee on Medical Ethics, vol. 1* (London: HMSO).

Hughes, Julian C. (2001). 'Views of the Person with Dementia', *Journal of Medical Ethics* 27: 86–91.

Humber, James M. and Robert F. Almeder, eds. (2000). *Is There a Duty to Die?* (Totowa, N.J.: Humana Press).

Hume, David (1770). 'On Suicide'.

Humphry, Derek (1981). *Let Me Die Before I Wake: Hemlock's Book of Self-Deliverance for the Dying* (Los Angeles: The Hemlock Society).

— (1996). *Final Exit: The Practicalities of Self-Deliverance and Assisted Suicide for the Dying* (New York: Dell, 2nd edn).

Humphry, Derek and Ann Wickett (1978). *Jean's Way* (London: Fontana).

Jackson, Emily (2004). 'Whose Death Is It Anyway?: Euthanasia and the Medical Profession', *Current Legal Problems* 57: 414–442.

Jackson, Jennifer (1994). 'Determining Incompetence: Problems with the Function Test' in Grubb (1994): 53–65.

Jacobs, Sandra (2003). 'Death by Voluntary Dehydration – What the Caregivers Say', *The New England Journal of Medicine* 349: 325–326.

Jansen, Lynn A. (2004). 'No Safe Harbor: The Principle of Complicity and the Practice of Voluntary Stopping of Eating and Drinking', *The Journal of Medicine and Philosophy* 29: 61–74.

Jaworska, Agnieszka (1999). 'Respecting the Margins of Agency: Alzheimer's Patients and the Capacity to Value', *Philosophy and Public Affairs* 28: 105–138.

Jennett, Bryan (2002). *The Vegetative State: Medical Facts, Ethical and Legal Dilemmas* (Cambridge: Cambridge University Press).

Johnston, Mark (1987). 'Human Beings', *The Journal of Philosophy* 84: 59–83.

Kagan, Shelly (1988). 'The Additive Fallacy', *Ethics* 99: 5–31.

— (1989). *The Limits of Morality* (Oxford: Clarendon Press).

— (1998). *Normative Ethics* (Boulder, Colorado: Westview Press).

Kahneman, Daniel, Paul Slovic and Amos Tversky, eds. (1982). *Judgment Under Uncertainty: Heuristics and Biases* (New York: Cambridge University Press).

Kamisar, Yale (1958). 'Some Non-Religious Views Against Proposed "Mercy-Killing" Legislation', *Minnesota Law Review* 42: 969–1042.

— (1991). 'When is There a Constitutional "Right to Die"? When is There No Constitutional "Right to Live"?', *Georgia Law Review* 25: 1203–1242.

— (1995). 'Against Assisted Suicide – Even a Very Limited Form', *University of Detroit Mercy Law Review* 72: 735–769.

Kamm, Frances Myrna (1991). 'The Doctrine of Double Effect: Reflections on Theoretical and Practical Issues', *The Journal of Medicine and Philosophy* 16: 571–585.

— (1996). *Morality, Mortality, vol. II: Rights, Duties and Status* (New York: Oxford University Press).

— (1998). 'Physician-Assisted Suicide, Euthanasia, and Intending Death' in Battin, et al. (1998): 26–49.

— (1999). 'Physician-Assisted Suicide, the Doctrine of Double Effect and the Ground of Value', *Ethics* 109: 586–605.

— (2000a). 'Nonconsequentialism' in Hugh La Follette, ed., *The Blackwell Guide to Ethical Theory* (Oxford: Blackwell): 205–226.

— (2000b). 'The Doctrine of Triple Effect and Why a Rational Agent Need Not Intend the Means to His End', *The Aristotelian Society: Supplementary Volume* 74: 21–39.

Kant, Immanuel (1780). *Lectures on Ethics*.

— (1785). *Foundations of the Metaphysics of Morals*.

Kass, Leon (1989). 'Neither For Love Nor Money: Why Doctors Must Not Kill', *The Public Interest* 94: 25–46.

Kennedy, Ian and Andrew Grubb (1994). *Medical Law: Text With Materials* (London: Butterworths, 2nd edn).

Kenny, Anthony (1983). *Thomas More* (Oxford: Oxford University Press).

Keown, John (1993). 'Hard Case, Bad Law, "New" Ethics', *Cambridge Law Journal* 52: 209–212.

— (1994a). 'Some Reflections on Euthanasia in The Netherlands' in Gormally (1994): 193–218.

— (1994b). 'Further Reflections on Euthanasia in The Netherlands in the Light of the Remmelink Report and the van der Maas Survey' in Gormally (1994): 219–240.

— ed. (1995a). *Euthanasia Examined: Ethical, Clinical and Legal Perspectives* (Cambridge: Cambridge University Press).

— (1995b). 'Euthanasia in The Netherlands: Sliding Down the Slippery Slope?' in Keown (1995a): 261–296.

— (2002). *Euthanasia, Ethics and Public Policy: An Argument Against Legalisation* (Cambridge: Cambridge University Press).

Kimsma, Gerrit K. and Evert van Leeuwen (2004). 'Assisted Death in The Netherlands: Physicians at the Bedside When Help Is Requested' in Quill and Battin (2004): 221–241.

King, Nancy M. P. (1991). *Making Sense of Advance Directives* (Dordrecht: Kluwer).

Kirschner, Kristi L., Carol J. Gill and Christine K. Cassel (1997). 'Physician-Assisted Death in the Context of Disability' in Weir (1997): 155–166.

Kittay, Eva Feder (2005). 'At the Margins of Moral Personhood', *Ethics* 116: 100–131.

Kitcher, Philip (2002). 'Creating Perfect People' in Justine Burley and John Harris, eds., *A Companion to Genethics* (Oxford: Blackwell): 229–242.

Kleinig, John (1991). *Valuing Life* (Princeton, N.J.: Princeton University Press).

Korsgaard, Christine (1983). 'Two Distinctions in Goodness', *The Philosophical Review* 92: 169–195.

— (1989). 'Personal Identity and the Unity of Agency: A Kantian Response to Parfit', *Philosophy and Public Affairs* 18: 101–132.

Kuflik, Arthur (1979). 'Morality and Compromise' in J. R. Pennock and J. Chapman, eds., *Compromise in Ethics, Law and Politics: Nomos XXI* (New York: New York University Press): 38–65.

Kuhse, Helga (1987). *The Sanctity-of-Life Doctrine in Medicine: A Critique* (Oxford: Clarendon Press).

— (1996). 'Sanctity-of-Life, Voluntary Euthanasia and the Dutch Experience: Some Implications for Public Policy' in Paul Bayertz, ed., *Sanctity of Life and Human Dignity* (Dordrecht: Kluwer): 19–37.

— (1999). 'Some Reflections on the Problem of Advance Directives, Personhood, and Personal Identity', *Kennedy Institute of Ethics Journal* 9: 347–364.

— and Peter Singer (1985). *Should the Baby Live?: The Problem of Handicapped Infants* (Oxford: Oxford University Press).

—, Peter Singer, Peter Baume, Malcolm Clark and Maurice Rickard (1997). 'End-of-Life Decisions in Australian Medical Practice', *The Medical Journal of Australia* 166: 191–196.

Lanham, David (1993). *Taming Death by Law* (Melbourne: Longman Professional Publishing).

Law Reform Commission of Canada (1983). *Report No. 20: Euthanasia, Aiding Suicide and Cessation of Treatment* (Ottawa: Law Reform Commission of Canada).

Lee, Melinda A., Heidi D. Nelson, Virginia P. Tilden, Linda Ganzini, Terri A. Schmidt and Susan W. Tolle (1996). 'Legalizing Assisted Suicide – Views of Physicians in Oregon', *The New England Journal of Medicine* 334: 310–315.

Lemos, Noah M. (1994). *Intrinsic Value: Concept and Warrant* (Cambridge: Cambridge University Press).

Lidz, Charles W., Alan Meisel, Eviatur Zerubavel, Mary Carter, Regina M. Sestak and Loren H. Roth, eds. (1984). *Informed Consent: A Study of Decision-making in Psychiatry* (New York: The Guilford Press).

Lifton, Robert Jay (1986). *The Nazi Doctors: Medical Killing and Psychology* (New York: Basic Books).

Locke, John (1706). *An Essay Concerning Human Understanding.*

Lockwood, Michael (1988a). 'Quality of Life and Resource Allocation', *Philosophy (Supplementary Volume)* 23: 33–55.

— (1988b). 'Hare on Potentiality: A Rejoinder', *Bioethics* 2: 343–352.

Mack, Eric (1980). 'Bad Samaritanism and the Causation of Harm', *Philosophy and Public Affairs* 9: 230–259.

Magnusson, Roger, with Peter H. Ballis (2002). *Angels of Death: Exploring the Euthanasia Underground* (Melbourne: Melbourne University Press).

Malm, Heidi (1992). 'In Defense of the Contrast Strategy' in John Martin Fischer and Mark Ravizza, eds., *Ethics: Problems and Principles* (New York: Harcourt Brace Jovanovich): 272–277.

Mangan, Joseph T. (1949). 'An Historical Analysis of the Principle of Double Effect', *Theological Studies* 10: 41–61.

— (1991). 'Reply to Joseph Boyle's "Who Is Entitled to Double Effect?"', *The Journal of Medicine and Philosophy* 16: 511–514.

Marquis, Don (1998). 'The Weakness of the Case for Legalizing Physician-Assisted Suicide' in Battin, *et al.* (1998): 267–278.

Mason, J. K., R. A. McCall Smith and G. T. Laurie (2002). *Law and Medical Ethics* (London: Butterworths, 6th edn).

Matthews, Merrill Jr. (1998). 'Would Physician-Assisted Suicide Save the Health-care System Money?' in Battin, *et al.* (1998): 312–322.

Mayo, David J. and Martin Gunderson (2002). 'Vitalism Revitalized: Vulnerable Populations, Prejudice, and Physician-Assisted Death', *Hastings Center Report* 32, no. 4: 14–21.

McFall, Lynne (1987). 'Integrity', *Ethics* 98: 5–20.

McHaffie, Hazel E., Ian A. Laing, Michael Parker and John McMillan (2001). 'Deciding for Imperilled Newborns: Medical Authority or Parental Autonomy?', *Journal of Medical Ethics* 27: 104–109.

McIntyre, Alison (2001). 'Doing Away With Double Effect', *Ethics* 111: 219–255.

McKie, John, Jeff Richardson, Peter Singer and Helga Kuhse (1998). *The Allocation of Health Care Resources: An Evaluation of the 'QALY' Approach* (Aldershot: Ashgate).

McLean, Sheila A. M. (2006). 'From *Bland* to *Burke*: The Law and Politics of Assisted Nutrition and Hydration' in McLean, ed., *First Do No Harm: Law, Ethics and Healthcare* (Aldershot: Ashgate).

McMahan, Jeff (1988). 'Death and the Value of Life', *Ethics* 99: 32–61.

— (1993). 'Killing, Letting Die and Withdrawing Aid', *Ethics* 103: 250–279.

— (1998). 'A Challenge to Common Sense Morality: A Review Essay of Jonathan Bennett, *The Act Itself*', *Ethics* 108: 394–418.

— (2002). *The Ethics of Killing: Problems at the Margins of Life* (New York: Oxford University Press).

Menzel, Paul T. (1979). 'Are Killing and Letting Die Morally Different in Medical Contexts?', *The Journal of Medicine and Philosophy* 4: 269–293.

Miles, Steven (1991a). 'Informed Demand for "Non-Beneficial" Medical Treatment', *The New England Journal of Medicine* 325: 512–515.

— (1991b). 'Legal Procedures in *Wanglie*: A Two-Step Not a Side-Step', *Journal of Clinical Ethics* 2: 285–286.

— (1992). 'Medical Futility', *Law, Medicine and Health Care* 20: 310–315.

— (2004). *The Hippocratic Oath and the Ethics of Medicine* (New York: Oxford University Press).

Miller, Franklin G. and Howard Brody (1995). 'Professional Integrity and Physician-Assisted Death', *Hastings Center Report* 25, no. 3: 8–17.

— and Howard Brody (2001). 'The Internal Morality of Medicine: An Evolutionary Perspective', *The Journal of Medicine and Philosophy* 26: 581–599.

— and Diane E. Meier (1998). 'Voluntary Death: A Comparison of Terminal Dehydration and Physician-Assisted Suicide', *Annals of Internal Medicine* 128: 559–562.

Miller, Franklin G., Timothy E. Quill, Howard Brody, John C. Fletcher, Lawrence O. Gostin and Diane E. Meier (1994). 'Requesting Physician-Assisted Death', *The New England Journal of Medicine* 331: 119–123.

Mojica, S. L. and D. S. Murrell (1991). 'The Right to Choose – When Should Death Be In the Individual's Hands?', *Whittier Law Review* 12: 471–504.

Moore, G. E. (1903). *Principia Ethica* (New York: Cambridge University Press).

— (1922). *Philosophical Studies* (London: Routledge and Kegan Paul).

More, Thomas (1516). *Utopia*, Edward Surtz and J. H. Hexter, eds., *The Complete Works of Thomas More, vol. 4* (New Haven and London: Yale University Press, 1965).

— (1535). *A Dialogue of Comfort: Against Tribulation*, eds., Louis L. Martz and Frank Manley, *The Complete Works of Thomas More, vol. 12* (New Haven and London: Yale University Press, 1976).

Nagel, Thomas (1970). 'Death', *Nous* 4: 73–80.

New York State Task Force on Life and the Law (1994). *When Death is Sought: Assisted Suicide and Euthanasia in the Medical Context* (Albany, N.Y.: New York State Task Force on Life and the Law).

Newton, M. J. (1999). 'Precedent Autonomy: Life Sustaining Intervention and the Demented Patient', *Cambridge Quarterly of Healthcare Ethics* 8: 189–199.

Nitschke, Philip and Fiona Stewart (2005). *Killing Me Softly* (Melbourne: Penguin Books).

Norcross, Alastair (2003). 'Killing and Letting Die' in R. G. Frey and Christopher Wellman, eds., *A Companion to Applied Ethics* (Malden, Mass.: Blackwell): 451–463.

Nozick, Robert (1981). *Philosophical Explanations* (Oxford: Clarendon Press).

Nussbaum, Martha and Amartya Sen, eds. (1993). *The Quality of Life* (Oxford: Clarendon Press).

Nutton, Vivian (2004). *Ancient Medicine* (London: Routledge).

Oakley, Justin and Dean Cocking (2001). *Virtue Ethics and Professional Roles* (Cambridge: Cambridge University Press).

O'Neill, Onora (2000). 'Agency and Autonomy' in O'Neill, *Bounds of Justice* (Cambridge: Cambridge University Press): 29–49.

Oddie, Graham (1997). 'Killing and Letting Die: Bare Differences and Clear Differences', *Philosophical Studies* 88: 267–287.

— (1998). 'The Moral Case for Legalisation of Voluntary Euthanasia', *Victoria University of Wellington Law Review* 28: 207–224.

Olson, Eric (1997). *The Human Animal: Personal Identity Without Psychology* (New York: Oxford University Press).

Onwuteaka-Philipsen, Bregje D., Agnes van der Heide, D. Koper, I. Keij-Deerenberg, J. A. C. Rietjens, M. L. Rurup, A. M. Vrakking, J. J. Georges, M. T. Muller, Gerrit van der Wal and Paul J. van der Maas (2003). 'Euthanasia and other end-of-life decisions in The Netherlands in 1990, 1995 and 2001', *The Lancet* 362: 395–399.

Orentlicher, David (1998). 'The Supreme Court and Terminal Sedation: An Ethically Inferior Alternative to Physician-Assisted Suicide' in Battin, *et al.* (1998): 301–311.

Otlowski, Margaret (1997). *Voluntary Euthanasia and the Common Law* (Oxford: Clarendon Press).

Parfit, Derek (1984). *Reasons and Persons* (Oxford: Clarendon Press).

— (1986). 'Comments', *Ethics* 96: 832–872.

Pearlman, Robert A., Clarissa Hsu, Helene Starks, Anthony L. Back, Judith R. Gordon, Ashok J. Bharucha, Barbara A. Koenig and Margaret P. Battin (2005). 'Motivations for Physician-Assisted Suicide', *Journal of General Internal Medicine* 20: 234–239.

Pellegrino, Edmund (1999). 'The Goals and Ends of Medicine: How Are They to be Defined?' in Hanson and Callahan (1999): 55–68.

— (2001a). 'Physician-Assisted Suicide and Euthanasia: Rebuttals of Rebuttals – the Moral Prohibition Remains', *The Journal of Medicine and Philosophy* 26: 93–100.

— (2001b). 'The Internal Morality of Clinical Medicine: A Paradigm for the Ethics of the Helping and Healing Professions', *The Journal of Medicine and Philosophy* 26: 559–579.

— and David Thomasma (1988). *For the Patient's Good: The Restoration of Beneficence in Health Care* (New York: Oxford University Press).

Plato. *Phaedo.*

Post, Stephen G. (1995). *The Moral Challenge of Alzheimer Disease* (Baltimore: The Johns Hopkins University Press).

Prado, C. G. (1990). *The Last Choice: Preemptive Suicide in Advanced Age* (Westport, Conn.: Greenwood Press).

President's Commission for the Study of Ethical Problems in Medicine and Biomedical and Biobehavioral Research (1983). *Deciding to Forgo Life-Sustaining Treatment: Ethical, Medical and Legal Issues* (Washington, D.C.: Government Printing Office).

Price, David (1997). 'Euthanasia, Pain Relief and Double Effect', *Legal Studies* 17: 323–342.

Provoost, Veerle, Filip Cools, Freddy Mortier, Johan Bilsen, Jose Ramet, Yvan Vandenplas and Luc Deliens (2005). 'Medical end-of-life decisions in neonates and infants in Flanders', *The Lancet* 365: 1315–1320.

Quill, Timothy E. (1991). 'Death and Dignity: A Case of Individualized Decision Making', *The New England Journal of Medicine* 324: 691–694.

— (2004). 'Dying and Decision Making – Evolution of End-of-Life Options', *The New England Journal of Medicine* 350: 2029–2032.

—, Christine Cassel and Diane E. Meier (1992). 'Care of the Hopelessly Ill: Proposed Clinical Criteria for Physician-Assisted Suicide', *The New England Journal of Medicine* 327: 1380–1384.

—, B. Lo and Dan Brock (1997). 'Palliative Treatments of Last Resort: A Comparison of Voluntarily Stopping Eating and Drinking, Terminal Sedation, Physician-Assisted Suicide, and Voluntary Active Euthanasia', *Journal of the American Medical Association* 278: 2099–2104.

—, Rebecca Dresser and Dan Brock (1997). 'The Rule of Double Effect: A Critique of Its Role in End-of-Life Decision Making', *The New England Journal of Medicine* 337: 1768–1771.

— and I. R. Byock (2000). 'Responding to Intractable Terminal Suffering: The Role of Terminal Sedation and Voluntary Refusal of Food and Fluids', *Annals of Internal Medicine* 132: 408–414.

— and Margaret P. Battin, eds. (2004). *Physician-Assisted Dying: The Case for Palliative Care and Patient Choice* (Baltimore: The Johns Hopkins University Press).

Quinn, Warren (1989a). 'Actions, Intentions and Consequences: The Doctrine of Doing and Allowing', *The Philosophical Review* 98: 287–312.

— (1989b). 'Actions, Intentions, and Consequences: The Doctrine of Double Effect', *Philosophy and Public Affairs* 18: 334–351.

Rachels, James (1983). 'The Sanctity of Life' in J. M. Humber, ed., *Biomedical Ethics Reviews* (Clifton, N.J.: Humana Press): 29–42.

— (1986). *The End of Life: Euthanasia and Morality* (Oxford: Oxford University Press).

— (1994). 'Active and Passive Euthanasia' in Steinbock and Norcross (1994): 112–119.

Rakowski, Eric (1994). 'Review of Ronald Dworkin, *Life's Dominion: An Argument About Abortion, Euthanasia, and Individual Freedom*', *Yale Law Journal* 103: 2049–2118.

— (1998). 'Review of Frances Myrna Kamm, *Morality, Mortality, vol. II: Rights, Duties and Status*', *Mind* 107: 492–498.

Rhoden, Nancy K. (1990). 'The Limits of Legal Objectivity', *North Carolina Law Review* 68: 856–857.

Richards, Norvin (1992). 'Surrogate Consent', *Public Affairs Quarterly* 6: 227–243.

Rietjens, Judith A. C., Agnes van der Heide, Astrid M. Vrakking and Bregje D. Onwuteaka-Philipsen (2004). 'Physician Reports of Terminal Sedation Without Hydration or Nutrition for Patients Nearing Death in The Netherlands', *Annals of Internal Medicine* 141: 178–185.

Rodin, David (2002). *War and Self-Defence* (Oxford: Clarendon Press).

Rorty, Amelie Oksenberg (1999). 'Integrity, Political not Psychological' in Alan Montefiore and David Vines, eds., *Integrity in the Public and Private Domains* (London: Routledge): 108–120.

Rosenfeld, Barry (2004). *Assisted Suicide and the Right to Die: The Interface of Social Science, Public Policy and Medical Ethics* (Washington, D.C.: American Psychological Association).

Roth, Loren H., Alan Meisel and Charles W. Lidz (1977). 'Tests of Competency to Consent to Treatment', *American Journal of Psychiatry* 134: 279–284.

Russell, Bruce (1980). 'On the Relative Strictness of Negative and Positive Duties' in Steinbock (1980): 215–231.

Ryan, Cheyney C. (1983). 'Self-Defense, Pacifism and the Possibility of Killing', *Ethics* 93: 508–524.

Savulescu, Julian (1994). 'Rational Desires and the Limitation of Life-Sustaining Treatment', *Bioethics* 8: 191–222.

— and Donna Dickenson (1998a). 'The Time Frame of Preferences, Dispositions, and the Validity of Advance Directives for the Mentally Ill', *Philosophy, Psychiatry and Psychology* 5: 225–246.

— and Donna Dickenson (1998b). 'Response to the Commentaries', *Philosophy, Psychiatry and Psychology* 5: 263–266.

Schauer, Frederick (1985). 'Slippery Slopes', *Harvard Law Review* 99: 361–383.

Schermer, Maartje (2002). *The Different Faces of Autonomy: Patient Autonomy in Ethical Theory and Hospital Practice* (Dordrecht: Kluwer).

Schneiderman, L. J., N. S. Jecker and A. R. Jonsen (1990). 'Medical Futility: Its Meaning and Ethical Implications', *Annals of Internal Medicine* 112: 949–954.

— (1996). 'Medical Futility: A Response to Critiques', *Annals of Internal Medicine* 125: 669–674.

Schweitzer, Albert (1946). *Civilization and Ethics*, translated by C. T. Campion (London: A. and C. Black, 3rd edn).

Seneca. *De Ira.*

— *Epistulae.*

Shils, Edward (1968). 'The Sanctity of Life' in D. H. Labby, ed., *Life or Death: Ethics and Options* (Seattle: University of Washington Press): 2–38.

Sidgwick, Henry (1907). *The Methods of Ethics* (London: Macmillan, 7th edn).

Siegel, Mark C. (1998). 'Lethal Pity: The Oregon Death With Dignity Act, Its Implications for the Disabled, and the Struggle for Equality in an Able-bodied World', *Law and Inequality* 16: 259–288.

Silvers, Anita (1998). 'Protecting the Innocents from Physician-Assisted Suicide: Disability Discrimination and the Duty to Protect Otherwise Vulnerable Groups' in Battin, *et al.* (1998): 133–148.

Singer, Peter A. (1994). 'Disease specific advance directives', *The Lancet* 344: 594–596.

Singer, Peter (1972). 'Famine, Affluence and Morality', *Philosophy and Public Affairs* 1: 229–243.

— (1994). *Rethinking Life and Death: The Collapse of Our Traditional Ethics* (Melbourne: Text Publishing).

— (1995). 'Is the Sanctity of Life Terminally Ill?', *Bioethics* 9: 327–343.

Skene, Loane (1998). *Law and Medical Practice: Rights, Duties, Claims and Defences* (Sydney: Butterworths).

— (2006). 'Life-Prolonging Treatment and Patients' Legal Rights' in Sheila A. M. McLean, ed., *First Do No Harm: Law, Ethics and Healthcare* (Aldershot: Ashgate): 419–429.

Smart, J. J. C. and Bernard Williams (1973). *Utilitarianism: For and Against* (Cambridge: Cambridge University Press).

Somerville, Margaret (1994). '"Death Talk" in Canada: The Rodriguez Case', *McGill Law Journal* 39: 602–617.

Steinbock, Bonnie, ed. (1980). *Killing and Letting Die* (Englewood Cliffs, N.J.: Prentice-Hall).

— (2005). 'The Case for Physician Assisted Suicide: Not Yet Proven', *Journal of Medical Ethics* 31: 235–241.

— and Alastair Norcross, eds. (1994). *Killing and Letting Die* (New York: Fordham University Press, 2nd edn).

Stell, Lance K. (1998). 'Physician-Assisted Suicide: To Decriminalize or to Legalize, That Is the Question' in Battin, *et al.* (1998): 225–251.

Stocker, Michael and Elizabeth Hegeman (1996). *Valuing Emotions* (New York: Cambridge University Press).

Stone, Jim (1994). 'Advance Directives, Autonomy and Unintended Death', *Bioethics* 8: 223–246.

Stutsman, Eli D. (2004). 'Political Strategy and Legal Change' in Quill and Battin (2004): 245–263.

Sutherland, Stewart (1992). *Irrationality: The Enemy Within* (London: Constable).

Taurek, John (1977). 'Should the Numbers Count?', *Philosophy and Public Affairs* 6: 293–316.

Teichman, Jenny (1996). *Social Ethics: A Student's Guide* (Oxford: Blackwell).

Temkin, Owsei (1991). *Hippocrates in a World of Pagans and Christians* (Baltimore: The Johns Hopkins University Press).

The Age Newspaper (Melbourne) (2005). 'Pope Slams Mercy Killing of Newborns', 25 January 2005: 11.

Thomasma, David, Thomasina Kimbrough-Kushner, Gerrit Kimsma and Chris Ciesielski-Carlucci, eds. (1998). *Asking to Die: Inside the Dutch Debate About Euthanasia* (Dordrecht: Kluwer).

Thomson, Judith Jarvis (1976). 'Self-Defense and Rights', *The Lindley Lecture* (Lawrence, Kansas: University of Kansas Publications).

— (1991). 'Self-Defense', *Philosophy and Public Affairs* 20: 283–311.

— (1999). 'Physician-Assisted Suicide: Two Moral Arguments', *Ethics* 109: 497–518.

Tomlinson, Tom and Howard Brody (1990). 'Futility and the Ethics of Resuscitation', *Journal of the American Medical Association* 264: 1276–1280.

Tooley, Michael (1983). *Abortion and Infanticide* (Oxford: Clarendon Press).

— (1994). 'An Irrelevant Consideration: Killing versus Letting Die' in Steinbock and Norcross (1994): 103–111.

Trammell, Richard (1994). 'Saving Life and Taking Life' in Steinbock and Norcross (1994): 290–297.

Truog, R. D., A. S. Brett and J. Frader (1992). 'The Problem With Futility', *The New England Journal of Medicine* 326: 1560–1564.

Unger, Peter (1990). *Identity, Consciousness and Value* (New York: Oxford University Press).

— (1996). *Living High and Letting Die: Our Illusion of Innocence* (New York: Oxford University Press).

Uniacke, Suzanne (1994). *Permissible Killing: The self-defence justification of homicide* (New York: Cambridge University Press).

van der Burg, Wibren (1991). 'The Slippery Slope Argument', *Ethics* 102: 42–65.

van der Heide, Agnes, Paul J. van der Maas, Gerrit van der Wal, Carmen L. M. de Graaff, John G. C. Kester, Louis A. A. Kollee, Richard de Leeuw and Robert A. Holl (1997). 'Medical end-of-life decisions made for neonates and infants in The Netherlands', *The Lancet* 350: 251–255.

van der Maas, Paul J., Johannes J. M. van Delden, Loes Pijnenborg and Caspar W. N. Looman (1991). 'Euthanasia and other medical decisions concerning the end of life', *The Lancet* 338: 669–674.

—, Loes Pijnenborg and Johannes J. M. van Delden (1995). 'Changes in Dutch Opinions on Active Euthanasia', *Journal of the American Medical Association* 273: 1411–1414.

—, Gerrit van der Wal, Ilinka Haverkate, Carmen L. M. de Graaff, John G. C. Kester, Bregje D. Onwuteaka-Philipsen, Agnes van der Heide, Jacqueline M. Bosma and Dick L. Willems (1996). 'Euthanasia, Physician-Assisted Suicide and Other Medical Practices Involving the End of Life in The Netherlands, 1990–1995', *The New England Journal of Medicine* 335: 1699–1705.

van der Wal, Gerrit, J. Th. M. van Eijk, H. J. J. Leenen and C. Spreeuwenberg (1992a). 'Euthanasia and Assisted Suicide, I: How Often is it Practised by Family Doctors in The Netherlands?', *Family Practice* 9: 130–134.

— (1992b). 'Euthanasia and Assisted Suicide, II: Do Dutch Family Doctors Act Prudently?', *Family Practice* 9: 135–140.

—, Paul J. van der Maas, Jacqueline M. Bosma, Bregje D. Onwuteaka-Philipsen, Dick L. Willems, Ilinka Haverkate and Piet J. Kostense (1996). 'Evaluation of the Notification Procedure for Physician-Assisted Death in The Netherlands', *The New England Journal of Medicine* 335: 1706–1711.

van Hooff, Anton J. L. (1990). *From Autothanasia to Suicide: Self-killing in Classical Antiquity* (London: Routledge).

Varelius, Jukka (2006). 'Voluntary Euthanasia, Physician-Assisted Suicide, and the Goals of Medicine', *The Journal of Medicine and Philosophy* 31: 121–137.

Veatch, Robert (2001). 'The Impossibility of a Morality Internal to Medicine', *The Journal of Medicine and Philosophy* 26: 621–642.

Veldink, Jan H., John H. J. Wokke, Gerrit van der Wal, J. M. B. Vianney de Jong and Leonard H. van den Burg (2002). 'Euthanasia and Physician-Assisted Suicide among Patients with Amyotrophic Lateral Sclerosis', *The New England Journal of Medicine* 346: 1638–1644.

Velleman, J. David (1992). 'Against the Right to Die', *The Journal of Medicine and Philosophy* 17: 664–681.

— (1999a). 'A Right of Self-Termination?', *Ethics* 109: 606–628.

— (1999b). 'The Voice of Conscience', *Proceedings of the Aristotelian Society* 99: 57–76.

Verhagen, Eduard and Pieter J. J. Sauer (2005). 'The Groningen Protocol – Euthanasia in Severely Ill Newborns', *The New England Journal of Medicine* 352: 959–962.

Verhey, Allen (1998). 'A Protestant Perspective on Ending Life: Faithfulness in the Face of Death' in Battin, *et al.* (1998): 347–361.

Victorian Law Reform Commission (1984). *Working Paper No. 8: Murder – Mental Element and Punishment* (Melbourne: Victorian Law Reform Commission).

Walton, Douglas (1992). *Slippery Slope Arguments* (Oxford: Clarendon Press).

Warren, Mary Anne (1997). *Moral Status: Obligations to Persons and Other Living Things* (Oxford: Clarendon Press).

— (2000). 'The Moral Difference Between Infanticide and Abortion: A Response to Robert Card', *Bioethics* 14: 352–359.

Way, Jenny, Anthony L. Back and J. Randall Curtis (2002). 'Withdrawing Life Support and Resolution of Conflict With Families', *British Medical Journal* 325: 1342–1345.

Wear, Stephen (1998). *Informed Consent: Patient Autonomy and Physician Beneficence Within Clinical Medicine* (Dordrecht: Kluwer, 2nd edn).

— (1999). 'Patient Freedom and Competence in Health Care' in Cutter and Shelp (1999): 227–236.

—, S. Lagaipa and Gerald Logue (1994). 'Toleration of Moral Diversity and the Conscientious Refusal by Physicians to Withdraw Life-Sustaining Treatment', *The Journal of Medicine and Philosophy* 19: 148–149.

— and Gerald Logue (1995). 'The Problem of Medically Futile Treatment: Falling Back on a Preventive Ethics Approach', *The Journal of Clinical Ethics* 6: 138–148.

Weinrib, Lorraine (1994). 'The Body and the Body Politic: Assisted Suicide Under the Canadian Charter of Rights and Freedoms', *McGill Law Journal* 39: 618–643.

Weir, Robert F., ed. (1997). *Physician-Assisted Suicide* (Bloomington and Indianapolis: Indiana University Press).

Wellman, Carl (2003). 'A Legal Right to Physician-Assisted Suicide', *Social Theory and Practice* 29: 19–38.

White, Becky Cox (1994). *Competence to Consent* (Washington, D.C.: Georgetown University Press).

Wicclair, Mark (1991). 'Patient Decision-Making Capacity and Risk', *Bioethics* 5: 91–104.

— (2000). 'Conscientious Objection in Medicine', *Bioethics* 14: 205–227.

Wikler, Dan (1979). 'Paternalism and the Mildly Retarded', *Philosophy and Public Affairs* 8: 377–392.

Wildes, Kevin (1993). 'Conscience, Referral and Physician Assisted Suicide', *The Journal of Medicine and Philosophy* 18: 323–328.

Wilks, Ian (1997). 'The Debate Over Risk-related Standards of Competence', *Bioethics* 11: 413–426.

Williams, Alan (1996). 'QALYs and Ethics: A Health Economist's Perspective', *Social Science and Medicine* 43: 1795–1804.

Williams, Bernard (1985). 'Which Slopes Are Slippery?' in Michael Lockwood, ed., *Moral Dilemmas in Modern Medicine* (Oxford: Oxford University Press): 126–137.

Wilson, Bradley E. (1996). 'Futility and the Obligations of Physicians', *Bioethics* 10: 43–55.

Wineberg, Howard (2000). 'Oregon's Death with Dignity Act: Fourteen Months and Counting', *Archives of Internal Medicine* 160: 21–23.

Winkler, Earl R. (1995). 'Reflections on the State of Current Debate Over Physician-Assisted Suicide and Euthanasia', *Bioethics* 9: 313–326.

Wolf, Susan (1986). 'Self-Interest and Interest in Selves', *Ethics* 96: 704–720.

Wolf, Susan M. (1996). 'Physician-Assisted Suicide in the Context of Managed Care', *Duquesne Law Review* 35: 455–479.

World Medical Association (1992). 'Statement on physician assisted suicide', 44th World Medical Assembly, Marbella, Spain, September 1992.

— (2002). *Resolution on Euthanasia* (Washington, D.C.: World Medical Association).

Young, Robert (1976). 'Voluntary and Non-voluntary Euthanasia', *The Monist* 59: 264–283.

— (1979). 'Infanticide and the Severely Defective Infant' in R. S. Laura, ed., *Problems of Handicap* (Melbourne: Macmillan): 126–135.

— (1986). *Personal Autonomy: Beyond Negative and Positive Liberty* (London: Croom Helm).

— (1998). 'Informed Consent and Patient Autonomy' in Helga Kuhse and Peter Singer, eds., *A Companion to Bioethics* (Oxford: Blackwell): 441–451.

— (2006). 'Euthanasia, Voluntary' in Edward N. Zalta, ed., *Stanford Online Encyclopedia of Philosophy (Summer 2006 Edition)*, URL = <http://plato.stanford.edu/archives/sum2006/entries/euthanasia-voluntary/>.

Youngner, Stuart (1998). 'Commentary on Charland', *Philosophy, Psychiatry and Psychology* 5: 89–92.

Zimmerman, Michael J. (2001). *The Nature of Intrinsic Value* (Lanham, Maryland: Rowman and Littlefield).

Zohar, Noam J. (1998). 'Jewish Deliberations on Suicide: Exceptions, Toleration, and Assistance' in Battin, *et al.* (1998): 362–372.

Zuger, Abigail and Steven H. Miles (1987). 'Physicians, AIDS, and Occupational Risk: Historic Traditions and Ethical Obligations', *Journal of the American Medical Association* 258: 1924–1928.

Index of English-language legal cases

Index of names and subjects